THE NEW WORLD LOOKS AT ITS HISTORY

THE *New World*

LOOKS AT ITS HISTORY

Proceedings of the Second International Congress
of Historians of the United States and Mexico

EDITED BY **ARCHIBALD R. LEWIS**

AND **THOMAS F. McGANN**

UNIVERSITY OF TEXAS PRESS, AUSTIN
PUBLISHED FOR THE INSTITUTE OF LATIN AMERICAN
STUDIES, THE UNIVERSITY OF TEXAS

Library of Congress Catalog Card No. 62–14503

Copyright © 1963 by the University of Texas Press

Manufactured in the United States of America

CONTENTS

GENERAL INTRODUCTION

THE CONTENTS of this slender volume represent papers and comments which a group of distinguished historians delivered at the sessions of the Second International Congress of Historians of the United States and Mexico, held at the University of Texas on November 3–6, 1958.

At first glance the reader may well feel that the subjects presented here are to some extent unrelated—even of small interest except to historians who concern themselves with the history of the southwestern portion of the United States. Closer examination, however, should make it clear that the scholars from Mexico and the United States who planned this program were concerned with a broad purpose which had as its object an examination of the special nature of the history of the New World and the ideas which interest its historians. For instance, the first grouping of papers deals with the pre-Columbian culture of the Indians of the New World, as represented by those of the United States Southwest. Latin American historians, in contrast to those of the United States, have long understood the essential contribution which anthropologists and archeologists can make to the historians of the New World by explaining the Indian cultures which existed here before the coming of the white man. All too often, however, these anthropologists and archeologists have spoken a language so different from that of the historian that neither has understood the other. This section represents an attempt to bridge that gap.

It is equally important for historians of the New World to understand the nature of the European cultures that the settlers, arriving in the New World, brought with them, and the historical experiences that molded their thinking. A particularly good example of the nature of the culture and experience is dealt with in the second group of papers and comments, which are concerned with the medieval Spanish frontier. This frontier and the Spain which emerged as a result of it help to explain the way in which the Spanish and even the Anglo-Saxon settlers in the New World proceeded with their conquests and their settlements, as well as providing us with an interesting comparison between a European frontier in medieval times and those found later across the Atlantic.

When we turn to the third section we find the frontier in the United States and Mexico treated as a concept and as an actuality, with special attention to the hacienda of Northern Mexico and the ranch of Texas as concrete examples of the frontier. Though Latin American historians have, on the whole, been little interested in the concept of a frontier, in part because they have tended to view their own history in a rather different way, the frontier concept has claimed a major place in the thinking of United States historians. It is, perhaps, their unique contribution to historical study. Hence its inclusion here.

Next we find a group of papers and comment dealing with the "Great Frontier" concept, that attempt to generalize from the American frontier experience and give it a broader application on the world stage in modern times. Those historians who deal with this concept here endow it with a scope and describe it with a critical analysis which should interest a wide audience among the historians of the Americas.

Finally we find a section which is concerned with the way in which historians should view history and their craft and their responsibilities. It emphasizes the very different vision of history which one finds in the work of the scholars of the United States and that of their colleagues in Latin America. Whatever interests the historians of the New World as a whole—the American Indian, the Old World heritage, frontiers or the lack of them in their historical experience—this section clearly shows that they do not necessarily share the same attitude when they examine their past.

It may be worthwhile to emphasize that since the New World and its history are part of the wider world, the historians who speak in these pages are international in the widest sense of the word. The greater number of those who participated in the Congress and whose papers and comments are to be found here are from Mexico and the United States. But the reader will find contributions by distinguished American scholars who live in Canada, Brazil, and

Argentina. And since the New World is of concern also to the Old World, he will discover that the dialogue is joined by historians from Britain, France, Spain, and even distant Australia. As the New World looks at its history, then, it has invited the Old World to join in the examination, and to add its contribution to that continuing interchange of ideas and attitudes toward the historical process which marks the truly educated man.

The editors regret that they could not include in the volume many other aspects of the Second International Congress of Historians of the United States and Mexico. They had to omit discussions of the role of university presses in the United States and Mexico, comments on an exhibition of Mexican art which those attending the Congress enjoyed, and a stimulating view of higher education in the United States and Mexico which was a feature of the Congress' final session. They also regret that some of the participants did not make available to them their papers for inclusion in this volume and that some, like the late Jaime Vicens Vives, of Barcelona, at the last moment were unable to attend its sessions. They can only hope, however, that they have been able to include enough to stimulate historical interest and imagination on both sides of the Rio Grande and in the wider world.

The editors wish to express appreciation to the Rockefeller Foundation and Dr. John P. Harrison for assistance which helped make possible the Congress, and to Professor Lewis U. Hanke, whose enthusiasm did much to make the Congress a success. Our thanks go also to the Administration and to the Institute of Latin American Studies of the University of Texas and its Director, Dr. Eastin Nelson, for their interest and support and for their assistance in the publication of these *Proceedings*.

Finally, the editors wish to thank a number of scholars who took on the task of translating into English many of the papers and comments included in this volume, especially Dr. Pablo Max Ynsfran, Dr. Ramón Martinez-López, Dr. George Schade, and Mr. Charles Eastlack, all of The University of Texas. Their work of translation helped make the Congress a success and it allows the editors to produce a volume which is accessible to English-speaking scholars.

ARCHIBALD R. LEWIS
THOMAS F. McGANN

Austin, Texas

Part One
PREHISTORIC PEOPLES

Historians who deal with Mexico, Peru, Viking Scandinavia, the ancient Near East, and the Classical World have long been aware of archeologists' contributions to their understanding of the history they are attempting to reconstruct from other sources. On the other hand this has been less true of those scholars who are concerned with the history of the United States or of Medieval and Modern Europe, who have tended to neglect anthropology and archeology as disciplines which produce facts of value to their work. The following paper by Professor Campbell and the comment by Dr. Roberts should emphasize how it is possible for these disciplines to make an important contribution to our knowledge of the Indian past in the Americas and so assist historical research. It underscores the need for historians to have a grasp of these disciplines so that they can learn what investigators working in the fields of anthropology and archeology may contribute to historical study. If the past is prologue, then historians must begin to study this prologue to written history before the full documentation, which they feel is necessary for their work, is available to them. The archeologist and the anthropologist can help to bridge the gap in historical knowledge and give a deeper insight into historical materials.

The Present Status of Our Knowledge of Indian Civilizations West of the Mississippi

BY T. N. CAMPBELL
University of Texas

THIS ESSAY is addressed to historians and may be considered an attempt at communication between two disciplines that are concerned with human behavior through time and space but differ primarily in the kinds of evidence chosen for analysis and interpretation. I shall limit myself to a geographic area much smaller than is suggested by the assigned title. A literal interpretation of this title would lead to a consideration of prehistoric cultural developments in approximately the western two-thirds of the United States. It seems reasonable to reduce this area to somewhat more manageable proportions for the time allotted, and I will therefore focus attention on the area generally known as the American Southwest, plus its environs, and with an extension eastward to the lower part of the Mississippi Valley. This should bring about a more complementary relationship with studies of northern Mexico.

This area is marked by great physiographic, climatic, and biotic diversity. It actually includes parts of nearly all of the physiographic provinces that lie between Florida and California. Prehistoric Indian cultures in this particular area also show considerable diversity, reflecting to a certain extent these great ecological differences. Most archeologists would prefer to break this area up into at least three parts, particularly with respect to the later prehistoric cultures. They would speak of a small eastern part that is oriented toward the Southeastern cultural province, a larger middle area that exhibits Plains cultures, and a still larger western area that includes the cultures of the arid Southwest.

Archeological investigations have been going on in this area for at least eighty years, especially in the Southwest, where American archeology got off to a head start, and a tremendous body of empirical data has been accumulated in literally thousands of publications. It is doubtful if any one American archeologist today actually controls the literature of this entire area. Specialization has become inevitable, with all of its advantages and disadvantages. What I shall try to do here is summarize in a general way the major cultural units, call attention to a few of the newer archeological developments, and point to some of the problems that require attention in the immediate future.

As it is appropriate to this occasion, and very pertinent to the area under discussion, I would like to point out that one of the principal themes of American archeology is the comparatively early appearance of high culture or civilization in the Mesoamerican area and its effects on the less complex Indian cultures in what is now the United States. Mesoamerica is to the remainder of North America what early Mesopotamia was to a large part of the Old World, an area where an agriculturally based urban life appeared early and eventually affected less complex cultures at great distances. I think it is fair to say that one cannot properly evaluate the later developments in continental North American culture history without an understanding of Mesoamerica. The converse is also true. An understanding of the earlier cultures south of the Rio Grande depends upon knowing what happened in the United States and Canada. New World archeology, like New World historiography, has to be a cooperative enterprise.

During the past ten years there has been a growing interest in the formulation of schemes that describe the whole of New World prehistory in terms of stages of cultural development, an approach somewhat like that of the historian Toynbee. This is in accord with the present trend toward broad generalizations and syntheses in American archeology. Steward (1948, 1949) and Krieger (1953) have presented schemes of this type, although on a rather limited geographic basis. More recently Willey and Phillips (1958) have drawn up what they call a "historical-developmental sequence" for the whole Western Hemisphere and have made a serious but not entirely successful effort to apply it to the great welter of prehistoric cultures known to American archeologists.

The Willey and Phillips developmental scheme, which I shall use as a convenient framework for presentation in this paper, involves five stages: Lithic, Archaic, Formative, Classic, and Postclassic. The criteria used for stage determination are basically technological and economic, for data on these phases of prehistoric human life are the easiest to come by archeologically. The Lithic Stage includes the early migratory hunting and gathering cultures, with emphasis on hunting the big-game animals characteristic of the Pleistocene; the Archaic Stage covers the later hunting and gathering cultures, mostly after extinction of the big-game animals in early postglacial times, and is marked by a tendency to exploit fully the natural food resources of the local environment; the Formative Stage embraces cultures in which agriculture has become important enough to form the basis for sedentary village life; the Classic Stage is characterized by the development of urban life in cities built around ceremonial centers that include temple pyramids and palace platforms; and the Postclassic is a continuation of the Classic but marked by population movements, extensive warfare, and a general decline in the arts and religious architecture, ending with the European conquest.

This scheme is based on cultural development and is chronological only in a broad, general way. Archaic cultures, for example, may continue in an area where Formative cultures are already in existence. In some areas the Classic and the Postclassic stages never developed; in fact, in the scheme of Willey and Phillips these last two stages appear only in the area extending from Mexico to Peru. For cultures of the Classic and Postclassic stages Willey and Phillips use the term *civilization* in order to emphasize the greater cultural complexity that goes with urban life. As no one has yet provided us with a means for determining just when a village or town becomes large enough to be called a "city," that is, when urbanism begins, the terms *culture* and *civilization* can be used only in a contrasting sense. However, I am inclined to agree with Willey and Phillips that north of the international boundary between Mexico and the United States no real urban life ever existed in the prehistoric past. Hence west of the Mississippi there were no civilizations, only cultures of varying but lesser complexity.

We then have three developmental stages represented in the area west of the Mississippi, namely, Lithic, Archaic, and Formative. Actually, as the Lithic and Archaic both refer to hunting and gathering cultures, we have only two basic groups to consider, the hunters and gatherers on one hand and the sedentary village dwellers on the other.

Lithic Stage

The Lithic Stage, which among North American archeologists is also commonly referred to as Paleo-Indian, is characterized by the earliest known occupation of the Western Hemisphere, the first human movement into the great primal American frontier. It is assumed, in the absence of evidence to the contrary, that the first men came to the New World from Asia and that the most feasible route of entry was from northeastern Siberia through Alaska. This movement from Arctic Asia to America was essentially a land movement, most likely by hunters who followed the big-game animals of the Pleistocene (Eiseley, 1955). The time of original entry is not known, but there is general agreement that the Lithic Stage coincides with late glacial and early postglacial times. Stone artifacts constitute the bulk of the archeological evidence, hence the name "Lithic," and these artifacts frequently occur in association with remains of the extinct Pleistocene game animals.

Sites assignable to the Lithic Stage are fairly numerous in the Great Plains and the southwestern United States. Here a series of early complexes can be distinguished, but most of these are still not clearly defined and their relationships are poorly understood. This is largely because the archeological remains are meager, frequently consisting of spear or dart points and a few simple tools used for skinning, butchering, and processing hides. Wormington (1957) has recently grouped the various Lithic sites and complexes of the United States under two headings, a Paleo-Eastern tradition and a Paleo-Western tradition, with the Rocky Mountains serving as a rough dividing zone. In the Paleo-Eastern tradition there is emphasis on the hunting of big-game animals and the manufacture of distinctive, well-made spear or dart points of lanceolate form. In the Paleo-Western tradition more emphasis is placed on the gathering of wild plant foods, and the techniques of chipping flint are less complex. During the past few years some of the sites assigned to Wormington's Paleo-Western tradition have also been referred to as representing the earlier phase of the Desert culture of arid North America (Jennings and Norbeck, 1955). This Desert culture represents a long culture continuum that constituted the Archaic base on which were built the later, more complex Formative cultures of the Southwest. For the Paleo-Eastern tradition no comparable continuum has been established.

The best-known Lithic Stage cultures of our area belong to Wormington's Paleo-Eastern tradition. These are Llano and Folsom, which are characterized by distinctive types of fluted projectile points. The Llano, with its large Clovis-type point, is associated with mammoth hunting, and Folsom is associated with hunting of an extinct form of bison. These two cultures have been found stratigraphically separated at a locality near Clovis in eastern New Mexico. Folsom occurring in a higher and hence chronologically later stratum (Sellards, 1952). Only one radiocarbon date has been obtained for Folsom, and this date, about 8000 B.C., is from a site near Lubbock, Texas. Several radiocarbon dates from the stratigraphically earlier Llano culture give it a time range extending from over 35,000 B.C. to less than 5500 B.C. These dates are incompatible with other evidence and are not widely accepted at present. It is perhaps preferable to say that Llano is older than Folsom, which appears to go back at least to 8000 B.C.

In a central New Mexico cave Folsom artifacts have been found overlying remains of another but highly localized complex known as Sandia (Hibben, 1941), which is distinguished by single-shouldered lanceolate points. This stratigraphic position, as well as one questionable radiocarbon date of 18,000 B.C., seems to place Sandia in the same general time horizon as Llano.

In recent years evidences of other and later Paleo-Eastern Lithic complexes have been found, principally in the central and southern Great Plains. These are distinguished mainly by special types of parallel-flaked projectile points separately associated with extinct or near-modern forms of bison. Among these point types, which were formerly designated by the general term, "Yuma," are Plainview (Sellards, et al., 1947), Scottsbluff and Eden (Wormington, 1957, suggests that these be combined and called Cody points), Milnesand (Sellards, 1955), and Angostura (formerly known as "Long"; Hughes, 1949). These types appear to represent hunting groups that ranged over the Plains area between 8000 and 5000 B.C., or largely after Folsom.

Much more information is needed on Lithic Stage cultures in order to identify and define more clearly all recognizable units and to organize them in a more meaningful way. The radiocarbon dating technique has been helpful, but thus far has not told us much more about chronological placement of Lithic cultures than cultural stratigraphy and geological interpretation. A few widely scattered finds that could be earlier than Llano have been made, but the validity of these is still being debated (Krieger, 1953; Willey and Phillips, 1958). Much more excavation will have to be done before the Lithic cultures can be seen in clear perspective.

Archaic Stage

The Archaic Stage includes a great variety of hunting and gathering cultures that are not associated with extinct animals. For a time American archeologists had difficulty with what appeared to be a long time gap between Lithic and Archaic cultures. Since the development of radiocarbon dating, this gap has disappeared. In fact, it has been something of an embarrassment to discover that radiocarbon dates for some cultures designated as Archaic are actually older than many of the dates for Lithic cultures. This of course adds to the difficulties of those who formulate developmental schemes.

Two large blocks of Archaic cultures have been distinguished in the United States. One of these is known as the Eastern Archaic, which is well represented in the eastern United States and extends westward into the Plains. The other is now generally referred to as the Desert culture, which in its broadest sense extends from Oregon southward to the Valley of Mexico and from the eastern slopes of the Rocky Mountains westward to the Pacific. This Desert culture, or Western Archaic, has a great time range, lasting from about 7000 B.C. to 1000 B.C., and in some areas it seems to have continued into post-Columbian times. It is referred to small, widely dispersed, nonsedentary population groups who preferred to live in caves and subsisted by intensive use of all natural foods available in the generally arid environment. They seem to have specialized in the seasonal collection of plant foods, especially small seeds, which were pulverized on flat milling stones. They made baskets, matting, netting, fur cloth, fiber sandals, digging sticks, spears and spear-throwers, and flat, curved wooden clubs.

This Desert culture embraces remains found in widely scattered sites, among them Gypsum and Lovelock caves in Nevada (Harrington, 1933; Loud and Harrington, 1929); Danger Cave in Utah (Jennings, 1957); the Uncompahgre sites in Colorado (Wormington and Lister, 1956); the Cochise sites of Arizona (Sayles and Antevs, 1941); various caves in Trans-Pecos Texas (Suhm, *et al.*, 1954); and various caves in Coahuila, including the remarkable Cueva de la Candelaria with its array of mortuary materials (Aveleyra, *et al.*, 1956).

The formalization of the Desert culture by giving it a name and a generalized list of traits is recent (Jennings and Norbeck, 1955), but the concept has been expressed frequently in the past. Although the Desert culture is now known in broad outline and in localized detail here and there, its geographic spread is such that we actually have only a small sampling. As the evidence thus far indicates great cultural conservatism, that is, relatively little cultural change through time (Jennings, 1957; Taylor, 1956), techniques for discovering such changes as do occur must be improved or new ones developed. Here artifact typologies could be of value, especially a typology of projectile points for arid North America as a whole. Regional variants of the Desert culture need clearer definition. The earliest and the latest phases need concentrated attention. The earlier phase, if the radiocarbon dates are acceptable, shows an overlap in time with certain Lithic cultures, which calls for clarification of relationships. Likewise, at the other end of the chronological column, we need more precise documentation on just how local variants of the Desert culture developed into the various Formative cultures of the Southwest.

Still another problem is the relationship of the Desert culture to the Eastern Archaic. Attack on this problem will lead to the intervening boundary zone, where there are large gaps to fill. In the southern Plains area, from the lower Pecos River northward to Nebraska, the Archaic stage is virtually unknown, largely because archeologists have not focussed attention on the Archaic occupation of this region. At present the area of most immediate promise for investigating relationships between the Desert culture and the Eastern Archaic is a broad belt of territory extending from southern Texas northward into Oklahoma. Here sufficient work has been done to permit the recognition, if not clear definition, of a series of Archaic cultures that bridge the boundary zone between the Desert culture and the Eastern Archaic. In eastern Oklahoma and in eastern Texas occur several Archaic cultures, the Grove Focus (Bell and Baerreis, 1951), the Fourche Maline Focus (*ibid.*), and the East Texas Aspect (Suhm, *et al.*, 1954), which appear to be marginal developments of the Eastern Archaic. West and southwest in Texas other Archaic cultures have been recognized, among them the Trinity Aspect (Crook and Harris, 1952), the Edwards Plateau Aspect (Suhm, *et al.*, 1954), and the Big Bend Aspect (*ibid.*). The last-named culture, the Big Bend Aspect of Trans-Pecos Texas, appears to be a Desert culture, but it shares traits with the Edwards Plateau and other Archaic cultures to the east. Relations between eastern and western facies of the Archaic will undoubtedly be clarified by further studies in Oklahoma and Texas.

Formative Stage

The Formative Stage of the area under question is very complicated, and many of the cultures attributable to this stage have been intensively studied. In the Southwest the major Formative cultures are designated as Anasazi, Mogollon, Hohokam, and Patayan. Sometimes a fifth, the Sinagua, is indicated, but this appears to be a special blend or hybrid whose status is still controversial. These various Formative cultures all appear to have developed from some form of the Desert culture around the beginning of the Christian Era, although in some instances the transitional phases have not been demonstrated. The main additions to the Desert culture, particularly agriculture and pottery, appear to have come from outside the Southwestern area, and it is now well established that agriculture preceded pottery. The designated area of origin for Southwestern agriculture and pottery is Mexico, but details of the diffusion are not yet clear.

One of the more interesting developments in recent years is the discovery that the agricultural food plant complex—maize, beans, and squash—reached the Southwest much earlier than had been supposed (Jennings, 1956). Furthermore, botanical studies and archeological stratigraphy indicate that various forms of these plants diffused at different times and reached the Southwest by more than one route. Corn of a very primitive type was grown in the Southwest as early as 2500 B.C. This surprisingly early date has been supported by an equally early date for corn in a cave in Tamaulipas (MacNeish, 1955). Squash seems to have been cultivated in the Southwest as early as corn, but evidence thus far places the entrance of beans much later. It has also been of great interest to learn that these various food plants were part of Southwestern cultures some 2,000 years before they had any striking effect on the economy and social life of any Southwestern culture. Sedentary life did not immediately follow the introduction of agriculture; no cultural revolution occurred, only a slow evolution.

The best-known culture of the Southwest is the Anasazi, a more recent term for the culture also known as Basket Maker-Pueblo or simply Pueblo (Reed, 1946). Some 2,000 years of continuous occupation have been documented, the Pueblo Indians of today representing a contemporary phase of this same culture. The area occupied by the prehistoric Anasazi varies considerably through time, but the general locus of the culture is the high plateau area of northwestern New Mexico, northern Arizona, southern Utah, and southwestern Colorado. The culture history of the Anasazi has been developed in complex detail, thanks to an abundance of highly visible archeological remains, fortunate conditions of preservation in dry caves and shelters, tree-ring dating, and a large group of archeologists of diverse institutional origins. It was with this culture that Southwestern archeology began, and nearly all later developments grew out of this early interest.

The Anasazi is characterized by agriculture with little use of irrigation; pit houses that are later replaced by surface houses of stone masonry arranged in compact, cellular units, frequently with more than one story; ceremonial chambers, known as "kivas," mostly subterranean and apparently derived from the earlier pit houses; gray corrugated and black-on-white painted pottery; and burial of the dead in a flexed position. Nearly all of the really impressive archeological ruins of the Southwest represent the Anasazi.

A formal chronological framework for the Anasazi culture was first set up in 1927 (Kidder, 1927). This so-called Pecos classification divided the Basket Maker phase into three periods and the Pueblo into five periods, each period designated by a Roman numeral. This continues in use today, along with Roberts' suggested revision of 1935, which emphasizes developmental stages rather than chronological position. The Roberts' revision, with commonly used date ranges, is as follows: Basket Maker (? B.C.–A.D. 400), Modified Basket Maker (A.D. 400–700), Developmental Pueblo (A.D. 700–1100), Great Pueblo (A.D. 1100–1300), and Regressive Pueblo (A.D. 1300–1500).

As Taylor (1954) has pointed out, it was originally assumed that Anasazi was the only culture represented in the Southwest, and this had a retarding influence on the development of culture-historical studies in that area. Since other cultures with about the same time range have been recognized, the Anasazi has had to be viewed in a different perspective. It has, in effect, been reduced from a position of towering dominance to a position of merely one among equals in a much more complicated frame of reference. With respect to Mesoamerica it occupies a more distant marginal position than Mogollon and Hohokam, and received agriculture and pottery considerably later. After these earlier diffusions, Mesoamerican cultures seem to have had little effect on the Anasazi, although recently some archeologists have professed to see Mesoamerican influences in Great Pueblo architecture (Ferdon, 1955) and in Regressive Pueblo ceramics and kiva mural art (Brew, 1944).

One problem that has evoked much interest is why the whole northern or San Juan Anasazi area was completely abandoned in the latter part of the thirteenth century at the end of the Great Pueblo Period. Various explanations have been proposed (O'Bryan, 1952), such as prolonged drought with concomitant reduction of vegetation, erosion, and lowering of the water table; loss of soil fertility through overuse of the land; invasion of the area by nomadic raiding peoples, such as the Ute, Paiute, Navaho, and Apache; poor sanitation and disease epidemics; and even internal dissension. For none of these, except drought, is there much specific evidence, and debate on this matter continues. It seems likely that more than one factor was involved (Brew, 1946). This particular population shift was sudden and dramatic, and numerous spectacular archeological sites were left behind. What is often lost sight of is that this is merely the beginning of a series of population movements and areal shrinkages that continued into historic times.

Another feature of Anasazi archeology that has received much attention is the identification of archeological remains that represent the antecedents of the various surviving historic Pueblo Indians (Reed, 1955). This interest in local cultural continuities is likely to persist, for it coincides with the current trend toward ethnohistorical studies stimulated by the Indian claims against the United States government.

The Mogollon culture, first recognized in the early 1930's, is associated with the mountainous belt of southeastern Arizona and southwestern New Mexico, particularly the upper headwaters of the Gila and Salt rivers. The principal Mogollon traits are agriculture; villages of pit houses with tunnel-like entrances, later replaced by

stone masonry houses similar to those of the Anasazi; large ceremonial structures; polished brown and polished red pottery, with a
later red-on-brown painted pottery; and flexed burials.

Knowledge of the Mogollon has increased rapidly during the past
twenty years, and at least six regional variants have been identified.
Wheat (1955) has recently presented a chronological sequence
which divides the Mogollon into five phases comparable to the
period divisions of Anasazi and Hohokam. The periods and their
time ranges are as follows: Mogollon 1 (300 B.C.–A.D. 400), Mogollon 2 (A.D. 400–600), Mogollon 3 (A.D. 600–900), Mogollon 4 (A.D.
900–1000), and Mogollon 5 (A.D. 1000–circa 1500).

The Mogollon is clearly derived from the Cochise variant of the
Desert culture. From the very beginning its status has been controversial because it exhibits traits that link it with Anasazi. As Reed
(1955) has phrased it, Mogollon has been variously referred to as
"illegitimate, peripheral, hybrid, or transitional." Actually Mogollon
seems to have influenced Anasazi culture up until about A.D. 700,
after which the trend is reversed and eventually, in its final phase,
Mogollon becomes rather similar to Anasazi. These relationships are
rather complex and difficult to evaluate. At present Mogollon appears to have received status as a separate Southwestern culture,
but argument continues as to whether it should be thought of as a
parallel development to Anasazi in a broader culture that includes
both (Reed, 1955).

The Hohokam culture occupied the desert region of southern
Arizona, particularly along the Gila and Salt rivers in the Phoenix
area. It was first recognized in the 1930's, and a long sequence of
prehistoric occupation is now on record. This sequence is expressed
by four periods—Pioneer (300 B.C.–A.D. 550), Colonial (A.D. 550–
900), Sedentary (A.D. 900–1100), and Classic (A.D. 1100–1500).
These date ranges (Wheat, 1954) are estimates based largely on
cross-ties with the tree-ring–supported Anasazi sequence to the
north, and there is not complete agreement on their accuracy. The
Hohokam culture is characterized by intensive agriculture based on
canal irrigation, the main crops being corn, beans, squash, and cotton; villages of brush houses that include large, oval structures considered to be courts for ball games; red-on-buff pottery; superior
work in stone and sea shell; cremation of the dead and burial of
the ashes with quantities of pottery and a variety of other funerary
offerings.

The Hohokam also appears to have developed out of the Cochise variant of the Desert culture. In the Pioneer Period it is not too unlike other early Formative cultures of the Southwest, particularly the Mogollon, but beginning with the Colonial Period a series of changes slowly take place that transform the culture into something that is highly distinctive in the Southwest. This transformation is interpreted as the result of Mesoamerican contacts, so that in effect the Hohokam became a Mexicanized Southwestern culture.

The most interesting recent development in connection with the Hohokam is the identification of the source of many of the Mesoamerican traits of the Colonial and Sedentary periods. The Mesoamerican origin of these traits has been accepted for some time (Haury, 1945), but it has not been possible to name a specific Mesoamerican culture with which the Hohokam was in extended contact. As a result of Kelley's recent excavations near Durango, Mexico, relationships have been established between Hohokam and the Chalchihuites culture, a peripheral Mesoamerican culture of Zacatecas and Durango that flourished during the late Classic and Postclassic periods of the Mesoamerican sequence (Jennings, 1956). The contacts between Chalchihuites and Hohokam seem to have occurred during the early part of the Mesoamerican Postclassic. Eventually, through this link, it should be possible to bring the Mesoamerican and Southwestern cultural sequences into more precise alignment. During the Hohokam Classic Period the Chalchihuites culture came to an end, but Mesoamerican culture traits continued to reach the Hohokam through the Sinaloa and Culiacán cultures of the Pacific coast of northwestern Mexico. Among the more notable Mesoamerican increments to Hohokam culture are numerous ceramic forms and decoration motifs, copper bells, mosaic mirrors, urn burials, various forms of small carved shell ornaments, stone carving, courts for ball games, platform mounds and courts, and possibly canal irrigation.

On the western side of the Southwest is a vaguely defined basic culture known variously as Patayan (Colton, 1945) or Yuman (Rogers, 1945). Its somewhat meager remains, which include evidences of agriculture and the manufacture of pottery, are distributed over western and northwestern Arizona and portions of adjoining California and Nevada. It is especially associated with the valley of the Colorado River from the Grand Canyon westward and southward. Because this area roughly coincides with the geographic dis-

tribution of the historic Yuman-speaking Indians, it has been assumed that the Patayan culture is attributable to the prehistoric
Yumans. The Patayan culture, especially in northwestern Arizona,
was originally considered to be a peripheral development of the
Anasazi, but slowly increasing knowledge has made it possible to
interpret Patayan as an independent development modified on the
east by contact with other Southwestern Formative cultures. Several
local subdivisions or branches of the Patayan have been named and
to some extent described, among them Cohonina, Cerbat, and Prescott. Recent detailed investigations by Schwartz (1956), as yet not
fully published, indicate that the Cohonina branch south of the
Grand Canyon was in existence by A.D. 600 and that it survived into
historic times, when it is identifiable as the culture of the Havasupai
Indians. This appears to be the best demonstration on record that
the Patayan culture represents the prehistoric Yuman-speaking Indians of the Southwest. The Patayan is still very imperfectly known,
and there is debate over the proper cultural classification of some
of its suggested subdivisions. Studies similar to that of Schwartz, if
carried out in other parts of the Patayan area, would doubtless
reveal a rather complex culture history along the lower Colorado
River.

In the southern Plains just east of the Southwest only one Formative culture has thus far been defined, a late prehistoric Plains
sedentary culture known as the Panhandle Aspect. It is associated
with the large river valleys of the Texas and Oklahoma Panhandles
(Krieger, 1946). It is of special interest because its villages consist
of stone masonry houses and apparently represent the easternmost
extension of the Anasazi architectural complex. Otherwise this Panhandle culture is typically Plains and has been related to the Upper
Republican Aspect of Nebraska.

Farther east and southeast, both in Oklahoma and Texas, are a
number of late prehistoric cultures that do not seem to have achieved
sedentary village life. Among these, for example, are the Henrietta
Focus and the Central Texas Aspect (Suhm, et al., 1954), which
show some Plains traits and also some traits indicating contact with
Formative Stage cultures farther east.

Still farther east is the Caddoan area, whose Formative cultures
have received much study during the past two decades. This area
includes southeastern Oklahoma, northeastern Texas, northwestern
Louisiana, and southwestern Arkansas. Here a fairly long sequence

of occupation is represented, and its latest phases are linked firmly with the historic Caddo peoples of this area. Some thirteen foci of culture have been identified, and these are grouped into an earlier Gibson Aspect, possibly beginning as early as A.D. 500, and a later Fulton Aspect, ending with the removal of the Caddoans from the area (Suhm, et al., 1954). Prehistoric Caddoan culture is characterized by agriculture; earthen platform or temple mounds; large wooden houses covered with mud or thatch; complicated ceramics, with emphasis on incised and engraved decorative techniques; and burials of the dead, with an abundance of mortuary offerings, including pottery, pipes, and various ornaments of stone and shell. Difficulties have arisen in interpreting the prehistoric Caddoan phases, because so many of the excavated sites are cemetery sites only, few villages having been excavated and published. Furthermore, the chronology is not well established and there has been much debate over the correlation of the Caddoan phases with phases of the Lower Mississippi Valley sequence to the east.

The Caddoan culture is sometimes regarded as an entirely separate development (Griffin, 1952) and sometimes as a marginal southwestern development of the Mississippi culture that is so widely distributed over the southern and midwestern states (Suhm, et al., 1954). The Mississippi culture is characterized by intensive agriculture, sedentary village life, and large ceremonial centers with earthen platform mounds. Both the Mississippi and the Caddoan cultures have a number of traits of obvious Mesoamerican origin, and one of the major archeological problems in the eastern United States involves the identification of these Mesoamerican culture elements, tracing them northward from Mexico, and establishing the time of the various diffusions. Here the Caddoan area has been of special interest because it is nearest to Mesoamerica. But southward from the Caddoan area, in southern Texas and northeastern Mexico, lies a large region that seems to have been devoid of complex cultures at any time in the past. This discontinuity raises questions about the modes of cultural diffusion, and various hypotheses have been offered to explain how Mesoamerican traits were carried across this gap (Kelley, 1952; Krieger, 1945, 1948). It is doubtful that an early solution to this problem can be anticipated. Much more archeological information is needed on the area lying between the northern border of Mesoamerica in eastern Mexico and the Caddoan-Mississippi area of the eastern United States.

This review has presented in broad outline a picture of prehistoric human cultural development in the southwestern quadrant of the United States as it is known today. It indicates continuous occupation of the area from the close of the Pleistocene to the time of the European conquest. The first occupants of this area were hunting and gathering peoples whose cultures developed slowly until the introduction of agriculture from Mesoamerica set the stage for sedentary village life. Thereafter cultures of greater complexity appeared, developed traits of their own, influenced or were influenced by adjacent cultures, and at times received additional stimuli from Mesoamerica. As archeological work in this area continues, the picture of what happened in the past should become clearer, and in the meantime there is the great task of explaining why it happened that way.

REFERENCES CITED

Aveleyra Arroyo de Anda, Luis, Manuel Maldonado-Koerdell, y Pablo Martínez del Rio
　1956. Cueva de la Candelaria. *Memorias del Instituto Nacional de Antropología e Historia*, V. México, D.F.
Bell, Robert E., and David A. Baerreis
　1951. A Survey of Oklahoma Archaeology. *Bulletin of the Texas Archeological and Paleontological Society*, Vol. 22, pp. 7–100. Lubbock, Texas.
Brew, John Otis
　1944. On the Pueblo IV and on the Katchina-Tlaloc Relations. El Norte de México y Sur de Estados Unidos, Tercera Reunión de Mesa Redonda sobre Problemas Antropológicos de México y Centroamérica. *Sociedad Mexicana de Antropología*, No. 3. Castillo de Chapultepec.
　1946. Archaeology of Alkali Ridge, Southeastern Utah. *Papers of the Peabody Museum of American Archaeology and Ethnology*, Vol. 21, Cambridge, Massachusetts.
Colton, Harold S.
　1945. The Patayan Problem in the Colorado River Valley. *Southwestern Journal of Anthropology*, Vol. 1, No. 1, pp. 114–121. Albuquerque, New Mexico.
Crook, Wilson W., Jr., and R. K. Harris
　1952. Trinity Aspect of the Archaic Horizon: The Carrollton and Elam Foci. *Bulletin of the Texas Archeological and Paleontological Society*, Vol. 23, pp. 7–38. Lubbock, Texas.
Eiseley, Loren C.
　1955. The Paleo-Indians: Their Survival and Diffusion. New Interpretations

of Aboriginal American Culture History. *75th Anniversary Volume of the Anthropological Society of Washington.* Washington, D.C.

Ferdon, Edwin N., Jr.
  1955. A Trial Survey of Mexican-Southwestern Architectural Parallels. *Monographs of the School of American Research,* No. 21. Santa Fe, New Mexico.

Griffin, James B.
  1952. Culture Periods in Eastern United States. James B. Griffin, editor, *Archeology of Eastern United States,* pp. 352–364. Chicago.

Harrington, M. R.
  1933. Gypsum Cave, Nevada. *Southwest Museum Papers,* No. 8. Los Angeles.

Haury, Emil W.
  1945. The Problem of Contacts between the Southwestern United States and Mexico. *Southwestern Journal of Anthropology,* Vol. 1, No. 1, pp. 55–74. Albuquerque, New Mexico.

Hibben, Frank C.
  1941. Evidences of Early Occupation of Sandia Cave, New Mexico, and Other Sites in the Sandia-Manzano Region. *Smithsonian Miscellaneous Collections,* Vol. 99, No. 23. Washington, D.C.

Hughes, Jack T.
  1949. Investigations in Western South Dakota and Northeastern Wyoming. *American Antiquity,* Vol. 14, No. 4, pp. 266–277. Menasha, Wisconsin.

Jennings, Jesse D.
  1956. The American Southwest: A Problem in Cultural Isolation. Robert Wauchope, editor, Seminars in Archaeology: 1955. *Memoirs of the Society for American Archaeology,* No. 11, pp. 58–127. Salt Lake City.
  1957. Danger Cave. *Memoirs of the Society for American Archaeology,* No. 14. Salt Lake City.

Jennings, Jesse D., and Edward Norbeck
  1955. Great Basin Prehistory: A Review. *American Antiquity,* Vol. 21, No. 1, pp. 1–11. Menasha, Wisconsin.

Kelley, J. Charles
  1952. Some Geographic and Cultural Factors Involved in Mexican-Southeastern Contacts. Sol Tax, editor, *Indian Tribes of Aboriginal America: Selected Papers of the XXIXth International Congress of Americanists.* Chicago.

Kidder, A. V.
  1927. Southwestern Archaeological Conference. *Science,* Vol. 66, No. 1716, pp. 489–491. Washington, D.C.

Krieger, Alex D.
  1945. An Inquiry into Supposed Mexican Influence on a Prehistoric "Cult" in the Southern United States. *American Anthropologist,* Vol. 47, No. 4, pp. 483–515. Menasha, Wisconsin.
  1946. Culture Complexes and Chronology in Northern Texas, with Extension of Puebloan Datings to the Mississippi Valley. *The University of Texas Publications,* No. 4640. Austin.

1948. Importance of the "Gilmore Corridor" in Culture Contacts between Middle America and the Eastern United States. *Bulletin of the Texas Archeological and Paleontological Society,* Vol. 19, pp. 155–178. Lubbock, Texas.

1953. New World Culture History: Anglo-America. A. L. Kroeber, editor, *Anthropology Today,* pp. 238–264. Chicago.

Loud, L. L., and M. R. Harrington

1929. Lovelock Cave. *University of California Publications in American Archaeology and Ethnology,* Vol. 25, No. 1. Berkeley.

MacNeish, Richard S.

1955. Ancient Maize in Mexico. *Archaeology,* Vol. 8, No. 2, pp. 108–115. New York.

O'Bryan, Deric

1952. The Abandonment of the Northern Pueblos in the Thirteenth Century. Sol Tax, editor, *Indian Tribes of Aboriginal America: Selected Papers of the XXIXth International Congress of Americanists,* pp. 153–157. Chicago.

Reed, Erik K.

1946. The Distinctive Features and Distribution of the San Juan Anasazi Culture. *Southwestern Journal of Anthropology,* Vol. 2, No. 3, pp. 295–305. Albuquerque, New Mexico.

1955. Trends in Southwestern Archeology. New Interpretations of Aboriginal American Culture History. *75th Anniversary Volume of the Anthropological Society of Washington,* pp. 46–58. Washington, D.C.

Roberts, Frank H. H., Jr.

1935. A Survey of Southwestern Archeology. *American Anthropologist,* Vol. 37, No. 1, pp. 1–35. Menasha, Wisconsin.

Rogers, Malcolm J.

1945. An Outline of Yuman Prehistory. *Southwestern Journal of Anthropology,* Vol. 1, No. 2, pp. 167–198. Albuquerque, New Mexico.

Sayles, E. B., and Ernst Antevs.

1941. The Cochise Culture. *Medallion Papers,* No. 29. Gila Pueblo, Globe, Arizona.

Schwartz, D. W.

1956. The Havasupai, 600 A.D.–1955 A.D.: A Short Culture History. *Plateau,* Vol. 28, No. 4, pp. 77–85. Flagstaff, Arizona.

Sellards, E. H.

1952. *Early Man in America: A Study in Prehistory.* Austin, Texas.

1955. Fossil Bison and Associated Artifacts from Milnesand, New Mexico. *American Antiquity,* Vol. 20, No. 4, pp. 336–344. Menasha, Wisconsin.

Sellards, E. H., Glen L. Evans, and Grayson E. Meade

1947. Fossil Bison and Associated Artifacts from Plainview, Texas, with Description of Artifacts by Alex D. Krieger. *Bulletin of the Geological Society of America,* Vol. 58, pp. 927–954. New York.

Steward, Julian H.

1948. A Functional-Developmental Classification of American High Cultures. Wendell C. Bennett, editor, A Reappraisal of Peruvian Archaeology.

Memoirs of the Society for American Archaeology, No. 4, pp. 103–104. Menasha, Wisconsin.

1949. Cultural Causality and Law: A Trial of the Development of Early Civilizations. *American Anthropologist*, Vol. 51, No. 1, pp. 1–27. Menasha, Wisconsin.

Suhm, Dee Ann, Alex D. Krieger, and Edward B. Jelks

1954. An Introductory Handbook of Texas Archeology. *Bulletin of the Texas Archeological Society*, Vol. 25, pp. 1–562. Austin.

Taylor, Walter R.

1954. Southwestern Archeology, Its History and Theory. *American Anthropologist*, Vol. 56, No. 4, pp. 561–570. Menasha, Wisconsin.

1956. Some Implications of the Carbon-14 Dates from a Cave in Coahuila, Mexico. *Bulletin of the Texas Archeological Society*, Vol. 27, pp. 215–234. Austin.

Wheat, Joe Ben

1954. Southwestern Cultural Interrelationships and the Question of Area Co-tradition. *American Anthropologist*, Vol. 56, No. 4, pp. 576–586. Menasha, Wisconsin.

1955. Mogollon Culture Prior to A.D. 1000. *Memoirs of the American Anthropological Association*, No. 82. Menasha, Wisconsin.

Willey, Gordon R., and Philip Phillips

1958. *Method and Theory in American Archaeology*. Chicago.

Wormington, H. M.

1957. Ancient Man in North America. *Denver Museum of Natural History, Popular Series*, No. 4, 4th ed. Denver.

Wormington, H. M., and Robert H. Lister

1956. Archeological Investigations on the Uncompahgre Plateau in West Central Colorado. *Proceedings of the Denver Museum of Natural History*, No. 2. Denver.

Comment: Further Observations on Our Knowledge of Southwest Indian Civilization

BY FRANK H. H. ROBERTS, JR.
Smithsonian Institution,
Washington, D. C.

DR. CAMPBELL CHOSE WISELY when he restricted the area which he discussed, because there are so many different Indian peoples and cultures throughout the western United States that it would be virtually impossible to do more than make brief comments about each in the length of time devoted to this entire session. Because of the early Spanish relationships in California, many would no doubt have been interested in some consideration of that portion of the country. However, the situation there is such that it would require the time allotted to several papers to summarize the basic information about the tribes located there and the people who preceded them.

I was interested in hearing Dr. Campbell arrange his material and carry on his discussion in accordance with the framework proposed by Drs. Willey and Phillips in their recent volume on *Method and Theory in American Archeology.* This is the first time that I have been present when a paper pertaining to a specific area was prepared in accordance with their outline and I was somewhat doubtful that it could be done satisfactorily. Like many others, I personally don't agree with some of the suggestions and conclusions made by Willey and Phillips, but it seems to me that Dr. Campbell has handled the situation very well. The review and summary of existing knowledge concerning the archeology of the Southwest presents in good form the story as we now know it. His treatment of the several different early hunting complexes presents the case fairly. He did not suggest it but it seems quite apparent to me that the Llano and Folsom cultures are closely related. As a matter of fact, I think it well justified to derive the Folsom from the Llano. The projectile-point types and other implement types are quite similar and I am of the opinion that the smaller, more finely chipped Folsom point simply represents a refinement of the preceding Clovis point of the Llano and records the shift from hunting the large mammoth and mastodon to the hunting of the smaller bison. The large heavy Clovis points of the Llano Period perhaps were not as satisfactory for smaller game, and as a consequence the more efficient Folsom form became the fashion. Deriving Folsom from Llano would strengthen Dr. Campbell's statement about a possible cultural continuum over a long period of time in the Southwest.

Interesting new light on the Folsom-Sandia situation has recently been obtained from sites near Lucy, New Mexico, where archeologists have found a number of projectile points which have the general Sandia characteristics but which in addition also have facial fluting quite suggestive of that on the Clovis and Folsom points. There again, it would appear, is evidence for certain continuity in the ancient hunting complex in the New Mexico area.

Dr. Campbell has clearly pointed out some of the complexities and rather disconcerting problems pertaining to the Archaic culture scattered across the Southwest. In some cases the remains undoubtedly are of similar age, while in others there is considerable discrepancy. As a matter of fact, if one were to consider only such objects as would be found in an archeological site, it is quite possible that some of the very late Indian tribes in the area would be classified as Archaic. Such a situation has been somewhat confusing to the archeologists and it certainly must be more than confusing to historians and others less familiar with the material. There is no doubt, as Dr. Campbell mentioned, that further work will produce a much better understanding of what actually took place among the Archaic peoples.

The Formative Stage in the Southwest is also quite complex, but the various ramifications with respect to relationships between the Anasazi, Mogollon, Hohokam, and Patayan are becoming much clearer, and I believe that it will not be very long before a well-rounded story can be told about that stage of development in the Southwest.

In connection with the mention of trade relations with the Meso-american area, I was particularly interested by Dr. Campbell's mention of contacts between Chalchihuites and the Hohokam. When I was studying the ceramic material from the Chaco Canyon area in New Mexico I examined the large collection of pottery and potsherds obtained from Pueblo Bonito by the late George H. Pepper, which are now in the American Museum of Natural History in New York City. Those of you who are familiar with the Pepper report on Pueblo Bonito probably recall the various pieces of stone which bear encaustic decorations and which undoubtedly represent trade with the Mexico area to the south. In addition there were a number of potsherds which Pepper did not describe and about which there is now considerable mystery. The late Dr. Tozzer of Harvard University mentioned the particular sherds to me and on one of my visits to the American Museum in 1925 I was shown the fragments and given an opportunity to examine them carefully. As a matter of fact, Mr. Neil M. Judd, Director of the National Geographic Society Pueblo Bonito Expeditions, and I carried them down to the Mexican hall, where pottery from various areas was on exhibit. After studying each lot carefully we were thoroughly convinced that the sherds from Pueblo Bonito were Chalchihuites. I later mentioned our conclusion to Dr. Tozzer, who agreed that they certainly must be. Somehow or other in intervening years that particular lot of sherds was misplaced or lost at the American Museum and others wishing to examine them have not been able to do so. It is one of those embarrassing situations which occasionally develop in archeology. Several other people did see them and there is no question that at one time they were in the collection. Assuming that they were found under the same conditions as the stones, it would appear that they had reached Pueblo Bonito well in the Classic Period shortly after A.D. 1100. There was other evidence of course of trade relations with the Mexican area in the Macaw skeletons and copper bells found in Pueblo Bonito.

In view of the time available for his paper it is obvious that Dr. Campbell could not go into all of the Indian history of the area, but it would have been extremely interesting had it been possible for him to discuss briefly the late pre-Spanish groups of hunting Indians who presumably drifted into the region only a century or two before the first Spanish explorers reached Arizona and New Mexico and parts of Texas. That chapter in the aboriginal story has not been worked out as well as some of the others, but it does present some intriguing problems. It probably would be of particular interest to historians, who for the most part are concerned with more recent developments than those pertaining to the archeological complexes which have received and continue to receive most of the attention of the anthropologists working in the Southwest.

Part Two

THE MEDIEVAL IBERIAN FRONTIER

The Frontier and Castilian Liberties . . .
. . . . . Claudio Sánchez-Albornoz

The Castilian as Plainsman . Charles Julian Bishko

Comment: The Spanish Frontier and Medieval France
. . . . Philippe Wolff

The two papers and the comment presented here are concerned with the Spanish Medieval Frontier, of all the frontiers of Medieval Europe the one which most resembles those later developed in the New World. The first paper, by Don Claudio Sánchez-Albornoz, Spain's leading medieval historian, describes with his usual lucidity the effect which Castile's frontier had upon its history and development, and especially upon the freedom which the Castilians enjoyed in the High Middle Ages. The second, by Professor Bishko, gives us a picture of a little-known aspect of Medieval Spain, the cattle frontier which developed in Andalusia and nearby regions, where most of the elements which we later find in the cattle kingdoms of Argentina, Uruguay, Mexico, and the American West had already developed by the thirteenth century. Professor Wolff's trenchant comments help round out the picture by adding thoughts concerning the role which France played in serving as a back country to this Spanish frontier. Particularly notable in this section is the political role which Don Claudio Sánchez-Albornoz assigns to Castile's frontier, one that should delight those who still accept Turner's views concerning the significance of the frontier in American history.

The Frontier and Castilian Liberties

BY CLAUDIO SÁNCHEZ-ALBORNOZ
Universidad de Buenos Aires

THE HISTORY OF no other European peoples, including those of the Iberian Peninsula, has been so decisively modified by a frontier as that of Castile. The wide-open frontier of this region exercised an important influence century after century, as long as it continued to exist. The very birth of Castile as a historical entity was a result of frontier war. Whatever may have been the germinal force which, following the fall of the Roman Empire and the Kingdom of the Goths, brought together the explosive mixture of Cantabrians, Basques, Goths, and Celti-berians in the original Castilian homeland, Castile would not have taken form without the century-long (791–907) hammering of un-interrupted attacks, first on the part of the armies of Córdoba and later from the Banu-Kasi renegades of the Ebro Valley.

The dreadful blows which fell upon those lands of Castile and Alava constituting the eastern marches of the Kingdom of Oviedo— I have explained the causes more than once, most recently in my *España, un enigma histórico*—brought Castile forth upon the his-torical scene. The mountain Kingdom of Asturias was entirely pro-tected by its cordillera, by the desert which extended from its moun-tains as far as the Duero watershed, and by the valley of the Duero, itself a veritable fosse. Only Castile lay open south of the Cantabrian cordillera, exposed to attack from the valley of the Ebro. Since the juxtaposition of Castilians and Basques in an area not very distant from one of the few routes connecting France and Spain was a never failing source of anxiety among the Mussulmans, they un-ceasingly attacked the perennial allies, Alava and Castile.

The result of these struggles is documented in my study, *Alfonso*

III y el particularismo castellano. Because these lands drained by the upper Ebro and its affluents were on the frontier for more than a hundred years—a frontier characterized by the harsh will to resist and the iron will to fight of an entire people—the inhabitants acquired their unique national dynamic and a consciousness of their own strength which eventually provoked unrest and then secession.

The southern border of the County of Castile was the most hard-hit zone of the Kingdom of León during the following century; it was very near to Medinaceli, the military capital of the Caliphate in central Spain, while the Duero could be crossed more easily in Castile then further downstream. The Grand County of Fernán González and his successors took root as an autonomous entity and as a unique social phenomenon within the community of North Spanish Christian Powers.

The rise of Castile which followed during the twelfth century when, having been constituted an independent kingdom upon the death of Alfonso VII in 1157, it took from León the political primacy of Spanish Christendom, is also largely due to the continued existence of a long frontier with Moorish Spain, a frontier which extended from Placencia to the Aragonese border. After successive invasions from Africa by the Almorávides and the Almohades, this fiercely contested frontier was defended by Castile through the organization of a great military force, which gave rise to unprecedented social and political innovations.

The great advance of the frontier after the Battle of Las Navas (1212)—Castilian dominion was extended as far as the Tagus and the foothills of Granada—definitely joined Castile and León and brought about the political, social, and economic transformation of this united kingdom, making possible the decisive achievement of spiritual identity and converting Castile and León into the axis of the Hispanic world and a power on the European international scene.

Even the crisis of Castile in the late Middle Ages is due principally to the interruption of the southward advance for almost two centuries; to the disappearance, following the rout of the Benimerines at the Battle of Salado (1340), of the series of African threats which had menaced Castile from outside its boundaries since 1086; and to the stagnation of the frontier in Granada, although there was, of course, no end to the endemic war of surprise attacks, sieges, sackings, captivities, duels, and combats. Thus ceased the stimulus which great dangers, great battles, and great frontier advances had provided throughout the history of Castile from its earliest origins as a primitive county. Nevertheless, Castile could not dispense with the century-long armed watch along the Granada frontier, as had Aragón and Portugal. Castile could not redirect that warlike dynamism to which the struggle against the Spanish and African Moslem had given birth. Therefore this military energy, which had formerly been employed in great offensive and defensive actions along the uncertain and always changing frontier, was poured into fiendish and prolonged civil wars.

The Moorish frontier not only gave rise to the Kingdom of Castile, made it grow, and provoked its great crisis. The psychic and vital impact of the dramatic ups and downs of the frontier struggles upon the culture of Castile and León and the uniqueness of the social, economic, and political arrangements occasioned by the problems of defense and colonization of the zones reconquered from the Moors, these were the directing forces of Spanish history.

The centuries-long frontier struggle between Christians and Moslems, from the Battle of Covadonga to the fall of Granada, changed the very face of Castile. The Reconquest occasioned the wanton destruction of wooded lands by fire and by the construction of stockades; not only to desolate the environs of a besieged city, but also to avoid surprise attacks in the forests which had to be crossed in the advance and to assure the defense of a newly conquered stronghold by making it impossible for the enemy to hide himself in the undergrowth of nearby hills; or merely for vengeance against the Moors, who were no less effective in the deforestation of Christian lands. How many Spanish plains and mountains— heavily forested when discovered by the Greek and Roman geographers—are nowadays barren thanks to eight centuries of destructive border war. I am sure a most revealing book could be written by a zealous scholar who set about investigating exhaustively the question of the changes which occurred in the landscape of central Spain, and perhaps throughout all of Spain, during the Reconquest.

It is also certain that another zealous scholar might write another great book concerning the changes undergone by the urban centers on the peninsula as a result of those centuries of shocks and battles. Innumerable are the centers of population which suffered ruin and decay, and those which were founded or revived with the advance of the frontier: the disappearance of the former was caused by the destruction of war or loss of strategic value; the growth of the latter by their favorable defensive position. I will cite only two examples: of the great cities which fell from their former stature, Mérida; and of the villages which were metamorphosed into city-fortresses, Madrid.

But eight centuries of frontier war undoubtedly had even more decisive influence in the creation of Hispanic cultural values. It was not only necessary to resist the barbarous attacks which, year after year, decade after decade, century after century, fell upon León and Castile from south of the frontier. It was also inevitable that some organization be created for the defense and repopulation of the frontier lands liberated by the southward expansion of the dominions of Castile. This twofold enterprise contributed through the centuries to the formation of a psychology, a style of life, a characteristic temperament, a cosmology, a set of collective tastes and illusions, of values and aversions, a religious sensibility, a conception of morality, literary and artistic forms, a social organization, a political structure, economic organization, an equilibrium among power, wealth, and labor, a confrontation of man with man, a unique view of the past and the future, and a way of observing events beyond the frontier with a mixture of xenophobic pride and discipular admiration—all quite different from the characteristics of the other peoples of Western Europe.

Inasmuch as I believe that these differences are the key to the history of Spain, I have devoted two stout volumes to the study along the general lines of these influences of the struggles and problems of the frontier on the enigmatic past of my Spanish fatherland. It seems beside the point to recapitulate at the present time what I have already put down there in fifteen hundred pages which may be read by anyone who interests himself in the subject. Therefore I will limit myself today to the study of but one of the consequences of the great frontier duel of Medieval Spain, which made the Castilians the most free of European peoples of that day.

I believe that after my exhaustive proof of the extreme depopulation of the valley of the Duero there remains no doubt about it. We have the facts and we understand how it came about. It is documented by Christian and Islamic texts which go back to the ninth and tenth centuries. It is confirmed by the silence which envelops the archeological and linguistic past of that region, making it impossible for us to know its history under Rome and the Visigoths; the evident hiatus which in that area separates the ecclesiastic and urban life of the period before the Islamic invasion from that which followed the Reconquest and colonization; the peculiar characteristics of the toponymy of that region, which betray the renovation and comparative modernity of its centers of rural habitation; the singularities of the speech and economic and institutional life of the district and the quantity of information we possess concerning the repopulation of this zone. Once again I must refer to my *España, un enigma histórico,* where I have documented the proofs here adduced.

This demographic phenomenon was to have transcendental historical consequences for the social structure of the Kingdom of Castile and León. It was necessary to bring back to life an immense wilderness which was at that time the area most threatened by the Islamic armies. We know how this colonization was achieved. The king would send a prince, a magnate or a prelate to the region he wished to have repopulated. The royal delegate, who had received his lands *ad populandum,* would restore and fortify the ruined cities, would raise new castles, would found villages, fix the boundaries of rural holdings—farms or ranches—and would divide these among those who presented themselves for settlement. In other cases the sovereign would donate to a private citizen or a religious institution a more or less extensive terrain and would authorize the reception of settlers there, provided these did not come from within his own royal demesnes, and sometimes even without this restriction. Upon occasion the prince himself, or a representative of his authority, encouraged small groups of colonists to settle, and gave them title to the lands they had occupied, or ceded these lands to them by means of a sort of collective agrarian contract which, by reason of its perpetuity and other features, resembled entailment. Often the sovereign authorized either by edict or by general decree the occupation of the unsettled lands of a bishopric or other territory, or confirmed *a posteriori* property rights in lands individually or collectively reoccupied by squatters. I have published and collected many texts which prove these assertions and I am to study this theme at length in writing the history of the institutions and the life of the Kingdom of Asturia and León in the History of Spain under the general editorship of Menéndez Pidal. For the time being I will merely allude to the charters which inform us about the colonization of the environs of Astorga and Chaves, by Gatón and Odavio, and to the decrees of Alfonso III (866–910) concerning the resettlement of the diocese of Lugo and the Alfoz of León.

For approximately two centuries the reshuffling of the population was intense and continuous. From the old centers of the Kingdom in its maritime and mountain provinces great bands of colonists emigrated to the so-called *terra de foris,* the valley of the Duero. In this colonization of the wilderness the nobility could hardly have played a smaller role. In the northern homeland beyond the mountains there had never existed extensive latifundia; the primitive style of life had not permitted it in the beginning and it was not favored by the geography of the region. Then too, in Asturia, Cantabria, and the Basque country (if not in Galicia), there were lacking the great masses of servile population suitable for resettlement in the south under the control of a powerful lordly caste. Yet even if there may have been in Galicia powerful noblemen who had at their disposition many freedmen, tributaries, and serfs, it is doubtful whether they would have encouraged their dependents to migrate to the south, where they would run the great risks which threatened the frontier zone. On the contrary. The princes, magnates, and prelates were not accompanied on these great colonial undertakings by masses of villains or serfs. The nuclei of resettlement were groups of audacious men free in the lands they left behind. They were men connected by bonds of kinship, allegiance, friendship, or proximity to the chieftains of the resettlement. Or else folk who had no such relationship, who migrated to the frontier attracted by hopes or illusions of prosperity and good fortune, or who had fled northward from Islam to live as free men among men of their own race and faith. I do not know of a single documented case of colonization involving a large group subject to the power and patrimonial dominion of a magnate or prelate; on the other hand, I know of many groups who came together to form a settlement under the leadership of a royal delegate—groups of common folk from the north such as those described above. Astorga was populated by the village of Bierzo under the leadership of Count Gatón, and the Alfoz of Salamanca by citizens of León under Bishop Gonzalo. The necessary proofs exist in abundance of the migration, especially to the region of León, of large groups of Mozárabes, free men, of course. As an example we need only recall the case of the Toledan burghers who went north to found Zamora or the Cordoban weavers of silks and tapestries—*tiraceros*—who settled in León.

Nor can we conceive of vassals or serfs transplanted by their liege lords to the frontier zones in the initial nuclei of the rural communities located on royal lands or on the lands ceded by the king to church or magnate. Our doubts on this score are reinforced by the fact that the legal codes of the era deny admission of known serfs or villains to the new settlements, and also by the prohibition, in royal documents, of migration from royal lands to demesnes of church and nobility. The toponymy itself testifies to the frequent presence in the colonized areas of villages populated by groups who migrated together from the neighborhood of their common origin— I have reference to Galicians, Toledans, Asturians, Basques, and so on, who named not a few of the *villas* of León and Castile. And our doubts are confirmed by the liberties which we later find the inhabitants of these little towns in the resettled areas enjoying, those located on private lands as well as those on lands pertaining to the king. Not only the new proprietors, but even those who held their lands in entail—and here I am using the names of these legal fictions to signify situations and personal rights which approximate rather than coincide with the precise legal meaning of these terms—all enjoyed the status of free men. For in truth only those were accepted who by their social condition did possess freedom of movement—it was the common possession of the proprietors who had the right to select their own chief and of those who held their lands in entail: the *iuniores* of the Leonese fiefs, the peasants of Castile, and, with them, whosoever had won this liberty *de facto* in the course of his hazardous migration to the frontier—the so-called *advenientes* and *escotos* mentioned in the Laws of Castrojériz (984).

Still less could we suppose that men subjected to the condition of serfs or villains—by "villains" I mean Leonese or Galician *iuniores* dependent upon some lord as well as Castilian and Basque vassals—would play the part of the squatters who worked and planted at their own risk lands formerly uncultivated and without master, nor could we expect them to occupy without title the deserted lands, trusting in the royal decrees encouraging the increase of population in the frontier area and in the express or tacit confirmation *a posteriori* of the king or perhaps in some general and traditional right. I make all these distinctions because the diplomas of Asturia and León countenance all this casuistry, as I will show in a moment.

On the contrary, I am sure that the resettlement of the frontier wilderness of the Duero was not realized by masses dependent upon the dominating power of the king or of the lay or ecclesiastic lords; and I have been careful always to refer to masses of serfs and villains, because it is obvious that, as an exception to the general rule, individual vassals or serfs could have accompanied their masters—princes, nobles, and prelates who had received lands *ad populandum;* or the kings or private citizens could have employed some of their *pueri* or *iuniores* in carrying out material arrangements connected with taking possession or in the rough work of bringing the land under cultivation.

But if the initial movements of the resettlement implied the displacement of masses of population free of the harsh yoke of servitude or vassalage, the enterprise of repopulation accented the liberty of the colonists, of those who settled in the lands of the lay and ecclesiastic powers as well as of those who established themselves in the royal demesnes. As I have said before, a whirlwind of liberty shook the frontier of the *terra de foris,* that is, the valley of the Duero. No one dared place restrictions on the liberty of the new settlers, neither prince, nor those charged by the princes with the rehabilitation of some frontier area, nor the *comites* or *potestates* who in the name of the king subsequently ruled the nine ages of man, nor the private citizens—counts, princelings, prelates or abbots—who had been favored by the king with the gift of wild and almost deserted lands. Far from placing limits on this freedom, they were forced to bow to it. We can affirm this because we know that all the colonists who possessed liberty by birth or emancipation were careful to preserve it, while it was acquired by those who, after abandoning their old homes, came as *de facto* free men to the royal or private domains then being settled. The assurance that they would maintain their legal status while improving their fortune on the frontier and the hope that they would acquire liberty for themselves and their dependents upon moving to the newly colonized lands channeled into the valley of the Duero the masses who came to settle there.

The charters of the period confirm these conclusions in various ways. They betray the existence, in the region, of an enormous mass of small free proprietors, sometimes grouped together in tiny but free rural communities. And they bear unanimous witness to the freedom of movement of those who had settled on royal or noble property without having been forced to accept the status of serf or villain.

Documents contained in the churches and monasteries which were then rising in the valley of the Duero testify to the abundance there of small free proprietors. The freeholders appear in hundreds of charters of the ninth, tenth, and eleventh centuries, selling, yielding or exchanging land holdings of insignificant size and value. One document will concern a certain holding of seven, four, or even three *cuartillas* of arable land.[1] Another treats of a vineyard, an orchard, a piece of land, a flax field, or a quantity of fodder which is to be exchanged for a couple of shillings or a few measures of wheat. Another tells of a part of a flax field, of a vineyard, of a pasture, or of an orchard which is to be sold for a few bushels of wheat or a few pecks of rye. The records fill the parish archives of Cardeña and Sahagún and the town of León, to cite only the richest repositories among the old monasteries of Castile and León, and the cathedral and monastery archives through the kingdom.

In many documents we also find references to villages which are entirely free. Such must have been the towns which in the environs of León were dedicated to various industrial specialties and to supplying the markets of León; I have reference to the villages named Torneros, Olleros, Roderos, Macellarios, Grulleros—villages whose existence I proved more than three decades ago in my *Estampas de la vida en León hace mil años*. Free were the towns which appear making contracts, disputing with and entering legal causes against magnates and religious institutions; and also those which we discover in the possession of communal grazing lands, salt beds, mills, and community fields; those we find selling or donating these communal lands, salt beds, or mills or holding pasture in common with villages or with some monastery; and those which have achieved the privilege of immunity, thus converting themselves into future councils in embryo.

I have listed the names of many of these free Castilian towns in my *España, un enigma histórico*. I must add a few more to those already listed and not a few of these in the Province of León. And as I have said many times, most recently in the work just mentioned, the number of free towns in Castile at the beginning of the colonization of this area must have been so great that, in the fourteenth century, five hundred years after the beginnings of the Reconquest, in the census which Peter the Cruel had made in 1359 and which we know by the name of the *Becerro de las behetrías,* there still remained within the jurisdiction of Castile—leaving Rioja and Bureba out of the count—an enormous number of free men and free towns. Out of 1,359 villages, 659 were free villages, or villages inhabited by free men, possessing the privilege, rare in the Europe of that epoch, to choose their own patron and to change their leader. We possess early evidence that, not long after they settled in the *terra de foris,* the free colonists began to feel the all-absorbing influence of lay and ecclesiastic lords. If, after a five-century struggle with these insatiable parasites, there yet remained in Castile so large a number of villagers and towns which had preserved their liberty in face of the difficulties of the times, can we not affirm without a doubt that the Castilians of the times of the first resettlement were in large part small freeholders?

The *Becerro de las behetrías* itself tells us much more: it lists many villages and very, very many men who worked on the royal properties, and at times, to judge by the rights and tributes which they paid as individuals or as part of a municipal population, we can catch another intimation of their original status as free proprietors. And these masses, in giving allegiance to the *hombres de behetría,* who themselves were mostly descended from freeholders, help to confirm the erstwhile liberty and the former status of proprietors of many of the first colonists of the wilderness frontier.

And beyond this, it seems certain that the great majority of all the colonists were free men, including those who did not achieve proprietorship. This is evident, as I have said, from the freedom of movement and other civil rights enjoyed even by those who did not work their own land. It seems to me that the difference between the settlers who possessed proprietary rights to their lands and those who were mere villains of the king, the church, or the nobles can be more adequately traced not to the various types of settlement which were carried on simultaneously during the Reconquest, but rather to the different stages of the resettlement during which a participant might arrive. I see no reason to suppose that when Count Gatón moved with the people of Bierzo to resettle Astorga, or when any other royal delegate marched off with his followers, leaving the Asturian homeland in order to rehabilitate some zone of the valley of the Duero, he would make distinctions in settling his people on the land he was bringing back to life and would give to some proprietary rights while others received their lands in entail. This differentiation came later: it was because the king, or whoever governed in his name the lands reoccupied many a year before, would with the passage of time establish there some new group of colonists in accordance with a less liberal system, making them mere cultivators and not owners of the soil. For the prince in his own demesnes—which must not be confused with the royal dominion—or the nobility or the church in theirs, were slow to welcome these Johnny-come-lately colonists—those who had had no part in the first stages of resettlement—and so these late comers had to resign themselves to tilling lands in which they had no property rights. In these colonists of the rear guard I see the ancestors of the future vassals of king and abbot, the entailees of León and the peasants of Castile.

Nevertheless, full civil rights and full liberty of movement were possessed by all these rear-guard colonists, all these whom we have called "entailees"—not, of course, in the strict sense of the word. This is borne out by Leonese documents dating from before and after the promulgation of the Laws of León (1020) and Castilian documents of the tenth and eleventh centuries. It is confirmed by royal and noble patents of resettlement in both kingdoms, dating from the tenth to the thirteenth centuries, and by the legal codes of the Kingdom of Castile and León, beginning with the Fuero Real. The oldest texts recognize the possession of these rights by those whom we have supposed the descendants of the colonists who formed the rear guard in the resettlement of the valley of the Duero, and the more recent texts either maintain these rights or extend them. I will some day study this phenomenon in more detail.

In my *España, un enigma histórico* I demonstrated also that the southern zone of the valley of the Duero, the area between the river and the Cordillera Central, also underwent extreme depopulation, although a few centers of rural population carried on without interruption in the mountain valleys to the south and in isolated settlements on the plain. The time came when it was necessary to rehabilitate this newly reconquered southern land, which was given the name of *Extrema Durii,* a name which was eventually converted into a regional place name, and with the passage of time was ap-

plied to the southern frontier of the Kingdom of León, the Extremadura of modern Spain, the province which gave birth to the great
Conquistadors.

The resettlement south of the Duero got off to an early start. By
the tenth century a few advanced colonies had already been founded
within lands tributary to Salamanca and Sepúlveda. But these
colonies could not survive and the resettlement of this part of the
Duero Valley was interrupted for many decades. Colonization in
this area was revived with the decay of the power of the Caliphate,
but it was not carried out intensively until the capture of Toledo
in 1085. With the invasion of the Almorávides most of the lands
which had been reconquered to the south of the Cordillera Central
were lost again, with the exception of Toledo and the strongholds
which served to protect communication between Toledo and the
Duero Valley. The *Extrema Durii* were, therefore, on the frontier—
except during the Almorávid crisis—until the Battle of Las Navas
(1212).

During this period of more than a century the resettlement of
this frontier zone was carried out. This resettlement also helped to
contribute to the number of free men in the Christian kingdoms
descended from the Kingdom of Asturia and León and helped to
confirm these free men in the possession of their rights.

The colonization of the *Extrema Durii* differs in certain respects
from that of the lands resettled during the ninth and tenth centuries.
During this earlier period the colonization had been carried out
slowly, because the advances had been made step by step; and also
because in the homeland there were no centers of urban population.
The conquest of Toledo, however, occasioned the sudden advance
of the frontier from the watershed of the Duero to the valley of
the Tagus. And by the time this advance of the frontier took place,
a new civil institution had been invented: the town council.

In my book *Ruina y extinción del municipio romano en España*
I proved, and today no one contests my thesis, that the municipal
life implanted on the peninsula by Rome was extinguished during
the seventh century. In my *España, un enigma histórico*, I pointed
out how the first embryos of the Castilian town councils began to
appear before the year 1000 and I listed many which were organized in Castile before 1085. Some day I will make a listing of those
which during the eighty-five intervening years were founded in
León.

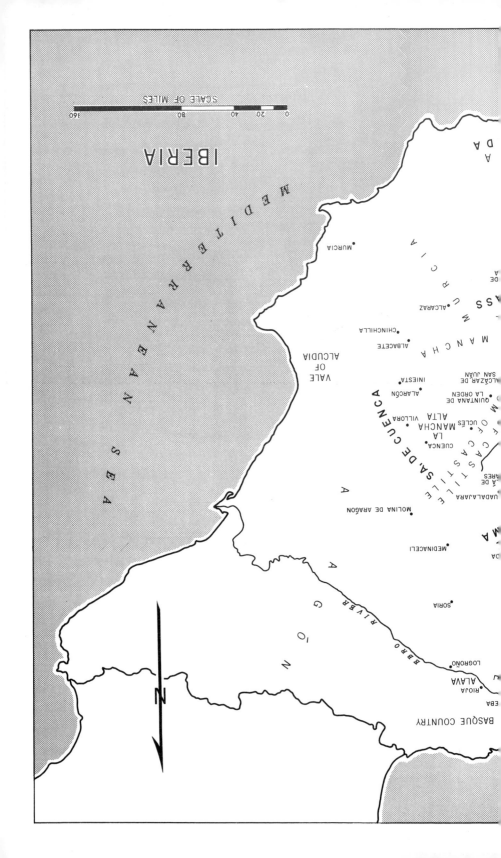

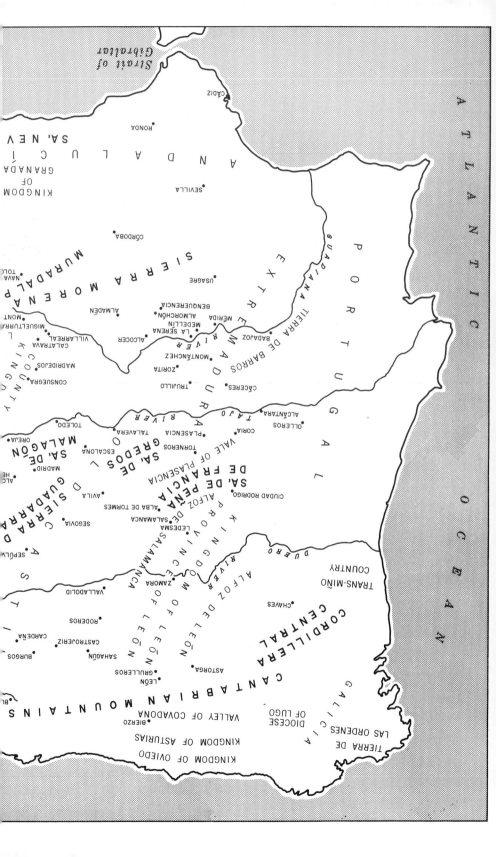

When Toledo was won and the repopulation of the original Extremadura and the recently occupied stretch of the Tagus Valley
was initiated, the municipality won for itself an important place
among the political machinery of the Kingdom of Castile and León.
The municipality had great possibilities for the revival of the enormous frontier zone which so urgently needed to be resettled. It was
necessary to create there fortified urban nuclei on those sites which
possessed strategic importance and were easily defensible. It was
necessary to guarantee to these urban centers the requisite supplies
and foodstuffs. This new legal fiction made it possible to grant these
urban nuclei relative autonomy and to confirm their inhabitants in
the possession of their goods and their liberties. By yielding to the
inhabitants the privilege of a municipal council, which enabled them
to control their own affairs in large measure, and by assuring them
a favorable legal and economic status, it was possible to attract
settlers to the strategic sites, to establish on these sites fortified cities,
and to increase the sense of responsibility and self-sufficiency of the
inhabitants, who thereby contributed the more effectively to the
defense and reoccupation of the frontier area.

So it is no surprise that a chain of municipal councils should have
sprung up from the Aragonese border to the very shores of the
Atlantic in Portugal, along both sides of the Cordillera Central,
which constitutes the spinal cord of Spain to this day. The ampli-
tude of public lands, the kind of municipal organization, and the
political power of these municipalities are without parallel. Many
of them were actually strong and extensive city-states which had a
decisive influence upon the life of Castile. We need not concern
ourselves with this influence here. It will suffice to point out the
effectiveness of their popular militias in the frontier struggles against
the Almorávides and the Almohades and the role these city-states
played in bringing Ferdinand III to the throne—the king who
pushed the frontier to the foothills of Granada. Among these councils that of my own Avila was outstanding. The Almohade Sultan
Abu Yacub had to mobilize an entire army and stage an ambush
in order to vanquish the *mesnadas* of Avila; and he was so proud
of his triumph over them that he sent a letter announcing his victory throughout the Afro-Hispanic Empire and had it celebrated in
a great poetic joust in Seville. And in the political turmoil at the
beginning of the reign of Ferdinand the Holy, the militia of Avila,
in league with that of Seville, routed the powerful magnate Don

Alvaro Núñez de Lara, theretofore regent of the kingdom, and took him prisoner.

A priori, we would suppose that those who lived under these town councils which could muster a cavalry and infantry capable of deciding the course of Castilian affairs were free men and masters of their own destiny. We have documents which prove this to have been the case. The municipal *fueros* of the twelfth century which regulated the life of some of these municipalities—Sepúlveda, Avila, Guadalajara, Madrid, Escalona—and those which later governed Soria, Alcalá, Zorita, Cuenca, Alba, and Salamanca give evidence that the small as well as the great towns of the region between the Duero and the Tagus were inhabited by men enjoying complete individual liberty.

Distinctions were made among the citizens of these communes: on the basis of their localization within the urban center or in the villages which gradually grew up in the surrounding countryside, on the basis of their status as cavalrymen or footsoldiers in the struggle against the Moors, on the basis of contractual relationships which bound the less prosperous to work the lands and tend the herds of those who had made their fortune, or on the basis of occupation in the case of some exceptional artisans who dedicated themselves to various industrial or mercantile tasks rather than the traditional pursuits of farmer and herdsman. The upper class in the cities managed to win certain financial privileges—and thus arose the gentleman burgher. But all enjoyed the same legal status. The population was not divided into classes of free men, serfs, and villains. In fact, even the minorities which lived under these town councils were not deprived of their liberty, if we except the presence of an extremely small number of Moorish slaves. Even the *hidalgos* who lived within the territory governed by a municipal council did not enjoy a superior position before the law.

In this rehabilitated zone between the Duero and the Tagus we know of no lay or ecclesiastic demesnes until long after the reoccupation of Toledo. Even the institution of the *behetría*—an area dependent in perpetuity upon the magnates as a class—apparently did not take root here. The integration of the rural workers into the municipal organization and the protection which they received from this source assured them of their safety and freed them from the necessity of availing themselves of the sponsorship of some nobleman.

This new frontier was swept by the winds of liberty even more strongly than the *terra de foris* during the Reconquest and resettlement of that wilderness on the upper Duero. The impulse which created the town councils of the region between the Duero and the Tagus was felt in those lands colonized during the ninth and tenth centuries and even in the mountain and maritime fringe of Cantabria, from Galicia to the Basque country. It echoed southward to the Moorish province of Al-Andalus, with its population of Mozárabes and Jews, both groups then suffering from the persecution of their African masters. Once again men from the north and from the south left their homes to settle on the frontier. Once again they were attracted by the hope of a rapid increase in prosperity and the desire to live as free men among co-religionists of their own race. This time their number was considerably augmented by the Jews who fled the fanaticism of the Almorávides and the Almohades.

The kings welcomed those Jews and Mozárabes who settled in the recently colonized zone and they tried to attract northern Christians to settle in the most dangerous areas. In order to encourage them to run the risks which were involved in the struggle against the Moors—whenever a stronghold fell the inhabitants were either liquidated or sold as slaves—the sovereigns did not stint special privileges and liberties. This is made perfectly clear by the provisions of the Fuero of Oreja, to which I have already referred several times. In this document, promulgated by Alfonso VII in 1139, the King even offers amnesty to those who have seduced women or otherwise incurred the royal displeasure if they will take up residence on the frontier; he relinquishes his right to tax the properties of those who settle in Oreja; he frees them from tolls and renounces his claim to the royal fifth of any booty taken from the Moors; in case internal struggle should arise he guarantees the life of each settler with a ransom of a thousand shillings and of their livestock at twice its real value.

Oreja was located on the Tagus frontier, facing Almorávide territory in a position of strategic importance for the defense of Toledo. It was natural that the Emperor would be liberal in his efforts to resettle it rapidly and effectively. The necessity for liberality had arisen many times since the beginnings of the Reconquest under the Kings of Oviedo. It continued to be necessary as the area policed by Castilian military power extended southward to the boundary of the Kingdom of Granada, to that province which sacramentally preserves its historic denomination: Frontera. The repetition of these circumstances must always have led to similar concessions.

The liberties which were gradually granted to those who settled in the frontier areas first made of Castile an island of free men in the midst of feudal Europe and later the kingdom of this feudalized Europe where municipalities played their most decisive role. In my *España, un enigma histórico* I presented a map of the municipal councils of Castile in 1188. Neither to the north nor to the south of the Pyrenees can any other nation show such a density of powerful free rural councils possessing such an important influence in the political equilibrium of the state. Nowhere else do we find such a network of municipalities under royal patronage, a network so dense that it hardly leaves room for the appearance of feudal holdings.

Not even in the allied Kingdom of León do we observe this phenomenal density. León had a much smaller frontier area propitious for the generation and proliferation of such municipal entities. It was held back by the dead weight of Galician feudalism. Even in the Leonese highlands feudal holdings were more in evidence than in the adjacent areas of Castile, as a natural result of the presence there, until 1157, of the political center of the realm, the royal seat at León.

Even so, the example of the liberties possessed by the Castilian councils and their influence on the political set-up of the monarchy forced the young King of León, Alfonso IX, during the disturbances which accompanied his accession to the throne, to grant to his subjects, in 1188, the Magna Carta guaranteeing their civil and public rights and their right to take part in the government of the state. These laws were promulgated twenty-five years before John Lackland was forced to sign the English Magna Carta in 1213. In my *España, un enigma histórico* I have compared the zeal which the English nobility displayed in the preservation of their privileges and rights and in limiting the authority of their sovereign with the popular movement in León, in 1188, "to guarantee peace and general justice against the attacks, violences, pride and injustice of the powerful, rather than against the king, although it also tried to guard against the royal power, extracting from the king the promise to respect the laws, not to listen to the wiley accusations of the grandees, not to consent to the decrease of his own income in favor of the clergy, and to govern the kingdom in accordance with the wishes of the three estates from which it was constituted."

We can explain the authorization of these Leonese laws—and we cannot study them here in greater detail—only as the result of the awareness of king and court of the strength of the free municipalities which had arisen under royal patronage in the lands which had been or were then on the frontier. This same awareness had moved Alfonso VIII of Castile, not long before, to ask many of the municipal councils of his kingdom to approve the marriage of his daughter Berenguela to Prince Conrad of Germany. I doubt that any other kingdom of feudal western Europe could have produced in 1188 two similar instances of popular political intervention.

As an essential feature of Castilian life the frontier had a powerful influence on the Castilian mentality of the first half of the thirteenth century. It suggested strange metaphors to the pious poet who sang the virtues of Mary and the saints in Rioja, far to the north of the frontier then being pushed southward from the Tagus to the mountains of Granada. In praising the excellences of Saint Dominic, Berceo wrote: "Bien sabía al diablo tenerle la frontera." [2] And when Beelzebub has him say to the holy man: "Aun agora quieres far otro poblamiento: Bien me ten por babieca si yo te lo consiento." [3]

The social projections of the frontier struggles and the resettlement of the frontier did not cease with the reconquest and the rehabilitation of the lands between the Duero and the Tagus. The battles and the process of colonization continued. But from here on the phenomenon of mass liberation no longer took place, because there were no large servile groups left in the kingdom; yet these further conquests, by confirming less numerous bands of colonists in the possession of freedom and relative prosperity, helped to assure the institutionalization of personal liberty.

Between the victory of Las Navas at Tolosa (1212) and the conquest of Seville (1248) the southern boundary of the kingdom advanced from the shores of the Tagus to the mountain bulwark of Granada; just a few years later Alfonso X pushed it forward to Cádiz. As in the case of the advances which had taken place within the province of Castile, these were accompanied by a considerable displacement of population. La Mancha and Extremadura were almost depopulated, and almost all of the Andalusian cities were evacuated before the oncoming Castilian forces. The Moors who had remained in the country rebelled against Alfonso the Wise, who obliged most of them to emigrate. After this fabulous expansion of

Castilian dominions to the south, doubling the territory of the monarchy in less than fifty years, it became necessary once again to colonize the depopulated lands of the new frontier, for the islands of Islamic population which remained in both zones were small indeed.

Here in these regions newly gained from the Moor there arose new and powerful town councils under the royal patronage. To name these centers of resettlement is to name the great urban nuclei of the Extremadura, Murcia, Andalucía and La Mancha of our own day. But in this reconquered area, from Toledo to the shores of the Atlantic and the Mediterranean, the municipalities were not permitted to monopolize the spoils of the process of resettlement. In the old homelands of Castile and León a powerful oligarchy had been growing up in the course of the eleventh, twelfth, and thirteenth centuries. The defense against the dreadful pressure of the Almohades and the conquest of Andalucía had made necessary the organization of the effective storm troops of the era, the Religious Orders of Knighthood, and the granting of special privileges to them. These two political powers took part in the division of the immense territories incorporated under the Castilian crown during this fifty-year period. Such was the size of the newly occupied zone that there was enough for all: for the oligarchy, for the military orders, and for the municipalities. Accordingly, in La Mancha, Extremadura, Andalucía, and Murcia, along with the many free municipalities under royal patronage, arose many estates belonging to magnate, clergy, or the masters of the Orders of Santiago, Calatrava, or Alcántara.

If, then, for these reasons the inhabitants of the municipalities directly dependent upon the monarch constitute but a part of the population which together formed the social fabric of these new lands, the weight of the municipal tradition of Castile and León, the necessity to attract settlers to this new frontier, and the ecological demands imposed by the geography of the area gave rise to a series of urban centers which, excepting a few entirely inhabited by Moors—and these could not survive unchanged—soon became the seats of town councils which, if they depended upon some member of the lay or clerical oligarchy or the master of one of the military orders, nevertheless preserved for their inhabitants full individual freedom, including rights of property and inheritance and many political liberties. The *fuero de señorío* of Usagre is typical of the documents which testify to the freedoms enjoyed by the inhabitants of even the dependent municipalities. Consequently, the third great advance of the frontier of Castile once again affirmed the freedom which had become the right of all Castilians, whether by birth or by conquest.

The stagnation of the frontier from the times of Alfonso X until the reign of Ferdinand and Isabella—only the fortifications of the Strait of Gibraltar and a few frontier strongholds were won during this period—interfered with the process of consolidating and perfecting Castilian personal and political liberties. I have studied the decay of liberty during this period in my *España, un enigma histórico*. Without a doubt one of the factors which contributed to the decline of liberty during this era was the long interruption of the alarms which, century after century, had reached the ears of the citizens of Castile and León from their southern frontier.

This silence and that interruption influenced the change of program which can be noted in the Castile of the late Middle Ages, the appearance of new historical processes, such as the fight against the Jews, which were to cast tragic shadows upon the history of modern Spain. But the great task of Reconquest, the defense and resettlement of the frontier, these had lasted too long and were too enduring not to cast their shadows also far beyond the chronological limits of the period of their greatest activity. One of these projections was the conquest and colonization of America; another, the literary formation of the Cervantine couple, Don Quixote and Sancho, the authentic incarnation of the lineage of Castile, crystallized during times of eruptive dynamism on the Castilian frontier.

"The people of Castile," I wrote in my *Raíces medievales del Quijote*, which has been published in my recent book *Españoles ante la historia*, "were for century after century a people with a frontier spirit. . . . For many a century all of Castile must have dreamed of the conquest, at the same time easy and difficult, of wealth by force of arms. . . . Sometimes the waiting lasted for decades, new lands were not won and the Moorish dogs could be seen upon the horizon. . . . But in the end fair winds would prevail and the great change of fortune, so long dreamed of and yearned for, would take place. . . . For this reason, and because for many centuries the Sanchos of Castile had been listening to opportunity knocking on their doors with a promise of riches and well-being through the magic of victory in war, the authentic

Sancho, neighbor of a rural hidalgo who had discovered his authentic ancestral ego as he lost his mind, allowed himself to be
seduced by the promises of Alonso Quijano and decided to set forth
with him in search of adventures."

"*Hamlet*," I wrote, "arose in the England of Elizabeth, tortured
by the necessity of choosing between Catholicism and the Reform;
Don Juan was born of the all-conquering Spain of the sixteenth century, overflowing with cosmic force, and *Faust* was engendered by
the philosophically intellectual Germany of the *Aufklärung;* Don
Quixote and Sancho were the sons of the frontier spirit of medieval
Castile, populated with heroic warlike fantasies and hallucinated by
sudden, half-fantastic hopes."

NOTES

1. A *cuartilla* is equivalent to approximately 1/3 acre.
2. "He knew well how to hold the frontier against the Devil."
3. "So even now you want to make another settlement: You must think me a
fool if you suppose I will let you."

The Castilian as Plainsman: The Medieval Ranching Frontier in La Mancha and Extremadura

BY CHARLES JULIAN BISHKO
University of Virginia

FEW GENERALIZATIONS in Spanish historical thought command readier assent than that which affirms the profound influence of the Reconquest on the making of Castile. Yet it is only in recent decades that scholars like Claudio Sánchez-Albornoz, J. M. Lacarra, Julio González, and others have established the thesis that those eight centuries of now slow, now rapid southward advance against the Moors were not merely an Iliad of military and political combat, but above everything else a medieval *repoblación*, or recolonization, of the Iberian Peninsula.[1] From this standpoint, the Reconquest appears as a frontier movement in the authentic American sense—the occupation and development of relatively empty territories on the margin of an expanding society.

Like all new historical interpretations, this frontier approach to medieval Iberian history raises many questions for investigation. Furthermore, it imposes the necessity of advancing beyond traditional lines of political, constitutional, and juridical research into the as yet little explored fields of medieval peninsular demography, ecology, anthropogeography, and agrarian history. At the same time it suggests the great utility of exploiting, on a comparative basis, the rich body of methods and interpretations evolved by frontier historiography in the study of other frontiers, medieval and modern, and not least that of the United States, where the subject of the frontier has been pursued more intensely, more heatedly, and surely more fruitfully, than anywhere else.[2]

It is in the light of such reflections as these that the frontier historian might reappraise what has always been one of the obscurest, least understood, and most hastily treated of all the major geographic and chronological subdivisions of the Castilian Reconquest. This is the great region of the southern tableland or *meseta* of inner Iberia, the rolling plains and flat steppelands between the valley of the Tajo and the Sierra Morena that constitute the historic provinces of La Mancha and Extremadura. Historians concerned with more typical elements of medieval European life—agriculture and land tenures, peasants and nobles, secular churchmen and monks, towns, middle classes, and urban economy—have tended to dismiss this curious part of Spain where all these things were either lacking or of secondary importance. But it is precisely here, under such conditions, that a fresh approach in terms of the frontier holds much promise.

From this point of view, the Guadiana River Basin can be seen as one of the most interesting stages in the long advance. Its problems and their solutions are significant not only for Spanish history but also for the pastoral-plains society which the Castilian eventually transplanted to Northern Mexico and Texas, the Orinocan Llanos, the Chilean Central Valley, and the limitless pampas of the Río de la Plata.

North American historians are familiar with the classic work of Walter Prescott Webb, *The Great Plains*, which so brilliantly traces the institutional and psychological adaptations made by American frontiersmen moving from the humid, forested, agricultural East into the level, timberless, semiarid spaces of the plains.[3] Medieval Castilian frontiersmen, on both the northern and southern halves of the *meseta*, as again in Andalusia, confronted parallel difficulties in establishing a new society in a dry plains environment of climatic extremes, insufficient water, limited cultivable soil, treelessness, and xerophytic brush vegetation; but in La Mancha and Extremadura these conditions were more widespread, more intense, more hostile to human occupation than anywhere else between the Cantabrians and the Sierra Nevadas. In addition, the land was virtually unpeopled—the desert of the Guadiana is a southern frontier counterpart to Sánchez-Albornoz' desert of the Duero—and under the shadow of Almorávid and Almohade military power, which halted or slowed the Reconquest here for a significant century and a half.

The Guadiana Basin, still today the least populated major region of Spain, is a land of long, parching summers and cold, snowless winters; of an inadequate and irregular rainfall (ranging from under sixteen inches in eastern La Mancha to thirty-two inches in favored parts of Extremadura), the effects of which are aggravated by a high evaporation rate and an extreme permeability of the soil; and of a drainage system of lakes and rivers which, like long stretches of the broad, shallow Guadiana itself, become in summer dry arroyos or mere trickles.[4] To a limited degree, the high watertable offsets the surface shortage, permitting the sinking of wells and the raising of ground water through the *noria,* the vertical waterwheel with pots fastened to its rim which is turned by animal power; such wells determined in large part the distribution of frontier settlements, but they never became the basis for more than a very limited *regadío* or irrigated farming system. Throughout the year the wind blows, raising in the dry season from the grey, bleak Manchegan steppes the dust-haze of the *calina;* but not until the end of the Middle Ages, with the expansion of cereal production, was it apparently deemed profitable to introduce the medieval invention, the windmill, into this area naturally suited to its use.

Climatic conditions and the lateritic Mediterranean red earth soils of clayey, sandy or saline structure account for the advanced treelessness of most of the basin, not, as so often alleged, medieval deforestation. The predominant vegetation is the *matorral,* which includes various woody, aromatic, deep-rooted, leathery-leaved, evergreen, drought-resistant bushes and shrubs—broom, gorse, heather, sage, rosemary, cistus, and others. Ignacio Olagüe, who attempts to explain Spain's decline in the later sixteenth century as due to an alleged radical change in *meseta* climate, attributes forests, extensive grasslands, and flourishing crop farming to medieval La Mancha and Extremadura, but his thesis rests more on personal conviction than factual proof.[5] It seems highly probable, however, that in medieval times the region's grasslands were much more extensive than today, after centuries of overgrazing and spring burnings, for it is upon grass, not *matorral,* that the medieval documents on grazing rights lay stress. In La Mancha this grass was to be found at its richest in the Murcian plains around Chinchilla and Albacete, on the *campos* of Montiel and Calatrava, in the sheltered Sierra Morena valleys near Alcaraz and the Vale of Alcudia; and in Extremadura, in the renowned pastures of La Serena, the Tierra de Barros, the *campos* of Badajoz, Cáceres, Alcántara, and Coria, and the Vale and Vera of Plasencia. One characteristic of Guadiana Valley grass is especially to be noted: it grows not only in the spring, when grass is available in most of the Peninsula, but abundantly in the fall rainy season. This fact accounts for the great drives of transhumant sheep and cattle from the north, stock movements that play a central role in the history of the Manchegan and Extremaduran frontier period.

The other major factor in shaping the course of Castilian occupation of the Guadiana plains was military: the fact that between 1085 and 1235 La Mancha and Extremadura were the invasion corridor and battleground of Berber armies based in Andalusia and of Castilian-Leonese forces raised on both sides of the Central Sierras.[6] For a century and a half frontier warfare swept the plains, in four principal phases: (1) the Almorávid period, 1085–1150, which commenced disastrously, but under Alfonso VII in the early 1140's saw the first permanent establishments in the plains country at Coria in Extremadura and Calatrava in La Mancha; (2) the two extremely critical decades, 1155–1175, when ferocious Almohade offensives wiped out Ferdinand II's gains in León and recovered virtually all of La Mancha except the key fortress of Calatrava; (3) the period 1175–1212, of long-delayed Leonese arrival in the Tajo Valley and steady Castilian advance in La Mancha, culminating in the victory of Las Navas; and, finally, (4) the period 1212–1235, when the Almohades were driven from the remaining portions of La Mancha and Extremadura.

Carrying on this prolonged struggle imposed important changes upon Castilian military organization, changes that were to have lasting effects upon the methods of colonizing the plains.[7] For both Moors and Castilians, the endless warfare itself was a typically plains affair, where occasional major campaigns aimed at conquest of the settled territory on the other side of the *despoblado*; but it was normally characterized by incessant raids and hit-and-run attacks (*algaras, correduras*) which sought to surprise the enemy, devastate and pillage his towns and farms, and then swiftly withdraw across the intervening plains with captured humans, livestock, and other booty. In consequence the Guadiana zone forced Castilian and Leonese rulers into a costly defense in depth by means of castles and towns, and into desperate efforts to maintain control of strategic routes and mountain passes, such as Muradal, also called Despeñaperros.

In the first half of the twelfth century the kings depended increasingly upon the powerful municipal militias, such as those of Sala-

manca, Avila, Segovia, Madrid, Toledo, and Cuenca, which came
to be characteristic of the new *concejos* or towns of the region
between the Duero and the Tajo. From the Fuero de Cuenca (1189–
1190) and similar sources, it can be gathered that these urban
armies, adapting themselves to the exigencies of plains warfare, included a cavalry of *caballeros villanos* or petty nobles resident in
the town; an infantry of *peones,* the free but non-noble citizen-
soldiers; and archers, both mounted and foot. Elaborate procedures
were developed for defense of the town during the army's absence;
the siting and layout of encampments; the use of scouts and spies;
compensation for wounds and losses of equipment; and division of
spoils. Thus, in a very literal sense, urban frontier warfare was economic warfare. On campaigns, to judge by Cuencan practice, it was
customary for the host to divide itself into equal halves; one, called
the *azaga,* constructed a defensible base-camp, from which the other
half, the *algara* proper, departed to launch its lightning thrust into
enemy country, and to which it returned to await the inevitable
counterattack.[8]

But by the second half of the century, the advent of the Almohades
and continuous bitter fighting in the Guadiana Basin proved con-
clusively that the frontier military needs of the crown could not be
adequately met by municipal armies and nobles, resident at often
considerable distances from the scene of combat, slow to muster,
privileged in respect to length and frequency of service, and dis-
inclined to take up homesteads or promote settlements in the plains.
What was required in addition to these regular forces, as the Almohade crisis of 1155–1175 revealed, was fighters stationed in close
proximity to frontier defense points in or below the Tajo Valley,
capable of garrisoning exposed castles and fortresses, constantly
alert for instant action against raiders, and willing to undertake the
permanent conquest and colonization of La Mancha and Extremadura. This is the background for the sudden rise to prominence in
Castilian-Leonese history of the six great military orders of the
Templars, Hospitalers, Calatrava, Alcántara and the two branches
of Santiago, San Marcos in León and Uclés in Castile. Before the
mid-twelfth century, significantly enough, the older Temple and
San Juan had not fought the infidel in the two western kingdoms
of Spain; and it was the two decades of dire Almohade peril that
brought into existence all the native orders, whose founding members were nearly all well-blooded in Guadiana Valley fighting. These

paramonastic warriors, the *freires caballeros* of the orders, whom the *Rule* of Calatrava pictures as sleeping dressed and armed, ready at a moment's notice to mount their chargers and ride against the Moor, along with the vassal *caballeros* and *peones* of their patrimonies, henceforth become the standing protectors of the frontier settlements and a persistent scourge of the Almohades.[9]

The Castilian conquest of the Guadiana Basin, except in the lowest reaches of the river, was terminated by 1235; but the era of colonization extends to at least the end of the thirteenth century.[10] Throughout this period, royal efforts to promote settlement and economic development of the area depended almost exclusively upon two agencies, the town and the military order. Compared with its striking predominance in the twelfth-century colonization of the Duero-Tajo belt, where it served as the principal basis of political, ecclesiastical, social, and economic life, the royal *concejo* plays a distinctly secondary role in La Mancha and Extremadura. To be sure, towns founded by the king on his crownland (*concejos de realengo*), and largely self-governing under a royal *fuero* defining municipal laws and liberties, sprang up both in Extremadura, where we find notable examples in Coria, Cáceres, and Badajoz, and also in La Mancha, for example, Alarcón, Alcaraz, Chinchilla, and Villarreal (modern Ciudad Real). Yet such towns were comparatively few in number, partly because urban agglomerations remained scattered in the plains country, partly because so much of the territory was entrusted to the military orders. It is noteworthy that of these royal towns, only two, Coria and Badajoz, attained the level of episcopal sees.

Far more important than the *concejos de realengo* as colonizers were the military orders, which throughout La Mancha and Extremadura directed the settlement and Castilianization of the frontier. The military was but one of four vital functions these great corporations performed. From the governmental standpoint their broad patrimonies constituted palatine lordships, outside the law and jurisdiction of the king and his officials, lands where the orders ruled and administered justice through their capable directorate of grand masters or priors, and subordinate district *comendadores*. Over much of the Guadiana Basin, until the days of the Catholic kings, government was thus the monopoly of the orders, as the royal laws and charters recognize when the king speaks of "mi tierra e la de las ordenes." But the orders largely replaced not only the king's government, but also that of the secular church. The new Extremaduran bishoprics carried on the ecclesiastical policy followed in the Duero-Tajo settlement; but all La Mancha remained part of a huge diocese of Toledo, where the orders, secure in their papal, Cistercian, or Compostellan exemptions from episcopal control, administered their domanial churches, providing clergy and collecting tithes. No less startling, the orders entirely prevented monasticism from establishing itself in the Tierra de las Ordenes, and because Cáceres, Badajoz, and other towns in *realengo* prohibited the gift, sale, or exchange of land to religious orders, the plains country was a strangely monkless land, the one large subdivision of the medieval West where monasticism—Benedictine, Cluniac, Cistercian, Carthusian, Franciscan, Dominican—plays no part whatsoever in religious life.

Lastly, the orders were active colonizers of the Guadiana frontier, making grants to nobles who undertook settlement projects, and establishing towns and villages to which they conceded, in order to attract colonists, liberal *fueros*, often those of Cuenca or Cáceres. Alcázar de San Juan, Consuegra, Madridejos, Calatrava, Almadén, Quintanar de la Orden, Mérida, Usagre, Alcocer, Medellín, Montánchez, Trujillo: such are some of the many pueblos sponsored by the orders. Yet most of these towns remained small and overwhelmingly rural in social and economic composition, partly again because of environmental handicaps to urban growth, but also because the often more limited rights of self-government allowed by the orders, the retention of various seigneurial rights and monopolies, the exclusion of royal law, and prohibition of appeals in judicial cases to the crown repelled settlers.[11] The well-known case of Cáceres, where the colonists compelled Alfonso IX to swear that the town would never be transferred to an order, is indicative of the hostility frontiersmen felt.[12]

Population in all the plains towns, whether of the orders or of the crown, belonged mostly to the two social classes characteristic of the Castilian meseta frontier: the *caballeros villanos* and the *peones*.[13] Each charter member of the town, of either class, received a town lot, and often a piece of arable land just outside it, at the time of its foundation; a land distribution or *repartimiento* was effected, either by the order's *comendador* (as at Madridejos in 1238), or, in the royal towns like Cáceres, through a two-stage partition by *cuadrelleros* to soldiers of the conquest and subsequently by *sex-*

meros to later arrivals.[14] These land cessions, in line with Castilian frontier practice, were full allodial grants. After at most a three-year period, the settlers could sell, exchange, or give them away, although both the crown and the royal *concejos* forbade land transfers to religious orders, and the military orders required prospective owners to promise vassalage to them.[15]

That farming, particularly the raising of grain, was carried on in the land close to the town is evident from references in the sources to units of arable land and to wheat, barley, and the like; to plowteams of oxen and mules, the latter probably a Moorish carryover; and to various tithes and taxes levied on crops. Olive culture is rarely mentioned, but viticulture on the other hand was obviously widespread and the subject of promotion by at least one order, Calatrava. This order, in establishing Miguelturra near Ciudad Real in 1230, compelled *caballeros* to plant two *arranzadas*, and *peones* one, of vineyard under threat of losing their allotments.[16]

Far more economically significant, however, than cereal agriculture or viticulture was stock raising in that advanced form, more fruitfully developed in the Iberian Peninsula than anywhere else in the medieval world, which is properly called ranching.[17] The systematic ranging of large numbers of sheep, cattle, horses, and other livestock on the open *meseta* plains had first developed above the Duero River; all the way from the Rioja and Burgos westwards to León, Zamora, and the trans-Miño country there occurred in the late ninth and the tenth centuries, as part of the Asturoleonese—Castilian colonization of the desert of the Duero, a shift towards the pastoral side of the balance in the old Cantabrian-Pyrenean mixed farming system of crops and livestock. After 1085 both the limited arable and water resources of the northern *meseta*, and the military conditions of the Reconquest that favored mobile property over easily destroyed crops and orchards, promoted the rapid expansion of ranching into the new frontier settlements of the Duero-Tajo region such as Segovia, Sepúlveda, Avila, Valladolid, Salamanca, and Ciudad Rodrigo above the Central Sierras, and Soria, Guadalajara, Madrid, Cuenca, Toledo, and Talavera beyond them.

From the middle twelfth century this flourishing Castilian pastoralism, made aware of the rich pasturage resources of the trans-Tajo plains, must have acted as a powerful if now little-mentioned factor in Castilian southward expansion. Certainly by the second half of the century towns like Cuenca, Toledo, and Plasencia, and

the military orders of Calatrava, the Hospital, and Uclés, were send-
ing their herds and flocks into the Guadiana Basin in spite of the
ever-present danger of Almohade attack. With the final expulsion
of the Moors under Alfonso IX, Ferdinand III, and Alfonso X in the
succeeding century, and the opening up of the richest Manchegan
and Extremaduran grasslands, there occurred, simultaneously with
a parallel development in Lower Andalusia, an explosive expansion
of the ranching industry of the plains. This movement is strongly
reflected in the extraordinarily numerous chapters which such *fueros*
as those of Coria and Cáceres devoted to pasturage rights, stock
taxes, and tithes, disputes among stockmen, compensations for crop
damage, and similar topics; and it appears also in the many pastoral
references of the charters of the military orders and the Guadiana
towns.[18]

These sources also throw considerable light upon three central
questions in the rise of frontier ranching in La Mancha and Extremadura: the social status of the stockmen themselves; the grazing
system upon which the industry was based; and the evolution of
new regulatory institutions. Aside from a small number of seigneurial
ranchers, of whom we know next to nothing, the frontier stockmen
of the Guadiana Basin were either the orders with their great flocks
and herds, or the many small and middle-sized ranchers living in
the towns. Early in their history, as their records prove, the orders
became heavily engaged in stock raising; as usual, figures are hard
come by, but the Templar-Alcántara quarrel in 1243 over 42,000
sheep in the vicinity of the Tajo Valley town of Ronda, is suggestive.[19] Thirteenth-century Calatrava diplomas show that great
Manchegan order protecting its brand against use by others, and
driving its animals eastward into the pastures of Uclés and north-
wards into the Sierras of Guadarrama and Malagón, where they
aroused the opposition of Segovia and Avila.[20] Ferdinand III's
generous grants to the Templars of wide pasturelands around Almorchón, Alcocer, and Capilla, in the heart of the most prized
grazing ranges; Sancho IV's extension to Uclés of free pasturage
rights throughout the realm; and the appointment of special pastoral
administrators, *frayles veedores* and *comendadores de las vacas*, by
Calatrava, Uclés, and San Marcos, all bear witness to the basic importance of pastoral enterprise in the economic activity of these
corporations.[21]

On the other hand, there were numerous small and middle-sized

ranchers, the townsmen, both *caballeros villanos* and ordinary free-
men. In the Guadiana region even more than above the Tajo, it is
patent that the majority of such townsmen were in no significant
sense landed proprietors; although they possessed small holdings in
or near the town, their real wealth was not in land but in livestock,
and in the cherished right of access to the grazing grounds not only
of the town, but very commonly also of either the military orders
or of the crown. Such stipulations as those of the Fuero de Cáceres
requiring stockmen to combine their separate herds of animals into
cabañas of 400 cattle, 200 mares, or 2,000 sheep, and the royal provisions on exemption of herdsmen from military service, which contemplate ranchers owning fewer than 40 cows or 100 sheep, or
between 40 and 100 cows and 100 and 1,000 sheep, prove that
the small-ranching class, which is also typical of northern *meseta*
ranching, was strongly established throughout La Mancha and
Extremadura.[22]

In the more northern centers of Castilian ranching, on both sides
of the Duero, the grazing of livestock was normally carried on
through seasonal rotation of pastures within the confines of the municipal bounds; lowland pastures near the town served in the winter,
while the summer months saw the stock driven into the upland
grazing grounds of the nearest sierra. Such a pasturage system,
which is really more sedentary than truly transhumant, required a
minimum of special institutions. *Pastores* and *vaqueros* at the duly
specified times drove the stock to or from the pastures and kept it
under constant herding; *montaneros* might be named to patrol the
municipal *montes* or pastures against entry of outsiders; and the
regular alcaldes or other town officials, on the basis of provisions in
the *fuero* or unwritten custom, handled all questions of stray animals, pasturage rights, and stock damage to vineyard or arable, the
wages and misdeeds of herdsmen, the settlement of disputes, and
the imposition of penalties.

When the frontier moved southward, from the reign of Alfonso
VI on, municipal grazing and pastoral regulation under the control
of the alcaldes remained the general rule in the new *concejos* of the
Duero-Tajo region. But certain important changes soon appear.
These were due chiefly to the fact that many of these towns, particularly those near the Central Sierras, like Avila, Segovia, Madrid,
and Escalona, came to possess much larger municipal territories
than were common hitherto. These often stretched far up into the

Guadarramas and Sierra de Gredos, where were the highly desirable *agostaderos,* or summer pastures. At the same time, other towns
on the edge of the plains, among them Cuenca, Toledo, and Talavera, began to winter their livestock southwards in the Guadiana
Valley. Thus, for the first time, absence from the town during several
months on the part of herdsmen driving sheep and cattle in far parts
of a town's own territory or, on the southern plains, completely outside it, became a frequent occurrence; and this in turn naturally
raised new problems of protecting the livestock and the herders, and
of municipal control over the latter.

One consequence of this, in the towns of the Central Sierras, and
on the margins of the Guadiana plains, was the introduction of an
organized escort of armed riders and men on foot, who accompanied
the animals during their sojourn in distant feeding grounds, with
the function of guarding both them and their herders. The oldest
and fullest description of such a pastoral military escort survives in
the Fuero de Cuenca, a frontier town only a dozen years old in
1189–1190, which, although located up in the Serranía de Cuenca,
stood on the very edge of La Mancha Alta. According to the Fuero,
each year at the beginning of December the sheep and cattle of the
Cuencan ranchers were placed under the formal guard of what is
called the *esculca,* which was clearly a company of armed, mounted
men who were provided by the stockowners on the basis of one
caballero for each herd of cattle or for every three flocks of sheep
they owned. Accompanied by these *esculqueros,* who elected
alcaldes de la esculca as their officers, and by the *pastores* and
vaqueros, the sheep and cattle were driven southward onto the
plains of La Mancha, very likely as far down as Villora, Tabarrosas,
and Iniesta, points mentioned elsewhere in the Fuero as limits
within which Cuencan livestock might be found. Here four and a
half months were spent in winter grazing. By mid-March the whole
outfit returned to the environs of Cuenca, where the *esculca* dis-
banded and the *concejo,* between that time and St. John's Day
(June 24), supervised what must have been the spring branding of
calves and lambs, and the cutting out of animals for sale or slaughter.
On St. John's Day the herds were driven north into the summer
pastures high in the Serranía; this time, however, they were escorted
only by sixty herdsmen on foot, supplied by seven of Cuenca's villages, who were commanded by the *alcaide* of Cuenca. By the first
of November, when the *alcaide's* term of office expired, the herds

were once again trailed back to Cuenca, presumably for some sort of fall roundup and in readiness to be entrusted at the start of December to the protection of the *esculca*.[23]

This Cuencan innovation of an armed guard for herds and *pastores* on the plains was certainly in use among plains towns that adopted the Fuero de Cuenca; these would include not only *concejos de realengo*, such as Alarcón, Alcaraz, and Plasencia, but also many settlements of the military orders which used it either in its original form or in the adaptations of the Fueros of Consuegra and Montiel. Furthermore, the existence of an armed pastoral escort, this time under the name of *rafala*, can be discovered in a number of ranching towns well to the west of Cuenca. The *rafala* first turns up, so far as we now know, in the pasturage agreements made ca. 1200 among the *concejos* of Plasencia, Escalona, and Avila; and in the Fueros of Coria and Cáceres a few years later.[24] The latter codes give us some data regarding the terms of service of the mounted *rafaleros*, and certain regulations governing them during the months when the *rafala* was away from the town on duty. So, too, the Fuero de Salamanca refers to a *rafala* guarding the municipal herds of swine when they were driven across the sierra, doubtless the Sierra de Peña de Francia.[25]

The *rafala-esculca*, however, was not the only new institution developed by Castilian municipal pastoralism to meet the frontier conditions of long-range grazing. Historically more important is the concomitant evolution of a system by which the herdsmen and their armed guards could be governed during their now prolonged seasonal absence from their homes. In his able book on the Mesta, Julius Klein assumes that from a very early date medieval Iberian towns possessed a kind of local stockmen's association called the *otero* or *mesta*, which met two or three times a year to restore stray animals to their owners, regulate the hiring of shepherds and cowboys, and punish violations of pastoral law. These meetings, which he sees continuing throughout the Middle Ages, Klein distinguishes carefully from what he regards as their institutional offshoot, the celebrated Real Mesta, or national association of Castilian stockmen which Alfonso X founded in the thirteenth century.[26] But the existence before the middle of the twelfth century of such local pastoral organizations is highly dubious, and indeed contradicts the many *fuero* references we have to the regulation of all aspects of stock raising, including specifically the restoration of strays to their

owners, by the regular town officials, normally the alcaldes. Why
are not such assemblies ever mentioned in the Leonese-Castilian
fueros of the tenth to thirteenth centuries, such as those of Soria,
Molina de Aragón, Guadalajara, Alcalá de Henares, Zamora, Salamanca, Alba de Tormes, Ledesma, and other pastoral centers? To
assume that *otero* and *mixta* or *mesta*, place names common in
northern Spain, designate the customary meeting places of these
hypothetical assemblies would be unwarranted.[27] The truth is rather
that so long as municipal stock raising operated within the more or
less narrow territories of northern Castilian and Leonese towns, the
ability of local officials to handle pastoral matters was adequate;
but, as with the *rafala-esculca*, it was the growing practice of transhumant grazing and its southward extension that produced changes
from the traditional pattern.

The earliest sure instance of this innovation appears in the Fuero
de Cuenca, which shows that before starting south in early December the *caballeros* forming the *esculca* chose special alcaldes, and
that these *alcaldes de la esculca* exercised not merely military but
judicial and general governmental authority over herdsmen and
esculqueros, serving in fact as substitutes for the ordinary alcaldes
to enforce the pastoral and other provisions of the Fuero. This authority, furthermore, was final, decisions of these special alcaldes
not being open to appeal or rehearing when, on returning home in
mid-March, they surrendered their authority to the *concejo*. The
arrangement was quite different from the one Cuenca followed for
the summer interval, when in the upland grazing grounds the sixty
village herders were subject to the authority of the *alcaide*. The
principle, in the case of the *esculca* and the winter herdsmen (who
were men of Cuenca, not villagers) is the same as that which other
sections of the Fuero show governed the organization of the town
army, and even of the town hunt club (*recloba*). That is to say: a
collective group of townsmen, absent from municipal territory on
official business, remained subject to the rights and obligations of
the Fuero, and continued to be governed by it under what were in
effect itinerant alcaldes.[28]

Whether, or how often, the whole company of guards and herdsmen assembled for special meetings at which the *alcaldes de esculca*
gave judicial decisions and distributed strays, we are not told; but
in the Fuero de Cáceres, which unlike that of Coria mentions both
rafala and *otero*, some additional light is thrown on what must have

been a growing practice where long-distance grazing was involved. The Cáceres *fuero* in several chapters speaks of the compulsory assembly of *rafala* guards and herdsmen, apparently three times a year, for the holding of an *otero,* at which judicial matters were settled.[29] So too the Fuero de Salamanca's chapter on the *rafala* that guarded the driving of pigs across the sierra mentions the *otero,* only in this case the *otero* meets daily, doubtless out of the need for frequent re-deployment of lithe but distinguishable porkers.[30] Presumably, Mérida, Usagre, and other towns using the Cáceres *fuero* followed the same pattern, so that at least here in Extremadura, if not in La Mancha, the existence of municipal pastoral assemblies in the thirteenth century seems certain.

In none of these texts, it may be noted, is the term *mesta* applied to meetings of herdsmen and guards; indeed, the use of the word in the Fuero de Cáceres to mean a stray animal shows that at least in northern Extremadura the terms were by no means synonymous.[31] What would appear to be the oldest documentary occurrence of *mesta* in the sense of an *otero*-like pastoral assembly is to be found in two diplomas of Alfonso X, issued at Seville on the same day in 1266; in these the king authorizes the holding of *mestas* at Seville and at Alcaraz in deep southern La Mancha.[32] The Seville charter, which thus sets up the later famous municipal *mesta* of Seville, has not yet been published, but was probably of the same tenor as the Alcaraz text, which has been. In the latter document the king orders that compulsory *mestas* of the sheepmen and cowmen of Alcaraz be held (literally 'made') three times a year at the forks of the Guadalmena River; and lays down a number of brief rules regarding the handling of strays, brawling among the herdsmen, and similar topics. Pretty clearly, this is what in Extremadura would have been called an *otero*; on the other hand, no less clearly, it hardly reflects the necessity of having regulations for stockmen who are encamped on ranges some distance away from their regular municipal government, since the Guadalmena forks are not far from Alcaraz. Whether the background for this was Andalusian is uncertain; Alcaraz possessed the Fuero de Cuenca, and the king advises the Alcaraz stockmen to consult Cuenca or Alarcón if problems arise, which suggests that before 1266 such *mestas* were to be found at those two places. The prime mystery here is why the king intervened to establish a *mesta*—which, unlike *otero,* seems to be the royal term for a pastoral organization—at Alcaraz; whereas, so far as we know, he did not do so in the case of the *oteros* already cited. The matter is not without wider implications. First, because from this type of royal-founded municipal *mesta* is descended a series of others in later medieval and early modern Spain, which are the prototypes of those eventually founded in a very few towns of the Indies, principally Santo Domingo and Mexico City.[33] Elsewhere in the New World pastoral matters were handled, according to the older tradition, by the town governments, or *cabildos.* Secondly, the Alcaraz and Seville *mestas* are somehow linked with the earliest evolution of the great Real Mesta of Alfonso X. If we hypothesize that these *privilegios* represent royal assent to local *mestas* and, in effect, exempt these from inclusion in the Real Mesta, then we may assume that the latter was already in existence before 1273, the usually assigned date of foundation, as is also indicated from other quarters.

The solution to this question, if it can be found, is involved in an even larger problem of the Castilian ranching frontier in La Mancha and Extremadura, that of the origins of the Real Concejo de la Mesta itself. In its main lines, the history of the Real Mesta has been admirably surveyed in Julius Klein's standard work on the subject, which, although published in 1920, stands up remarkably well after many years. Yet Klein's treatment of the Mesta's beginnings leaves something to be desired, especially when one attempts to determine to what extent the Mesta was really the product of the Guadiana Basin frontier.

The origins of the Mesta are more obscure than commonly supposed. What is often called Alfonso X's foundation charter is in fact four separate documents, dated in 1273 but claiming to replace older ones worn out by hard usage.[34] These texts do not set up an organization; they assume its existence and grant it royal protection and certain grazing and other privileges. Thus the Mesta must have existed before 1273, and its beginnings can be postulated not so much in the wide period 1212–1273, as Klein suggests, but more narrowly in the interval between the conquest of the Extremaduran pasturelands and a date as much before 1273 as it might have taken to wear out the original parchments. If we set 1230–1263 as approximate limits, we shall not be far wrong.

Now within this period the most important development leading towards the creation of the Mesta was certainly the initiation by northern stockmen in Galicia, Asturias, León, and Old Castile, of the great autumnal transhumant drives of sheep and cattle into Extremadura and La Mancha. Klein's assumption that these drives had been going on for centuries before the conquest of the plains on the basis of agreement with the Moors seems completely without foundation; his chief proof-text, a Cuencan charter of 1200, actually deals with the driving of stock south for sale in Moorish markets, a very different thing.[35] The *Chronicle of Alfonso VII* and other sources, which depict the incessant warfare of the plains and the no less incessant cattle and sheep lifting by both sides, emphatically contradict this view.[36]

To ignore the novelty of the northern entry into the Guadiana ranges is to misunderstand what happened. That this entry began immediately on the morrow of the Reconquest is manifest. Ferdinand III's charter of 1237, authorizing the Templar towns to collect grazing fees (*montazgos*) on the transhumants, follows by only one year his grant to the Templars of Almorchón, their earliest big southern Extremaduran acquisition. This document, along with Alfonso X's establishment in 1253 of Alcántaran and Templar toll-collecting stations at Capilla, Alcocer, Benquerencia, and an unidentifiable "Burgo" in the same region, and his 1255 *privilegio* to Logroño exempting that town's livestock from tolls except at Toledo, Murcia, and Seville, show a rapid development of transhumant drives along fairly fixed routes, the historic *cañadas*.[37] It must be remembered that these drives southward involved large numbers of animals; the *montazgo* payments were calculated on the basis of flocks of sheep numbering between 500 and 5,000, and cattle herds of 50 to 500. In accordance with the century-old custom, small urban ranchers would bunch their individual holdings into a municipal herd, so that the *cañadas* must have presented the colorful spectacle twice a year of one municipal herd after another, trailing along, under the command of its alcaldes and surrounded by its herdsmen and guards. Under these circumstances, mix-ups of strays between different town outfits and disputes among townsmen appealing to different *fueros* must have multiplied, and stressed the need for new regulatory machinery on a supra-municipal level.

But the handling of interurban strays and disputes was not the only or most serious problem confronting transhumant stockmen in their southern drives. Even more pressing was assurance of grazing rights, and defense against attack by Guadiana Basin stockmen who could hardly be expected to welcome these annual encroachments on their grass and water. Current views, largely shared by Klein, that it was farmers in general, or townsmen everywhere defending their liberties, who opposed transhumant pastoralism, and that Alfonso's Real Mesta was a nationwide association of stock raisers set up in reaction, are particularly distorting.[38] The plain fact is that the violent antagonism to the transhumants was largely Extremaduran and Manchegan. It was the military orders, and the towns of the Guadiana Basin—not those of trans-Tajo Castile, which were mostly members of the Mesta—which became the bitterest enemies of the northern stockmen and, after its formation, of the Real Mesta. This hostility, as the earliest Mesta charters make plain, found outlet in various forms, violent and nonviolent: in excessive impositions on the transhumants of *montazgos, portazgos,* and restrictions designed to impede passage or pasturage of the livestock; in seizures of animals, including breeding rams and the indispensable bell-wethers, and the killing or dispersal of whole flocks and herds; in armed attacks upon the herdsmen, resulting in injuries and deaths; and in the deliberate closing of *cañadas* by converting sections of them into enclosed pastures across which transit was forbidden. The struggle was basically one between two competing groups of cowmen and sheepmen, northern and southern, each fighting for possession of the winter grass in the choice pasturelands of the southern plains. It was a conflict in which the northerners, far from home and faced with determined opposition, welcomed royal intervention.

By just what steps, and in what chronological order, events led to royal recognition of the Mesta, it is at present impossible to determine. The more eastern towns, trailing through Cuenca into the grasslands of La Mancha, Murcia, and Andalusia, became united at some time in the second half of the thirteenth century in what was called the *concejo de la mesta de la cañada de Cuenca,* which held meetings attended by representatives from the towns using this *cañada.*[39] But did the towns or the king take the initiative in establishing it? We cannot now say, anymore than we can in the parallel case of Extremadura, the region primarily the subject of Alfonso X's pre-1273 charters. Several trunk *cañadas* terminated in Extremadura; whether, as in La Mancha, single *mestas* first developed for each route, is uncertain. The king was to name royal itinerant justices (*entregadores*) for each *cañada,* but whether this action preceded or followed a union of northern stockmen wintering in Extremadura is at present unanswerable. All we can be sure of is that out of the autumnal influx into Extremadura there emerged, probably between 1260 and 1265, the Real Concejo de la Mesta. And in this sense, the Mesta can be recognized as the product of the ranching frontier of the Guadiana Basin.

It lies beyond the bounds of this paper to estimate the full significance of the Guadiana Basin frontier, but certain broad consequences may be briefly suggested. For Iberian frontier history the Guadiana chapter presents unique features of considerable interest: the successful Castilian adaptation to semi-arid plains conditions unsuited to normal medieval agrarian and urban institutions; the development more than anywhere else in the Peninsula of an intensely pastoral society of small towns and small stockmen ranching great numbers of sheep and cattle on the open ranges; the supremacy—military, governmental, and religious—of the military orders at the expense of town, crown, and church; the transhumant invasions that produced the fateful establishment of the Mesta. In some measure the predominance of pastoralism, and of the Mesta, in sixteenth- and seventeenth-century Spanish economic life may be traced to the very success of the Guadiana Valley frontier; when, in the eighteenth century Jovellanos attacked pastoralism and the Mesta as responsible for most of the ills of Spanish society, he represented the reaction to the undue degree to which for so long the world of the plains, and notably that of La Mancha and Extremadura, had dominated the economic life of the nation.[40] For America also the Guadiana frontier has its implications, and not only in the conquistadores, Pizarro, Valdivia, and thousands of others, whom the region early sent to the Indies and who there created New Extremaduras in Mexico and Chile.[41] We are often told how in the New World the Spaniard succeeded only where he could conquer and exploit Indian agrarian societies, and critics lament his supposed failure to fill American plains regions from Texas to Argentina with farms and bustling urban communities. But it should be remembered that the development of a plains country through ranching was a Castilian frontier experience, as rule over great subject masses was not; that pastoralism has its own legitimate claims to respect in the early civilization of many regions and the permanent economy of some; and that where, from the sixteenth century on, the New World frontier of the Americas has fostered the rise of pastoral societies, they have been—with all their own many original contributions—deeply indebted to the way of life and institutional patterns of an Iberian plains background in which the Guadiana Basin was a central and integral element.

NOTES

Research grants from the Institute for Research in the Social Sciences and from the Research Committee, both of the University of Virginia, materially aided the preparation of this paper and are gratefully acknowledged.
1. C. Sánchez-Albornoz, *España, un enigma histórico* (2 vols. Buenos Aires, 1956), II, Chap. xii; José María Lacarra, ed., *La reconquista española y la repoblación del país,* Escuela de Estudios Medievales, Estudios XV (Zaragoza, 1951); J. González, "Repoblación de la 'Extremadura' leonesa," *Hispania,* III (1943), 195–273; J. González, *Repartimiento de Sevilla,* Escuela de Estudios Medievales, Textos XV–XVI (Madrid, 1951); and cf., despite its errors, Jean Gautier, "Le repeuplement de l'Espagne au moyen âge (régions du nord, du centre et du sud)," *Revue de Géographie Humaine et d'Ethnologie,* I (1948–1949), No. 2, pp. 91–94.
2. For the evolution, bibliography, and foreign applications of American frontier methodology, see, most recently, Gene M. Gressley, "The Turner Thesis—a Problem in Historiography," *Agricultural History,* XXXII (1958), 227–249.
3. W. P. Webb, *The Great Plains* (Boston, 1931).
4. For the geography of the Guadiana Valley see especially Juan Dantín Cereceda, *Regiones naturales de España* (2nd ed., Madrid, 1942), I, 11–84; G[onzalo] de R[eparaz] R[odríguez], Vol. I of José Gavira, ed., *España, la tierra, el hombre, el arte* (Barcelona, 1943), pp. 300–304, 340–342, 344 ff., 451–452, 469 ff.; Hermann Lautensach, "Spanien und Portugal," in Fritz Klute, ed., *Handbuch der geographischen Wissenschaft,* IX (Potsdam, 1936), 426–557; and the virtually inaccessible E. W. Gilbert, R. P. Beckinsale, and S. da Sá, *Spain and Portugal,* British Admiralty, Naval Intelligence Division, Geographical Handbook Series (4 vols. Oxford, 1941–1944), Vols. I and III. On La Mancha there is the excellent study by Otto Jessen, "La Mancha: Ein Beitrag zur Landeskunde Neukastiliens," *Mitteilungen der geographischen Gesellschaft in Hamburg,* XLI (1930), 123–227; also published as "La Mancha: Contribución al estudio geográfico de Castilla la Nueva," *Estudios Geográficos,* VII (1946), 269–312, 479–524. Unfortunately, there is no comparable geographic survey of Extremadura.
5. See his *La decadencia española* (4 vols. Madrid, 1950–1951), IV, Chaps. 24–25; and "El paisaje manchego en tiempos de Cervantes," *Anales Cervantinos,* III (1953), 215–279.
6. On the military history of the Guadiana Basin in the twelfth and thirteenth centuries, see Luis G. de Valdeavellano, *Historia de España,* (2nd ed., Madrid, 1955), I, Part 2, Chaps. xvi–xxi; A. de Ballesteros, *Historia de España* (2nd ed., Barcelona, 1943–1956), II, 307–407; III, Part I, pp. 1–13; Julio González,

Regesta de Fernando II (Madrid, 1943); González, *Alfonso IX* (2 vols., Madrid, 1944).

7. No good study of the organization and tactics of the medieval Castilian army has yet appeared, but certain aspects are well treated, largely from the juridical standpoint, in A. Palomeque, "Contribución al estudio del ejército en los estados de la reconquista," *Anuario de Historia del Derecho Español*, XV (1944), 205–251; cf. also Jaime Oliver Asín, *Origen árabe de rebato, arrobda y sus homónimos* (Madrid, 1928) and Ferdinand Lot, *L'art militaire et les armées au moyen âge* (2 vols., Paris, 1946), II, 260–297.

8. Rafael de Ureña y Smenjaud, ed., *Fuero de Cuenca* (Madrid, 1935), Chaps. XXX–XXXI.

9. Of the early history of the military orders in Castile only that of the Hospitalers has yet been carefully scrutinized: Santos A. Garcia Larragueta, *El Gran Priorado de Navarra de la Orden de San Juan de Jerusalén* (2 vols., Pamplona, 1957) I, 35–61; García Larragueta, "La Orden de San Juan en la crisis del imperio hispánico del siglo XII," *Hispania*, XII (1952), 483–524. For the native Castilian orders I have depended chiefly upon I. J. Ortega y Cotes, *et al.*, *Bullarium ordinis militiae de Calatrava* (Madrid, 1761); Francisco Uhagón y Guardamino, "Indice de los documentos de la Orden Militar de Calatrava existentes en el Archivo Histórico Nacional," *Boletín de la R. Academia de la Historia*, XXXV (1899), 5–167; A. F. Aguado de Córdova, *et al.*, *Bullarium equestris ordinis s. Iacobi de Spatha* (Madrid, 1719); Consuelo Gutiérrez del Arroyo de Vázquez de Parga, *Privilegios reales de la Orden de Santiago en la edad media* (Madrid, 1946); I. J. Ortega y Cotes, *et al.*, *Bullarium ordinis militiae de Alcántara* (Madrid, 1759).

10. For colonization by both crown and military orders in southern New Castile and Extremadura, the basic guides are the *Colección de fueros y cartas-pueblas de España, Catálogo,* edited by Tomás Muñoz y Romero for the R. Academia de la Historia (Madrid, 1852), and the *Bullaria* of the orders cited in n. 9 above.

11. Illustrations in FMonreal [Fuero de Monreal], granted in 1207 by Uclés (Luis Salazar y Castro, *Historia genealógica de la Casa de Lara* [4 vols., Madrid, 1636], IV, 678 [bis]); FMiguelturra, 1230, Calatrava (Eduardo de Hinojosa, *Documentos para la historia de las instituciones de León y de Castilla* [Madrid, 1919], pp. 148–150); FMérida, 1235, San Marcos de León and Archbishop Bernard of Compostela (*Bullarium s. Iacobi*, p. 106); FMadridejos, 1238, San Juan (Hinojosa, pp. 151–152); FSalvaleón, 1253, Alcántara (Hinojosa, pp. 158–160; *Bullarium de Alcántara,* p. 68); FVillas-buenas, 1256, Alcántara (*Bullarium de Alcántara,* p. 91).

12. Latin Fuero de Cáceres, 1229: Gónzalez, *Alfonso IX*, II, 691–692.

13. Claudio Sánchez-Albornoz, "Las behetrías," *Anuario de Historia del Derecho Español*, I (1924), 196–205; Sánchez-Albornoz, "El precio de la vida en el reino astur-leonés hace mil años," *Logos: Revista de la Facultad de Filosofía y Letras*, Universidad de Buenos Aires, III (1944), 244–249; Sánchez-Albornoz, *España, un enigma histórico*, II, 7–55; Sánchez-Albornoz, "La frontera y las libertades de los castellanos," in these *Proceedings*.

14. Hinojosa, pp. 151–152; Antonio C. Floriano, "Cáceres ante la historia:

El problema medieval de la propiedad de tierra," *Revista de Estudios Extremeños.*
V (1949), 3–29, especially pp. 7–10; Esteban Rodríguez Amaya, "La tierra en
Badajoz desde 1230 a 1500," *op. cit.*, VII (1951), 395–497.

15. Cf., for example, FCuenca, II, 2; the *reales privilegios* of Alfonso X to
the Concejo of Badajoz (A. Tomás González, *Colección de cédulas, cartas-
patentes, provisiones, reales órdenes y otros documentos* [6 vols. Madrid, 1829–
1833], VI, 112, 116); and the *fueros* of Mérida, Madridejos, Salvaleón and
Villasbuenas, cited above, n. 11.

16. FMiguelturra, c. 6 (Hinojosa, p. 150).

17. For what follows, and for bibliography on medieval Castilian ranching
of sheep and cattle, see Julius Klein, *The Mesta* (Cambridge, Massachusetts,
1920; Spanish translation, Madrid, 1936); C. J. Bishko, "The Peninsular
Background of Latin American Cattle Ranching," *Hispanic American Historical
Review*, XXXII (1952), 491–515.

18. *El Fuero de Coria*, ed. José Maldonado y Fernández del Torco (n.p.,
1949), *passim*; *Fueros y privilegios de Cáceres*, ed. Pedro Ulloa y Golfín (n. p.,
ca. 1657 ?); Antonio C. Floriano, *Documentación histórica del Archivo
Municipal de Cáceres* (Cáceres, 1934); Esteban Rodríguez Amaya, "Inventario
general de los Archivos de la S. I. Catedral y Ciudad de Badajoz, formado
por D. Ascensio Morales en 1753–1754," *Rev. Estud. Extrem.*, VIII (1952),
389–492; *Fuero de Usagre*, ed. Rafael de Ureña y Smenjaud and Adolfo Bonilla
y San Martín (Madrid, 1907), títulos 432 ff.; Miguel A. Ortí y Belmonte,
"Las conquistas de Cáceres por Fernando II y Alfonso IX de León y su
fuero latino anotado," *Rev. Estud. Extrem.*, III (1947).

19. *Bull. de Alcántara*, pp. 51–53.

20. Uhagón, *Indice de documentos de Calatrava*, p. 22, No. 104 (1255);
Bull. de Calatrava, pp. 683–686 (1221); Antonio Benavides, *Memorias de D.
Fernando IV de Castilla* (2 vols., Madrid, 1860), II, 813–815, Nos. dlii–dliii
(*reales* of 1311 but referring to reigns of Alfonso X and Sancho IV).

21. *Bull. de Alcántara*, pp. 73–75 (1236, in *inspeximus* of Alfonso X, 1255);
A. López Ferreiro, *Fueros municipales de Santiago y de su tierra* (2 vols.,
Santiago, 1895), I, 365; Gutiérrez del Arroyo, *Privilegios de Santiago*, No. 495
(1282); *Bull. de Calatrava*, p. 685 (1221), pp. 150–151 (1293); Benavides,
Fernando IV, II, 728, Col. 2 (1310).

22. FUsagre (= FCáceres), títulos 456, 464; *Memorial Histórico Español*, I
(1851), 178, 225; Hinojosa, *Documentos*, p. 169; Benavides, II, 292, Col. 1.

23. FCuenca, cc. XXXIX, 1–3; XXXI, 16.

24. Texts published by Luis Suárez Fernández, "Evolución histórica de las
hermandades castellanas," *Cuadernos de Historia de España*, XVI (1951), 47,
49; FCoria, título 163; FUsagre (= FCáceres) títs. 167, 443–466, 479, 482,
498–505.

25. FSalamanca, tít. 196, in Américo Castro and Federico de Onís, *Fueros
Leoneses* (Madrid, 1916), p. 148.

26. Klein, *The Mesta*, pp. 9–13.

27. Pending a careful philological examination of Iberian pastoral nomen-
clature in its historical as well as etymological aspects, it seems unwise to
attempt as yet any inferences based upon philological evidence alone. Juan

Corominas, *Diccionario crítico etimológico de la lengua castellana* (4 vols., Berne, 1954) regards *esculca* as of Germanic origin (II, 369); *rafala* as probably Arabic (III, 1069–1071, s.v. "rehala"); and *otero* (I, 173 s.v. "alto") and *mesta* (III, 358–359) as from the Latin. But his retention of Klein's mistake (*The Mesta*, p. 12, n. 3; p. 74) about the *rafala* at Cáceres as being concerned primarily with horse trading, his almost certainly erroneous derivation of *mesta* in its pastoral sense from Latin, *mixta*, and his surprising failure to discuss the well-known equation of *mesta* with Berber *mechta*, a winter encampment of nomadic shepherds (Klein, p. 10), all sufficiently underline the need for a study of Spanish pastoral vocabulary on the scientific level of, e.g., Y. Malkiel, "Estudios de léxico pastoril: 'piara' y 'manada'," *Bulletin Hispanique*, LIII (1951), 41–80.

28. FCuenca, XXXIX, 1–3; XXX, 1, ff.; XXXIX, 4.

29. FUsagre (= FCáceres), títs. 448, 451, 467; note the reference in tít. 448 to the "dia de la descamia" on which the "caualleros de rafala" are required to attend the *otero.*

30. FSalamanca, tít. 196.

31. FUsagre (= FCáceres), tít. 463.

32. González, *Repartimiento de Sevilla*, II, 347; González, *Colección de cédulas*, VI, 142–145.

33. Klein, *The Mesta*, pp. 8–9; José Miranda, "Notas sobre la introducción de la Mesta en la Nueva España," *Revista de Historia de América*, No. 17 (June 1944), pp. 1–26.

34. The texts have been published by Klein, "Los privilegios de la Mesta de 1273 y 1276," *Bol. R. Acad. Hist.*, LXIV (1914), 202–219.

35. *The Mesta*, pp. 166–170.

36. See, for example, *Chronica Adefonsi imperatoris*, ed. Luis Sánchez Belda (Madrid, 1950), cc. 36, 39, 88, 122, 131, 187; E. Lévi-Provençal, "Un recueil de lettres officielles almohades," *Hespéris*, XXVIII (1941), 52–53.

37. Klein's description and map of the *cañadas* (*The Mesta*, pp. 18–20) have been corrected in various respects by the much more detailed studies of the geographer Juan Dantín Cereceda, "Las cañadas ganaderas del Reino de León," *Boletín de la R. Sociedad Geográfica*, LXXVI (1936), 464–499; "Cañadas ganaderas españolas," *Congresso do mundo português, Publicações* (Lisbon, 1940), XVIII, 682–696; "La cañada ganadera de La Vizana," *Bol. R. Soc. Geog.*, LXXVIII (1942), 322–335. See Robert Aitken, "Routes of Transhumance on the Spanish Meseta," *The Geographical Journal*, CVI (1945), 59–69. It should however be noted that both Klein and Dantín Cereceda draw chiefly upon nineteenth-century accounts of the cañada system as then still surviving rather than upon the medieval documentation for the original network of the thirteenth and fourteenth centuries.

38. Klein, pp. 75 ff., 301 ff., 351–352; in certain passages, e.g., p. 98, where he seems to recognize that the conflict centered in the Guadiana Valley, Klein fails to reckon with the predominantly pastoral character of the Mesta's southern opposition.

39. Benavides, *Fernando IV*, II, 222–224.

40. Gaspar Melchor de Jovellanos, *Informe de la Sociedad Económica de*

Madrid . . . en el Expediente de Ley Agraria [1795] in *Biblioteca de autores españoles,* Vol. L (Madrid, 1898), 80–98.

41. See the suggestive comments on continuities between the medieval Iberian and the Ibero-American frontier by Silvio Zavala, "The Frontiers of Hispanic America," in Walker D. Wyman and Clifton B. Kroeber, eds., *The Frontier in Perspective* (Madison, Wisconsin, 1957), pp. 35–58; and "Las fronteras de hispanoamérica," *Cuadernos Americanos,* XVII (July–Oct., 1958), 374–384.

Comment: The Spanish Frontier and Medieval France

BY PHILLIPE WOLFF
Université de Toulouse

THE REMARKABLE PAPERS which have been presented by Claudio Sánchez-Albornoz and Charles J. Bishko have interpreted the frontier in two different ways: one in the old, European sense of a political and military boundary between two countries; the other in the American sense of "relatively empty territories being occupied and developed on the margin of an expanding society." I would like to add here a third: the frontier as a zone of material and cultural contacts between two worlds. In this last sense the movement seems a double one, for if it was European society which expanded at the expense of Islam, it was Islam, more rich and cultivated, which influenced Europe in its turn.

In a study which has become a classic, Claudio Sánchez-Albornoz has shown to what extent the phenomena of the frontier and the Reconquista have separated the Iberian Peninsula from the rest of Europe. Few would question his well-founded and suggestive views. But one sees in addition that the presence of such a frontier in a neighboring country was not entirely without influence in France. And this is what I wish to show here in a brief survey.

As a matter of fact the political and military frontier between Islam and Christianity might well have been established in France itself. At the beginning of the eighth century Moslem armies began the occupation of France. The victories of Charles Martel and the reconquest of Septimania by Pepin the Short decided matters differently. And it was from Toulouse that William, Charlemagne's own cousin, conquered and organized the Spanish March, that is to say, the future Catalonia. It has been suggested that the Frankish warrior class, established in Toulouse and other towns of lower

Languedoc, may well have been the forbears of that urban nobility which appeared later in the cities of southern France. Besides, the beginning of the ninth century saw developed, with the aid of Goths who were refugees from Spain, a colonizing movement in lower Languedoc which represented the frontier in the American sense of the word. Finally, the wars of Charlemagne and William against the Moors strongly stimulated the imagination. Two or three centuries later they gave birth to French epic poetry. In this sense, however, viewing the origins of the *chansons de geste*, one can assert that French literature at the beginning was a frontier literature.

In the eleventh century numerous French knights fought in Spain. They helped the kings of Aragon extend their domains into the plains. They assisted at the birth of Portugal. They came to the assistance of Alfonso VI of Castile when he was attacked by the Almorávides. The importance of such intervention has been a subject of disagreement, as we know. Nevertheless, when we note that it was in France that the idea of a crusade crystallized, and when we see that it was the French who furnished the main body of the First Crusade, we might well ask in what measure this represented the result of their Spanish experience. The question has been raised by my friends and colleagues, Dr. and Mrs. John H. Hill, in connection with Raymond IV of St. Gilles, whose military experience seems more extensive and richer than can be explained by local quarrels in Languedoc.

The fact that the most turbulent French knights could fight so advantageously along a nearby frontier could not help but assist the French Monarchy, and spare France from feudal wars. It also allowed the Spanish monarchs to call on the French back-country for help in the most critical moments of their struggle. Papal legates also favored a policy of marriage alliances which effectively reinforced dynasties like that of the counts of Barcelona but which brought them into internal disputes in France. The conflict between the counts of Barcelona and Toulouse and the intervention of Aragon in the Albigensian affair of 1213 illustrate the problems which can grow out of a relationship between a powerful frontier and its back-country.

But let us proceed with the role of the frontier in the American sense of the word. The French participated in the colonization of these vacant lands. M. Defourneaux has devoted a study to these "French in Spain in the Eleventh and Twelfth Centuries," a suggestive title indeed, without mentioning the works of Spanish historians, and in particular those of my friend and colleague J. M. Lacarra. We know the role which the Order of Cluny played in the ecclesiastical organization of reconquered land; one is not surprised therefore to find it established firmly in the French Southwest, which controlled routes leading into Spain, in such power that the Cluny Reform Movement often opposed the Gregorian Reform Movement and gave a unique aspect to the religious life of the region. One should also lay stress on feudal colonization which brought into Spain a portion of the feudal class, especially from Normandy and Burgundy, and so assisted peace in these regions. There was, finally, a movement of bourgeois and peasants, mainly coming from the Southwest. Marc Bloch suggested that this emigration may have delayed the settling of the French Southwest and retarded the founding of Gostides. More recently, in an interesting article published in the review *Les Annales*, M. Higonnet has studied such population movements more carefully. They could result in close relationships. Thus in 1230 in Lérida a man, descended from an emigrant from Toul, in his will left a building to be used as a hostelry by merchants of Toul who were still coming to this town.

This leads us to our final consideration. In what measure did France benefit from contacts of every sort which developed between Christian and Moslem in that frontier zone? The problem has been raised along several lines. In economic aspects no decisive proof has yet been furnished of important relations between Moorish Spain and France—let alone the entire West. But we do have some indications, like the customs duty at Jaca, published by M. Lacarra, the Arab texts cited by M. Lombard, and the abundance of money as seen in mints near the Pyrenees like that of Moralas. In the artistic realm it would be interesting to catalogue influences transmitted by way of Mozarab churches. In the domain of literature we know the arguments, often convincing, which have been advanced to base the literature of the troubadours on certain forms of Spanish Arabic poetry. Finally, one must not forget the decisive role played by Moslem and Christian Spain in the transmission of classical science and philosophy to France and the entire West.

All this shows the significance, the variety, and the complexity of the questions which have been raised. The Spanish frontier pro-foundly affected the destiny of the countries of the Iberian Peninsula. But it was also not without effect on neighboring France (and especially her Southwest) and even upon the entire Christian Occident.

Part Three

THE FRONTIER AND RANCHING IN THE UNITED STATES AND MEXICO

Here we find papers and comment which deal with the frontier and ranching in the United States and Mexico. The first contribution, by Professor Billington, is a classic statement of the frontier as it developed in the United States. It is critically analyzed, at the end of Part Three, by Professor Hogan, who seems to feel that the frontier thesis in its classic form leaves something to be desired. We find presented in Professor Chevalier's study, following Professor Billington's paper, a picture of the little-known but extremely important Northern Mexican frontier as it existed in the eighteenth and nineteenth centuries. The careful reader might well compare the vast differences which seem to exist between the frontier which Professor Billington describes for us and that which Professor Chevalier shows us existed to the south, in Northern Mexico. Finally, this section ends with Mr. Dyke's description of the Texas ranch, where the Northern Mexican and United States western frontiers met and merged. Mr. Dykes' paper brings us up to date by describing in considerable detail the Flat Top Ranch, which is certainly one of Texas' most interesting present-day ranches. Thus the author helps to explain the problems which ranchers face both north and south of the Rio Grande.

The Frontier in American Thought and Character

BY RAY ALLEN BILLINGTON
Northwestern University

SINCE THE ENUNCIATION of Frederick Jackson Turner's "frontier hypothesis" sixty-five years ago historians have generally agreed that many of the unique features of American thought and character can be ascribed to the nation's pioneering experience. If this is the case, why do the traits and institutions of its people differ from those of other frontier countries whose evolution has been roughly similar? The answer to this question can be found in three factors that have made the frontier process in the United States virtually unique: 1) the environment offered an unrivaled opportunity for *individual* self-advancement, 2) its early settlers were unusually well equipped to utilize this opportunity to the full, and 3) its resources were so abundant that their continued exploitation allowed a frontierlike atmosphere to persist long after the frontier was closed. This combination of forces, providing as they did a distinctive relationship between man and his environment, goes far to explaining the most exceptional aspects of American civilization.

Certainly the area of the present United States, unlike that of other lands opened during the Age of Discovery, was unusually well suited to utilization by individuals with a minimum of capital. The eastern half of the continent was covered with dense forest growth that not only attested to the richness of the soil but provided the pioneer with fuel, shelter, furniture, fencing, and farm implements. Further westward where prairies predominated more capital was needed for fencing and fuel, but the sums required were so nominal that they were within the reach of the frontier-oriented farmers who peopled the Mississippi Valley. Still farther westward individual enterprise could skim off the surface mineral wealth hidden in streams or lodes, and could fashion a giant pastureland from the Great Plains. In their constant progression westward, the pioneers recurringly discovered riches that could be extracted with the utilization of a minimum of capital or cooperative effort.

Other frontier countries were not similarly blessed. Canada's lush St. Lawrence Valley provided comparable opportunity for its French exploiters in the seventeenth century, with a resulting alteration in traits and institutions similar to that occurring in the English settlements,[1] but beyond lay the barren Laurentian Shield to halt the westward march and disrupt the continuity of the frontier experience. When this barrier was finally pierced by railroads in the late nineteenth century, the latter-day pioneers lacked the frontiering experience to respond to the environment in the normal fashion.[2] Similarly Latin America, with its rugged mountains, high plateaus, and dense jungles, provided few areas where individual enterprise was powerful enough to combat nature's forces. Only in the Argentine pampa and the Brazilian plains did a temperate climate, navigable rivers, and good soil beckon exploiters, and even there government largess rather than private initiative governed the settlement process.[3] Australia's arid interior also proved useless to small farmers, confining settlement to the coastal lowlands where the relatively dense population concentration forced a transition to an urban-industrial pattern far earlier than in comparable nations.[4] Only on Russia's eastward-moving Siberian frontier did pioneers encounter conditions paralleling those that awaited the American farmer, and there the social order that evolved differed markedly from the individualized, democratic society that emerged in the United States.[5]

This was the case because the frontiering process can be explained only in terms of the interaction between man and nature—as the application of socio-economic-political experience and standards to the conquest of exploitable areas. Different men, with varying backgrounds, will respond in their own ways to identical environments; moreover all frontier areas are continuingly dependent for settlers, markets, and culture on the regions behind them. These interrelationships are constant and enduring; the ferment of America's moving frontiers was partially the product of the ferment of the democratic, commercial, and industrial societies evolving in the successive Easts from which they emerged. These produced settlers who, by training and instinct, were capable of unleashing the energies of individual enterprise to extract the abundant resources awaiting them. On the other hand, the pioneers of the other principal frontier nation in the Americas, New Spain, were handicapped by traditions and culture patterns that foreordained an entirely different civilization for the portions of the continent that they occupied.

For this difference, the chronology of settlement was partly responsible. New Spain was founded, and its institutions established, in the fifteenth and sixteenth centuries, when Europe was just entering its modern age. At that time Spain was a country in which a modern absolute monarchy had just been imposed on a feudal order of nobles, in which middle-class capitalism was in its primitive stages, in which church and state were bound together under the sway of the crown, and in which an explosive nationalism prevailed in the wake of the expulsion of the Moors. The resulting combination of royal absolutism, a militant national church, and a martial spirit created an atmosphere in the colonies in which the individual was allowed little freedom to exploit the New World's resources. Restricted politically by all-powerful viceroys, commercially by an inflexible mercantilistic system, and economically by the operation of the semifeudal *mita* and *encomienda,* the pioneer in New Spain was denied the opportunity for individual self-advancement present in England's colonies. Moreover a humane church policy which decreed conversion rather than extermination for the Indians created a native labor force that monopolized jobs on farms and in mines which would otherwise have been opened to Spanish immigrants. The result was a transplanted European civilization, administered by a centralized bureaucracy, and designed to enhance the wealth of the monarch and his favorites through the exploitation of native workers rather than to provide an opportunity for personal self-advancement to Spanish frontiersmen.

England, on the other hand, entered the colonial race in the seventeenth century, with institutions far more modern than those that Spain transplanted to the New World. The political theories of the Stuart monarchs were still those of royal absolutism and divine right, but both the promoters of the English colonies and the adventurers who settled in them were generally foes of this official theory and active proponents of parliamentary constitutionalism. Thus inclined, they were more ready to accord the colonists a degree of self-rule, as they did when Virginia received its House of Burgesses and Massachusetts its General Court. Political liberty in the colonies was further broadened by constitutional controversies in the mother country when the dependencies were still in their formative stage. Equally vital was the economic freedom allowed to them by promoters who had embraced the theories of commercial capitalism during England's first "industrial revolution" (1540–1640). The prevailing capitalistic philosophy, combined with a lack of centralized civil authority at home, meant that the English plantations could be established by quasi-public enterprises motivated by the hope of gain, and that within those colonies the restrictive controls of feudal land tenure, medieval guilds, or monopolistic trading concepts failed to establish permanence. Instead individual handicraft trades, apprenticeship, private contracts, indentured servitude, and the wage system—all hallmarks of an advancing capitalism—took root, and provided incentives and opportunities, however unequal, to planters, farmers, merchants, and craftsmen. Their economic horizons were further broadened by the failure of an impotent national church to force on them a humanitarian Indian policy, allowing the extermination of native populations when they interfered with the exploitation of natural resources. With a government partially responsive to popular pressures, an economy controlled by ambitious merchant-capitalists, and a social structure sufficiently fluid to allow a large degree of individual advancement, the English colonists were far better equipped to evolve an exploitive frontier system than their Spanish counterparts to the south.

The result was to unleash expansive forces that persisted for the three centuries required to settle the continent. As the pioneers marched westward, they created a succession of new societies, or frontiers, each differing from the other, and all from the established social orders from which they emerged. This repeated "beginning over again" was basic to the frontier process, for the corrosive impact of migration on established customs, the necessities of adjustment to unfamiliar environments, and the mingling of peoples from divergent backgrounds created an atmosphere so uncongenial to traditionalism that the social evolution which followed resulted in a civilization pattern noticeably different from that on which it was based. Only in the United States, where individuals were relatively free to pursue the limitless opportunity that beckoned them onward, did this rebirth of society recur often enough to alter the nature of lives and institutions. For man is a creature of tradition; he clings doggedly to the past and changes his habits only under repeated pressures. Nothing less than a constant recurrence of the pioneering experience could affect the changes wrought in the American character by expansion westward.

Both the corrosive effect of the wilderness environment and the tenacity with which pioneers clung to their civilized heritage can be demonstrated on any of the successive frontiers that marked the advance of settlement in the United States, but that which evolved in the Ohio Valley provides one of the better examples. There, as elsewhere, life was so startlingly different and the forces of nature so strong that a regression toward primitivism altered the social order to a remarkable degree. As immigrants moved into this virgin land they fell under the sway of its vast distances and gloomy forests, both creating the impression that the pioneers were entering a new world where the standards and values of civilization no longer applied. Once in their new homes, this impression was deepened. Society was atomized; the lone settler was stripped of the sense of social interdependence normal in areas where men lived through cooperative enterprise and felt himself so completely self-sufficient that he owed no obligations to those around him. Concerned largely with providing food and shelter for his family, and aware that he could no longer lean on society for protection or sustenance, each individual was inclined to give freer vent to his impulses than in a region where he was subjected to social pressures. His rebellion against discipline was heightened by the almost complete absence of law-enforcement machinery, and by the pattern of cruelty that was common in relations with the Indians. The result was a reversion to primitive behavioral patterns on the part of the less restrained portion of the population that led Easterners to view the whole West as a land of unregenerate savagery.

That the Ohio Valley frontiersmen deserved the "half-horse, half-alligator" label fastened on them by travelers is open to question; modern investigators recognize that this image was based on Western exaggeration and Eastern imagination rather than on fact.[6] Few Kentuckians deserved to be branded "one-eyed savages," "barbarians," or "a kind of humanized Ourang-Outang . . . recently divested of the unsightly appendage of a tail," as they were by Easterners.[7] Yet a surprisingly large number of these pioneers did celebrate their release from civilization's shackles by drinking to excess, adopting the ethical standards of the Indians, engaging in fights in which noses were bitten off, ears ripped to ribbons, and eyes gouged from their sockets, and in every other way outdoing the red men in savagery.[8] A visitor to pioneer Nashville found that the three prisoners in the village jail had been found guilty of a stabbing, a nose biting, and an eye gouging,[9] while in nearby Kentucky the legislature in 1798 decreed special penalties for all who bit an opponent's tongue, slit his nose, ear, or lip, or purposely pulled or "put out an eye, while fighting or otherwise."[10] That a majority of the settlers stooped to such practices was not true; most were pious, law-abiding men more concerned with perpetuating than flaunting civilization. Yet even these could not escape the blighting effect of their environment.

Their milder reaction assumed the form of a deep-seated anti-intellectualism that prevailed everywhere in Western society. The scale of values forced on them by primitive living conditions naturally glorified material pursuits essential to society's well-being, and relegated abstract thinking to a lower level. "Men must have bread before books," wrote a Westerner in justifying this attitude. "Men must build barns before they establish colleges. Men must learn the language of the rifle, the axe and the plough, before they learn the lessons of Grecian and Roman philosophy and history."[11] Materialistic attitudes were not alone in fostering frontier anti-intellectualism; equally influential was the Western tendency to equate learning with despised aristocracy and the emotional nature of the revivalistic religions that prevailed there. "Just get up, and look to God, and fire away" was the formula used by one pioneer preacher for his sermons,[12] while another boasted: "I am a poor humble man—and I doesn't know a single letter in the A B C's, and couldn't read a chapter in the Bible no how you could fix it, bless the Lord!—I jist preach like Old Peter and Poll, by the Sperit."[13] In such an atmosphere the typical frontiersman had little appetite for "book larnin'" beyond that needed to cipher his accounts and spell out a few passages in the Scriptures. Observed one who knew them well: "A wheat field is more pleasing to their taste than a flower garden. A well-ploughed lot is more satisfactory to their eye than the most exquisite painting of a Raphael or a Claude. They would prefer seeing a gristmill working on their own stream, to the sight of the sculptured marble of the Venus or the Apollo!"[14]

That the frontier experience did weaken the ties binding pioneers to their past there can be no question, but those ties were far from severed. Among a surprisingly large portion of the "better element" that migrated westward, the determination to perpetuate unchanged the civilization they had abandoned seemed to increase in proportion to the distance that they placed between themselves and that civilization. Unlettered sons of toil who had gained their sole education in the school of life were always ready to demand schools to provide their children with opportunities they had denied themselves. Rough backwoodsmen who could scarcely read were eager to contribute to subscription libraries or to join local debating and literary societies. Every American schoolboy knows that the youthful Abraham Lincoln trudged through the snow to borrow books, but few realize how readily available booklenders were. In the primitive hamlet of New Salem, which was only two years old and contained only 150 inhabitants when he moved there in 1831, there was a good subscription school, several sizeable private libraries, a flourishing debating society, a lyceum within easy walking distance, a temperance society, and a nonsectarian Sunday school. In the six years that he lived there, Lincoln read Shakespeare and Robert Burns, Kirkham's *Grammar,* six books of Euclid, and a smattering of Tom Paine, Volney, and Jefferson, as well as numerous newspapers.[15] No wonder that a pioneering woman later reminisced: "I have read in books that the people of the frontier kept moving westward to escape civilization. But if my experience counts for anything, such people were the exceptions. So eager were we to keep in touch with civilization that even when we could not afford a shotgun and ammunition to kill rabbits, we subscribed to newspapers and periodicals and bought books." [16]

For those with such appetites, a surprisingly rich fare was available. A visitor in early Louisville called on a friend who owned one of the six copies of *Ivanhoe* in the village; in the hour that they chatted two persons arrived to borrow the book and he was told that every copy was in constant use.[17] In nearby Lexington a coffeehouse maintained files of forty-two newspapers for its patrons.[18] For would-be purchasers no less than six Lexington merchants advertised books for sale as early as 1788, when the total population was less than seven hundred. One boasted a stock of "books of divinity, law, and physic; several entertaining histories; some English and Latin school books; a variety of books for the instruction and entertainment of children; American magazines and museums of the latest dates;"[19] three years later this enterprising tradesman was selling the works of Homer, Virgil, Cicero, and Ovid, as well as Ainsworth's *Latin Diction* and such lighter entertainment as Blackstone's *Commentaries*, *The Pilgrim's Progress*, Chesterfield's *Letters*, Vattel's *Law of Nations*, and Tom Paine's *Works*.[20] Nor was this unusual. In 1796 Cincinnati, then a hamlet of five hundred souls, had two merchants selling books and even distant St. Louis supported a book store by 1820.[21]

The wares dispensed at these emporiums revealed the frontier's cultural conservatism, for the books that most appealed to Westerners were those traditionally popular in the East: standard English authors and the classics. Sir Walter Scott and Lord Byron were their favorites, but Fitz-Greene Halleck, James G. Percival, Nathaniel P. Willis, Felicia Hemans, and Thomas Moore were more popular than James Fenimore Cooper or Washington Irving whose Western scenes aroused more contempt than admiration among frontiersmen.[22] Books printed in the Ohio Valley showed a similar tendency to parrot Eastern tastes although the emphasis was on practical works designed to improve the reader's lot in this world or the next; almanacs and gazetteers comprised almost one-third of the total, with religious and instructional books next in popularity and fiction lagging far behind.[23] In almost no instance did a pioneer printer attempt to break with the past by emphasizing western scenes and character. Perhaps there was only slight boastfulness in the journal of the young lawyer who, leaving Pittsburgh for the frontier hamlet of Butler, recounted that he took with him for "lighter reading" the works of Shakespeare, Homer, Horace and Molière, as well as Plutarch's *Lives* "and other classical productions."[24]

Institutions through which learning was dispensed in the Ohio Valley showed a similar tendency to perpetuate unchanged the culture of the East. Subscription libraries multiplied with amazing speed after the first was founded at Lexington in 1795; nearby Georgetown established one in 1800, when its population was only 225 persons and Danville followed a year later, when its inhabitants totaled only 170. The farm community of Belpré opened the first library in Ohio in 1796 and others followed,[25] although all were to be dwarfed in fame by the "Coonskin Library" near Marietta, where twenty-four subscribers in 1804 pooled the furs they had trapped and dispatched one Samuel Brown to the East to trade them for fifty-two books. Brown returned with solid literary fare: ten volumes of Goldsmith, Ramsay's *History of the American Revolution*, Playfair's *History of Jacobinism*, Harris' *Minor Encyclopaedia*, Morse's *Geography* and his *Gazetteer*, biographies, sermons, religious works, and a few bits of fiction.[26] In Indiana, Illinois, and Missouri the story was the same, with such enthusiasm shown for libraries that often the entire male population of a community could be listed as subscribers.[27] In view of these traditional literary interests, the experience of an English traveler who found that most of the men he visited in early St. Louis had "not only read all of the first Waverley novels, but even the last one, the *Fortunes of Nigel*, which had been published only a short time before I left England,"[28] was scarcely surprising.

Other forms of cultural activity aroused the same ardent enthusiasm and revealed the same basic conservatism. Newspapers multiplied rapidly, most of them weeklies that sprinkled their columns with essays and verse currently in vogue behind the mountains;[29] "every *American newspaper*," observed Mrs. Trollope after her visit to the West, "is more or less a magazine, wherein the merchant may scan while he holds his hand out for an envoice, 'Stanzas by Mrs. Hemans,' or a garbled extract from Moore's Life of Byron."[30] Magazines such as Timothy Flint's *Western Monthly Review* and James Hall's *Western Monthly Magazine* showed a similar, although less pronounced, tendency to extol English authors rather than foster a literary spirit among the pioneers.[31] Theatrical companies, both amateur and professional, found that Shakespeare appealed to backwoods audiences more than native playwrights,[32] while the infant colleges that sprouted in many towns made no compromise with the rigidly classical curriculum that had been in vogue for centuries.[33] A writer in the *Western Review* only mirrored the attitude of many of the West's "better sort" when he declared: "Should the time ever come when the Latin and Greek should be banished from our Universities, and the study of Cicero and Demosthenes, of Homer and Virgil should be considered as unnecessary for the formation of a scholar we should regard mankind as fast sinking into absolute barbarism, and the gloom of mental darkness as likely to increase until it should become universal."[34]

Westerners who wrote in this fashion were clearly not illiterate barbarians who had severed all cultural ties with their past, but neither were they transplanted Easterners who had been deposited unchanged in their forest homes. Like it or not, their values and traits had been altered by their migration westward and the environmental forces operating upon them. Their migration westward had convinced them that progress could be achieved through change rather than stability; never again would they be content with the *status quo* or willing to accept unquestioningly orthodox behavioral patterns. The environment, with its abundance of natural resources, similarly altered their social concepts. In such a land, where every man could achieve affluence by the use of his own brains and brawn, traditional values that stressed hereditary virtues and traditional techniques that emphasised tested methods seemed outmoded. Change, innovation, progress—these had become the new guideposts to a constantly improving future.

Equally important for an understanding of the modern American character was the fact that the forces responsible for these new value-scales did not disappear with the passing of each frontier westward. When this occurred, the communities left behind had scarcely scratched the surface in utilizing available natural resources. With their exploitive tendencies stimulated by the initial pioneering experience, and with the tendency toward innovation encouraged by prior experimentation, the people were quick to develop new means of employing still-abundant known resources or discovering new ones. Thus was created a secondary, or man-made environment, that continued to shower wealth on its exploiters. As the nineteenth century waned, the peoples' frontier-inspired exploitive tendencies were gradually transferred from the soil—or farm exploitation—to other resources that the frontiersmen had discovered: coal, minerals, oil, and all other products necessary to create an urbanized, industrialized society. In this secondary environment, which persists today, Americans are still so blessed with relatively unexhausted natural resources that the habits and institutions developed in pioneering days remain virtually unchanged.[35] The persistence of plenty in the United States has allowed frontier characteristics to endure long after the passing of the frontier.

Prominent among these is the mobility that characterizes American society today as it did when the westward movement was at its height. Underlying this restlessness, from colonial days to the present, has been the realization that opportunity in the form of exploitable resources lay nearby. Pioneers moved toward the frontier for many reasons, but none was so prominent as the hope of self-betterment; only this allowed them to forsake their homes, their friends, and even their families with an abandon not understood by Europeans. "Wandering about," wrote a colonial governor, "Seems engrafted in their Nature; and it is a weakness incident to it, that they Should for ever imagine the Lands further off, are Still better than those upon which they have already Settled." [36] Timothy Flint in the early nineteenth century remarked on his countrymen's "rooted attachment to a wandering life," and Lord Bryce a half-century later referred to them as "almost nomadic." [37] Some went to nearby communities, some to cities, but to many the beckoning call of the West was irresistible. Explorers of the Louisiana Territory in 1819 encountered a man of sixty summers who had just completed a cabin at the furthermost point of settlement on the Missouri River but who questioned them eagerly on the fertility of the Platte River Valley. "We discovered," wrote their chronicler, "that he had the most serious intention of removing with his family to that river." [38]

That frontier-bred urge to move has been permanently engrained in the American character. The census of 1930 showed that three times as many persons who had been born east of the Mississippi River were living west of that stream as had been born west and were living east; between 1940 and 1950 the seventeen western states gained 25.8 per cent in population as compared with a gain of 14.5 per cent for the entire nation. Since 1950 another 3.1 million people have migrated into California alone. This wanderlust afflicts farmers and urbanites alike. In 1937 the Department of Agriculture reported that the average farm family remained in the same spot only five or six years, while the 1950 census revealed that three-fourths of the city dwellers had changed residence during the past decade. In recent years one in every five persons has moved each twelve months, one in every fourteen has shifted from one country to another, and one in every thirty from one state to another. Today over 20 per cent of the people live outside of the state in which they were born; for those over fifty years of age the percentage increases to 40.[39] Americans today, like their pioneering ancestors, are willing to go wherever opportunity beckons.

This constant shifting about has affected both the social structure and the individual character. Migration has always been a selective process; the old, the timid, the deeply rooted, and the economically secure have stayed behind while the principal migrants have been young, impatient with tradition, and usually in the lower-income brackets. This has created what one student has called a "decapitated society," deprived of the contributions of the financially elite who traditionally lend their support to intellectual and cultural activities. Much of America's anti-intellectual, anti-artistic prejudice can be ascribed to the sifting process that has eliminated the culturally oriented from the westward march.[40] The migration process has also altered the migrants. Moving denies the individual the security provided by family groups in more stable cultures, dangerously testing his own self-reliance and tending to focus his emotional problems inwardly, with a corresponding increase in tensions. More tensions are created when the migrant attempts to adjust to a strange environment. Some of the less stable crack under the strain; admission rates to mental hospitals are significantly higher among movers than nonmovers.[41] Others strive so earnestly to integrate in their new communities that they subjugate their own behavioral patterns to those of the group; the emphasis on conformity so prominent in the American character is partially traceable to this urge. They are also inclined to meet new situations with temporary expedients rather than long-range solutions, for planning against a remote future holds little appeal to men who conceive themselves to be permanently transitory. Pragmatism, with its stress on short-term adjustments, is a typically migrant philosophy.[42]

Mobility on the frontier, and since, has been both horizontal and vertical; each shift in residence was made with the expectation of a corresponding rise in social status. As this went on class lines were blurred until the concept of individual self-advancement, both socially and economically, became part of the American creed. Sociologists, despairing of any analysis of class structure in a land where virtually every person ranks himself in the middle class, have been forced to substitute the term "stratification" and to emphasize the "open-endedness" of each level. America's class struggle, in the words of one eminent historian, is only a struggle to climb out of one class and into a higher one.[43]

This attitude developed naturally in frontier regions, where self-sustaining family units made unnecessary the graded social structure essential in compact communities where each group performed functions indispensable to the good of the whole. Amidst nature's plenty the individual, performing the tasks essential to his own subsistence, not only provided for society's needs but assaulted the whole concept of class divisions. This did not mean that a classless society took root in the West; the division into "common folk" and the "better element" was as marked there as in urban areas. A New Englander was guilty of some exaggeration when he noted that settlers on the Indiana frontier were divided into "the superior and the inferior; the former *shaved* once a week, the latter once in *two* weeks," [44] but a fellow observer in Kentucky was nearer the truth: "A small party of rich citizens," he wrote, "are endeavoring to withdraw themselves from the multitude. . . . The present better sort of persons consist of six or eight families who live in a handsome manner, keep livery servants, and admit no persons to their table of vulgar or suspicious character." [45] Another recorded that "some of the females of this class have styled themselves and their families the *Well born*, to distinguish them from those not quite so wealthy, forgetting that some among them could not tell who had been their ancestors in the second generation." [46]

The frontier social order, although far from classless, did differ from that of the East in the relative ease of access into the select group at its pinnacle. This could be accomplished in two ways. One was through migration, for the antecedents of every newcomer were known only to himself and each arrival could proclaim himself a member of the elite without fear of dispute. A study of the seventeenth-century migration of 330 self-labeled "gentlemen" into Maryland indicated that only 50 had been entitled to that designation in England and that 225 had used the opportunity of the voyage across the Atlantic to raise themselves one notch in the social scale.[47] More common on later frontiers was improvement in status by the acquisition of wealth. This was possible where plentiful opportunities for individual gain allowed all with adequate abilities to earn community respect by performing functions for which they were naturally suited, rather than those deemed proper in prior societies. "To be useful is here the ruling principle," wrote a Swedish observer in the early nineteenth century; "it is immaterial what one does so long as he is respected and does his work efficiently. The prerogatives of rank and such considerations have no value." [48] Under these conditions social fluidity became commonplace in Western society, with respect for traditional status as negligible as attachment to place. A Cincinnati editor only mirrored the attitude of his readers when he wrote in 1825: "There are no people, probably, in the world, who are so ready to make experiments respecting social relations . . . as those of the western country,—none who are so little fettered by established habits, who are less disposed to consider hereditary prejudices and heirlooms which cannot be parted with." [49]

This social equality was arrogantly, even belligerently, defended by the Westerners. Woe unto any newcomer who attempted to inflict Eastern class prejudices, or his own snobbery, on the freeborn frontiersmen. A stranger who asked a servant girl the name of her master was likely to be informed: "I have no master. My employer is so and so." Another found it impossible to secure household help until he abandoned use of the word "servant." "Did a girl, too, fancy herself undervalued?" he wrote, "—was she not asked to the first table with company?—not included in invitations sent us from 'big-bug' families?—not called Miss Jane or Miss Eliza—she was off in a moment!" [50] Another new arrival in the Ohio Valley neglected to invite laborers in his employ to breakfast with the family; within hours of this insult the whole group quit their jobs. [51] Equally resented in the West were any "pretensions to singularity, or to superior refinement," as one traveler put it. To use a silver fork, to sport gold buttons on a coat, to put on unnecessary airs—these were invitations to ridicule, slander, and even personal abuse; one visitor almost had the metal buttons ripped from his clothes by an irate keelboatman on the Mississippi. [52] When an Englishman chided a backwoodsman concerning the lack of pomp and ceremony in Western life he was told: "Yes, that may be quite necessary in England, in order to overawe a parcel of ignorant creatures, who have no share in making the laws; but with us a man's a man, whether he have a silk gown on him or not." [53]

Deep-grained attitudes such as these were too firmly implanted in the American character by the frontiering experience to be easily discarded. With the growth of a stratified industrial society, social distinctions have slowly solidified, but the public creed requires that they be seldom mentioned. The United States today boasts a virtually classless society in the opinion of its populace, partly because this attitude has persisted since pioneer days, partly because the continuing exploitation of resources has allowed a greater opportunity for self-advancement than in non-frontier countries. Recent studies indicate that the greatest job mobility today is in areas of lesser occupations where no training or other qualifications are required for entry; [54] this suggests that the social structure is solidifying at the top and that emerging class distinctions will eventually hinder mobility. But that is for the future; Americans of the present retain the frontier-induced belief that any individual may ascend the social ladder to the limits set by his own abilities.

Both the persisting social mobility of the American people and the physical mobility with which it is allied are functions of the abundance that awaited the pioneers on successive frontiers and that endures today as the secondary exploitation of natural resources continues. They, in turn, have fostered other traits no less significant. From continued contact with exploitable wealth the Americans have developed a belief in the idea of progress, an intense materialism with a corresponding anti-intellectualism, and habits of wastefulness that underlie their whole exploitive economy. Their physical mobility has bred in them a restlessness, and a tendency to innovate with little regard to orthodoxy or tradition, just as their social mobility has given them unusual respect for the individual and an enduring faith in the democratic process. So long as the United States remains a land of plenty these characteristics will continue to distinguish its people as a lasting heritage of their unique frontier origin.

FOOTNOTES

1. A. L. Burt, "The Frontier in the History of New France," Canadian Historical Association, *Report* (1940), pp. 93–99; A. L. Burt, "If Turner had Looked at Canada, Australia, and New Zealand When He Wrote about the West," in Walker D. Wyman and Clifton B. Kroeber, eds., *The Frontier in Perspective* (Madison, 1957), pp. 59–77. An essential introduction to the comparative study of frontiers is Paul F. Sharp, "Three Frontiers: Some Comparative Studies of Canadian, American, and Australian Settlement," *Pacific Historical Review*, XXIV (1955), 369–377.

2. G. F. G. Stanley, "Western Canada and the Frontier Thesis," Canadian Historical Association, *Report* (1940), pp. 105–117.

3. Víctor A. Belaúnde, "The Frontier in Hispanic America," *Rice Institute Pamphlets*, X (1923), 202–213.

4. A. L. Burt, "Broad Horizons," Canadian Historical Association, *Report* (1950), pp. 1–10; Fred Alexander, *Moving Frontiers: The American Theme and Its Application to Australian History* (Melbourne, 1947), p. 26.

5. Donald W. Treadgold, "Russian Expansion in the Light of Turner's Study of the American Frontier," *Agricultral History*, VI (1952), 147–152.

6. Richard M. Derson, *Jonathan Draws the Long Bow* (Cambridge, Massachusetts, 1946), pp. 9–15.

7. Richard Weston, *A Visit to the United States and Canada in 1833* (Edin-

burgh, 1836), p. 124; William Fay, *Memorable Days in America: Being a Journal of a Tour to the United States* (London, 1823), p. 331; Timothy Flint, "The Kentuckian in New York," *Western Monthly Review,* I (1827), 88.

8. R. Carlyle Daley, *The Old Northwest: Pioneer Period, 1815–1840* (Indianapolis, 1950), I, 318.

9. J. E. Alexander, *Transatlantic Sketches, Comprising a Visit to the Most Interesting Scenes in North and South America and the West Indies* (London, 1833), II, 107.

10. Quoted in Ralph L. Rusk, *The Literature of the Middle Western Frontier* (New York, 1925), I, 75 n.

11. William N. Milburn, *The Pioneers, Preachers and People of the Mississippi Valley* (New York, 1860), pp. 391–392.

12. Quoted in Everett Dick, *The Dixie Frontier* (New York, 1948), p. 191.

13. Baynard Rush Hall, *The New Purchase; or, Seven and a Half Years in the Far West* (New York, 1843), I, 141.

14. James N. Lemann, "The Progress of the Northwest," *Hunt's Merchants' Magazine,* III (1840), 39. The frontier was only one of several forces contributing to American anti-intellectualism. For excellent discussions of the subject see Merle Curti, "Intellectuals and Other People," *American Historical Review,* LX (1955), 259–282, and Merle Curti, *American Paradox: The Conflict of Thought and Action* (New Brunswick, New Jersey, 1956), pp. 33–65. A significant, if somewhat overdrawn, study of anti-intellectualism on the Kentucky frontier is Arthur K. Moore, *The Frontier Mind: A Cultural Analysis of the Kentucky Frontiersmen* (Lexington, Kentucky, 1957).

15. Benjamin F. Thomas, *Lincoln's New Salem* (Springfield, Illinois, 1934), pp 29–36.

16. Elise D. Isely, *Sunbonnet Days* (Caldwell, Idaho, 1935), p. 180.

17. James Flint, *Letters from America* (Edinburgh, 1822), p. 272.

18. Fortesque Cuming, *Sketches of a Tour of the Western Country* (Pittsburgh, 1810), pp. 166–167.

19. Quoted in Howard H. Peckham, "Books and Reading on the Ohio Valley Frontier," *Mississippi Valley Historical Review,* XLIV (1958), p. 652.

20. Louis B. Wright, *Culture on the Moving Frontier* (Bloomington, Indiana, 1955), pp. 71–72.

21. John F. McDermett, "Private Libraries in Frontier St. Louis," Bibliographical Society of America, *Papers,* LI (1957), 22–24.

22. Rusk, *Literature of the Middle Western Frontier,* II, 1–30; Percy Boynton, *The Rediscovery of the Frontier* (Chicago, 1931), pp. 40–41; John F. McDermett, "Best Sellers in Early St. Louis," *School and Society,* XLVII (1938), 673–675.

23. Peckham, "Books and Reading on the Ohio Valley Frontier," *loc. cit.,* pp. 649–663, is a study of reading tastes based on western imprints. See also James M. Miller, *The Genesis of Western Culture: The Upper Ohio Valley, 1800–1825* (Columbus, Ohio, 1938), pp. 147–151.

24. H. M. Brackenridge, *Recollections of Persons and Places in the West* (Pittsburgh, 1834), p. 91.

25. An extended description of early libraries is in William H. Venable,

Beginnings of Literary Culture in the Ohio Valley (Cincinnati, 1891), pp. 129–160. Briefer accounts are in Rusk, *Literature of the Middle Western Frontier*, I, 67–68, and Wright, *Culture on the Moving Frontier*, pp. 117–119.

26. Sarah J. Cutler, "The Coonskin Library," *Ohio Archaeological and Historical Publications*, XXVI (1917), 58–77.

27. Peckham, "Books and Reading on the Ohio Frontier," *loc. cit.*, pp. 655–657; McDermett, "Private Libraries in St. Louis," *loc. cit.*, pp. 25–37.

28. Quoted in McDermett, "Private Libraries in St. Louis," *loc. cit.*, p. 19.

29. Rusk, *Literature of the Middle Western Frontier*, I, 131–203; Buley, *The Old Northwest*, II, 489–496.

30. Frances Trollope, *Domestic Manners of the Americans* (London, 1832), I, 128.

31. Venable, *Beginnings of Literary Culture in the Ohio Valley*, pp. 58–128; Rusk, *Literature of the Middle Western Frontier*, I, 64–131; Buley, *The Old Northwest*, II, 523–533.

32. Miller, *Genesis of Western Culture*, pp. 151–158; Rusk, *Literature of the Middle Western Frontier*, I, 352–457.

33. Buley, *The Old Northwest*, II, 384–415. The persistence of classicism in the colleges and intellectual life of the Ohio Valley frontier is explored in Walter A. Agard, "Classics on the Midwest Frontier," in Walker D. Wyman and Clifton B. Kroeber, eds., *The Frontier in Perspective* (Madison, Wisconsin, 1957), pp. 165–183, and Miller, *Genesis of Western Culture*, pp. 93–111.

34. *Western Review*, III (1820), p. 145.

35. The theory that continued abundance has been a principal force in shaping the American character is advanced in David M. Potter, *People of Plenty: Economic Abundance and the American Character* (Chicago, 1954).

36. Quoted in George W. Pierson, "The Moving American," *The Yale Review*, XLIV (1954), 100.

37. Timothy Flint, *Recollections of the Last Ten Years* (Boston, 1826), pp. 141, 204–207; James Bryce, *The American Commonwealth* (London, 1888), II, 251.

38. Edwin James, *Account of an Expedition from Pittsburgh to the Rocky Mountains, Performed in the Years 1819, 1820* (Philadelphia, 1823), I, 106.

39. Pierson, "The Moving American," *loc. cit.*, pp. 101–102; Peter H. Rossi, *Why Families Move* (Glencoe, Illinois, 1955), pp. 1–2.

40. Everett S. Lee, "A Sociological Examination of the Turner Thesis," unpublished paper read at the December, 1957 meetings of the American Historical Association; Pierson, "The Moving American," *loc. cit.*, pp. 108–109.

41. Benjamin Malsberg and Everett S. Lee, *Migration and Mental Disease* (New York, 1956).

42. Lee, "A Sociological Examination," p. 8.

43. Arthur M. Schlesinger, "What Then Is the American, This New Man," *American Historical Review*, XLVIII (1943), 239.

44. Barnard Rush Hall, *The New Purchase*, I, 72.

45. Thomas Ashe, *Travels in America Performed in 1806* (London, 1808), II, 150.

46. Cuming, *Sketches of a Tour of the Western Country*, p. 71.

47. William A. Reavis, "The Maryland Gentry and Social Mobility, 1637–1667," *William and Mary Quarterly*, 3rd Ser., XIV (1957), 418–428.

48. Franklin D. Scott, tr. and ed., *Baron Klinkowstrom's America, 1818–1820* (Evanston, Illinois, 1952), p. 132.

49. *Cincinnati Literary Gazette*, III (June 18, 1825), 193.

50. Barnard Rush Hall, *The New Purchase*, II, 11.

51. James Flint, *Letters from America*, pp. 142–143.

52. Alexander, *Transatlantic Sketches*, II, 63–64.

53. Simon A. Ferrall, *A Ramble of Six Thousand Miles through the United States of America* (London, 1832), p. 243.

54. Raymond W. Mack, "Occupational Ideology and the Determinate Role," *Social Forces*, XXXVI (1957), 37–44.

The North Mexican Hacienda: Eighteenth and Nineteenth Centuries

BY FRANÇOIS CHEVALIER
Institut Français d'Amérique Latine

THE NORTH OF MEXICO is defined as part of "Aridamerica," characterized by light rainfall, dry vegtation, and highlands where, of old, indigenous nomads wandered. This vast zone excludes the Sierra Madre to the west and the Huasteca to the east, but includes (or used to include) the plains of the Bajío in the south. We will not take examples from this last region since it was a frontier zone which also shared some of the characteristics of central and southern Mexico and since it was populated at a relatively early date by Spaniards and sedentary Indians.

Without going into the sixteenth and seventeenth centuries, which I have studied elsewhere,[1] I propose above all to describe the evolution of the northern hacienda during the two following centuries, principally marked, I believe, by two characteristics which were sometimes contradictory, at least in appearance. That is, the eighteenth and nineteenth centuries witness on the one hand the prolongation and, one might even say, the entrenchment of the semifeudal tradition of the great estates in the North, which sometimes attained to an autonomy greater than they would ever know after the Independence, due to the intensification of the nomadic incursions and, in certain periods, to the weakness of the central government. But, on the other hand, from the last third of the eighteenth century on one begins to notice on the part of some hacienda pueblos as well as on the part of the viceregal and national authorities a certain tendency to set up free villages independent of the local chief and in the very midst of the latifundia. It would seem that this new trend—which has never been studied nor, I believe, pointed out—was brought about principally by the growth of population, which sometimes transformed tiny nuclei of peons or tenant farmers into populous villages which naturally wanted to set up municipal governments for free self-administration such as other centers of population possessed. Then too, the civil and religious authorities felt the need to organize and improve the administration of these *"congregaciones"* located on the haciendas, setting them up as municipalities and parishes. In the zones exposed to Apache incursions they hoped that this development and the attendant liberties would encourage the settling of this always sparsely populated country. The ideas of the Enlightenment had their influence in this, thus prefiguring agrarianism, but a natural phenomenon also took place paralleling that which had forced the kings and grandees of Europe to grant privileges and liberties in order to attract colonists to wilderness zones.

And here I must thank a distinguished Mexican historian and investigator, Dn. Luis Chávez Orozco, who supplied me with some documents and references most important for the support of this thesis.

I. *The Prolongation of the Past*

The entire northern zone was exposed to constant incursions on the part of the nomads who, reacting to the Anglo-Saxon advance, infiltrated or migrated southward, on certain occasions even literally besieging such cities as Zacatecas. Many travelers describe these terrible Apaches or other Indian nations, who had become great horsemen, attacking the haciendas and even the small villages which they tried to burn, constantly interrupting communications, and, due to the resulting obstruction of commerce, interfering with the growth of the economy and the population. "Retablitos," *ex voto* paintings from the last century, show us these fearful indigenes: always on horseback, body naked, and sometimes painted in brilliant colors, directing their sure arrows against unwary travelers or herdsmen. Sometimes they had adopted some Mexican traits, such as the broad-brimmed hat or, worst of all, the rifle or the shotgun.

In addition, bands of robbers or outlaws used to wander these lands, even sacking, for example, the village of Sombrerete in 1832.

Therefore the haciendas of the North were always more or less fortified. Such, for example, was the one near Monclova which Padre Morfi describes to us in the eighteenth century: "The house, although not comfortable to live in, is well constructed for defense against the Indians; it has a large corral and a patio which is not smaller in which an enormous quantity of livestock would fit in case of attack, which occurs frequently; it is entirely surrounded by a new adobe wall, tall and strong enough; at the north-eastern corner an adobe tower was under construction, from which the artillery can play from under cover and protect the portals of the habitation." [2]

At the middle of the nineteenth century the novelist Payno, who always sticks close to reality, describes for us in the following manner a great northern hacienda: "The house of the Sauz hacienda was in fact a fortified castle. The façade was made up of a high, broad archway ending on both sides in two tall towers with loopholes, which were matched by two others guarding the back of the house. The *azotea* was surrounded by crenellations behind which a soldier could keep under cover; so that once the massive oak door reinforced with iron bands was closed a siege would be necessary to take that building. Within there were wells of fresh, potable water and supplies for three or four months, arms, munitions and everything necessary for defense. . . . When these country estates were formed from lands belonging to nations never subdued like the Mexicans by the Spaniard, the buildings were constructed like fortifications, sacrificing interior comfort and architectonic proportions to security. In the patio, which was large, three or four coaches, each with its own string of eight mules, could have entered, turned around as in a circus, and passed again through the portal which led to the open country." [3]

Padre Morfi described to us the curious invention of an *hacendado,* whose estate was located still farther to the north, near Santa Rosa, for protection against the constant and sudden attacks of the nomads in the open country: he "conceived of a sort of ambulating castle, constructed on a cart which follows the peons; within are kept some rifles, and at the least sign of attack the workers rush inside and, firing through the loopholes of the little fort, defend themselves against the shots of their enemies until the noise of the contest brings reinforcements to their aid; thus far this invention has freed him from surprise attacks and multiplied his wealth." The good father complains, however, that because of indolence and laziness, few of the neighboring landholders have such initiative.[4]

As is well known, most of these northern haciendas were settled either for the exploitation of silver mines or to furnish these mines with grain and meat, and sometimes with both objects in mind: only precious metals could attract settlers to these arid highlands and severe mountains of northern Mexico. Being often very distant from the principal centers of population, the haciendas formed little worlds capable for the most part of supplying their own needs. In addition to their herds and cultivated fields, they often had mills, workshops, orchards, and vineyards. Accordingly, in northern Durango the hacienda of Santa Catarina, then the property of the Conde de San Pedro del Alamo, contained in the last third of the eighteenth century two thousand inhabitants, whose little huts, along with the church and the main house, formed a vast square plaza. The Count possessed 130,000 sheep and 7,000 mares. There were lacking the sedentary Indians of the South, and the workers and servants were of the most varied origins, "from all the castes," at Santa Catarina; and in another place more to the north "Indians, *coyotes*, mulattoes, Pames, Tarahumaras . . . etc.: all are received without distinction, without inquiring who they are, nor whence they proceed." [5] Also, in 1787, the *intendente* of Durango complains that because of the lack of workhands in his immense district, the haciendas and royal mining concessions frequently became "the asylum where bums and bandits may come and go as they please on the pretext of looking for work without anyone inquiring whence and with whose permission they come"; but the excuse for this is that otherwise "it would not be possible to find workers, even bad ones." [6] Thus, peonage based upon retention for unpaid debts does not seem to be so common as in central and southern Mexico. On the haciendas of this same *intendencia* tenant farmers were living on their modest "ranchos"; they were "hard-up" people of various and frequently dubious origins who personally possessed, as did some servants, their own horses and small herds as well as the right to range these animals on the lands of the hacienda. [7]

The great isolated haciendas continued during this period to have their private jails and their own administration of justice, either because the *hacendados* or their henchmen had managed to obtain the offices of the local government, or because they simply exercised a *de facto* power which was not theirs by law. Thus Padre Morfi and a commandant who accompanied him noted near Parras the presence of "a lad in chains," whose master had "punished him by imprisonment" for a misdemeanor; the good Franciscan comments that "his Lordship was surprised by the tyranny and limitless jurisdiction which these *hacendados* appropriate to themselves, and he ordered him set free." In the mid-nineteenth century Payno shows us also the severe Marqués de Valle Alegre having one of his servants whipped without the judge of the village daring to intervene; nonetheless, in the later period such behavior provoked serious resentments among the peons of the hacienda.[8]

And finally, it would be a mistake not to study the private armies of the haciendas, which seem not to have been unusual, above all in the zones most exposed to the attacks of the nomads or of bandits. Sometimes they came into being by authorization or even command of the viceregal government, as in the case of Ciénega de Mata (S.L.P.). In other cases it was a *de facto* situation created in part by necessity and the lack of funds on the part of the government sufficient for such a vast country. Thus, during the period from 1810 to 1818 a henchman of the Conde de San Mateo Valparaíso, "nominated Colonel *ad honorem,* maintained for nearly one year eight hundred men on the northern frontier, whom he paid a peso a day," took part in the struggle for independence on the royalist side, and was routed in the end by the insurgents.[9] In addition, "all the Mexican aristocracy of the viceregal period thought it much to be a captain, and their descendants continued being captains within the home and even outside of it, without the independent government ever concerning itself about them," as Payno writes, who shows us his Conde del Sauz, in the mid-nineteenth century, donning the uniform of a Spanish *capitán de infantería* for a dinner at his hacienda, or before setting out to meet a relative.[10]

These great *hacendados* lived for most of the year in Mexico City or in other cities such as Durango, San Luis Potosí or Querétaro. But they would go to spend a season at their haciendas, where they gathered together at times many friends and relatives; then, too, they offered a generous hospitality to travelers and hikers, for whom a wing of the main house was generally held in readiness.[11]

When the rich *hacendados* traveled they liked to make a show of their military escort, for "those customs of the wealthy class of colonial times were preserved many years after the beginning of the republic, as one of so many ordinary things which nobody noticed except those whose business they were." Accordingly, Payno's Marqués de Valle Alegre, wishing to impress his future father-in-law, arrived at the latter's hacienda located in a northern state mounted on a magnificent stallion, dressed as a captain, and accom-

panied by "twenty-five buckskin knights armed to the teeth." Behind
them rolled "the coach of the house, a great spherical machine, the
color of the blue sky, with the arms of the Marquis on the doors,
supported by two husky gilded springs, enormous rear wheels, and
tiny front ones." The canvas cover which had guarded it against
the dust of the road had been removed, and the interior brushed so
that the lining of velvet, mistreated and worn with use, would show
to best advantage. "The coach of the Marquis was followed by that
of the servants, of the same style but less luxurious, . . . [with] eight
bay mules . . . and eight black mules kept in reserve," and in addition a magnificent "string of white mules, recently purchased, under
the care of seven or eight lads well mounted and with their lariats
close at hand." Finally, "the rear guard was formed by a squadron
of ten mules with their respective muleteers, their new furniture,
adorned with little tassels of vari-colored wool, and on their *atarrías*
lettering in white fabric upon a red ground which said: 'I serve
my master, the Marquis'." [12]

Clearly it was not always that the *hacendados* had such means as
this powerful marquis. Certain haciendas were abandoned because
of the constant attacks of the nomads. Not a few of the other landowners were debtors who had mortgaged their landholdings and did
not have the capital necessary to work their lands. [13] Sometimes their
indebtedness was caused by the luxury which they displayed. But
above all there were more modest proprietors, who resided throughout the year in the country, living a patriarchal and austere life with
their families. Such a man was the landowner near Zacatecas who
governed his hacienda by himself and with such good order, com-
posure, and good sense that his dependents enjoyed a much better
condition than those in other locales. Padre Morfi notes that "every
afternoon the master and the servants gather together in the chapel,
pray the rosary, the catechism is explained and, in short, the whole
breathes of economy, abundance and piety." [14]

In general, these *hacendados* were religious men who founded
chaplaincies and constructed churches where they arranged to have
themselves buried. Even the first Conde de San Mateo Valparaíso
became a hermit toward the end of his life, living in a grotto of the
hills near his principal hacienda. [15]

Among these great landholders not a few had a mentality comparable to that of the nobility of the Old Regime in Europe, showing
a certain disregard for money and economic return, carrying their

sense of honor to extremes, severe with their wives and daughters, who went abroad infrequently, even though the *hacendados* often fathered many illegitimate children—in sum, the enthusiastic heirs of a whole etiquette inherited from the old Spanish nobility.[16] But at the very time that this nobility seemed to be assuming a set character and to be arriving at its apogee, in the eighteenth century and even later, a wise observer could detect clear symptoms of the great changes which would, a century or more in the future, totally transform traditional Mexican society.

II. *Signs of Evolution and Antecedents of Agrarianism*

Beginning in the last third of the eighteenth century the great landed proprietors began to be criticized in Mexico, not only because of cases of monopolization of the land or local abuses, as formerly, but in addition because of the system of latifundia *per se.* This attitude is to be noted in the works of the bishops, of Fray Antonio de San Miguel, the Bishop of Michoacán, for example, or those of Abad y Queipo, for that matter. But possibly no one criticized more than the visiting Franciscan Fray Juan de Morfi the great haciendas of the North, which he got to know during the years 1777–1778.

Morfi was what we would call today a "progressive," visibly influenced by the ideas of the Enlightenment; he laments, for example, that so much money should have been spent in exaggerated decoration for a church instead of investing this money "in encouraging the industry of the poor" or in founding a new village within the parish of that sanctuary (Atontonilco, Guanajuato), "for there are abundant lands and water for this purpose, though it is true that the nearby haciendas tyrannize over that whole territory." Six leagues farther on he complains of a great hacienda (The R-ranch) because "everything is sacrificed to the inertia and obstructionism of the owners of these extensive holdings, whose lack of order is the principal cause of the underpopulation of America." [17] Morfi never ceases making such observations, whenever he encounters a great hacienda on his road: in Ciénega de Mata, for example, or in San Francisco de Patos, in the Marquisate of San Miguel de Aguayo (between Parras and Saltillo). Here, in spite of the excellent lands and water supply, the owner "does not earn his rents from his crops" but from his wool-bearing herd numbering two hundred thousand, and "there is not a sight in the world more sad than the environs of this hacienda," where the inhabitants, according to Morfi, "are wretched from the cradle, and working without interruption until they reach a most advanced age, they all die in misery." With but a part of the families here gathered one could make "a lovely town, but the vices of the methods employed in the civil economy of these haciendas makes them useless to the states." [18]

In short, it seemed to the good father that all evils stemmed from the latifundia, which leave great areas unpopulated, uncared for, and uncultivated, while it was so necessary to attract settlers to the far-flung territories of the North.

The *intendente* of Durango and the viceroy also insist upon the urgent need to people the northern zones in a correspondence carried on during the years 1787–1788. According to them it would otherwise be most difficult to resist the incursions of the nomads and there would be no possibility of economic development. It seemed necessary to attract and encourage settlers, creating a more secure environment, with more control, gathering the isolated inhabitants together, establishing parishes on the haciendas, and organizing their congregations into pueblos with their own administration of justice and economic and political government. Thus many crimes and robberies originating in the uncontrolled vagrancy of the inhabitants would be avoided. The situation had grown worse because of the pressure of the nomads and the bad policy of "those commissioned by the temporal power," who had taken the lands of the infrequent settlers away from them on the pretext that these lands had been property of the exiled Jesuits.

The *intendente* gives many concrete examples of haciendas where it would be desirable to found parishes and pueblos. In addition to the parish priest, each pueblo would have its *ayuntamiento* with "annual election of public officials," a school, a strong jailhouse, public properties, community lands, and so on.

Nevertheless the *intendente* as well as the viceroy note that the foundation of these pueblos on the haciendas should be brought about "without any prejudice" to the *hacendados* and "conserving the owners in all their exclusive rights and faculties." Thus the *hacendados* would in any case "benefit from a sure supply of peons and renters for their lands, which cannot cultivate themselves." [19]

In fact pueblos could not be founded without granting a minimum of lands and community property, as required by law: there could hardly be less than the modest "legal minimum" conferred to

Indian villages (600 varas, or 504 meters, square). In any case this would represent for a certain number of the inhabitants the possibility of gaining relative economic independence. Furthermore, commerce would no longer be limited to the *tienda de raya* of the hacienda. And finally, the *ayuntamiento,* elected by the locality, would be able to take over certain governmental functions which formerly fell to the *hacendado* or his foreman. This constituted, in the final analysis, a threat to the traditional hacienda system in the northern zones, where very few independent communities existed, whether because they had never been founded or because they had been absorbed within the latifundia.

Now, these projects for the erection of pueblos had not been born spontaneously of the imagination of an *intendente* or of a viceroy seeking ways to develop the northern territories, but had rather been suggested or imposed by the circumstances themselves. The population had grown during the eighteenth century; on certain haciendas the formerly tiny groups of peons or renters had grown considerably and were beginning to present administrative problems which the landowners could not always easily resolve, while the citizenry itself would have been glad to take charge of these matters, following the example of neighboring communities already possessing municipal organization. In other cases new nuclei of settlers and "the dispossessed" had established themselves on the unsettled lands of the latifundia, and were struggling to earn a living from the cultivation of their small fields. Accordingly, in the last third of the eighteenth century there was much discussion of the founding of pueblos, whether due to the spontaneous growth and division of the old groups of inhabitants or due to the desire of the authorities to encourage the settlement of the less-favored zones.

In fact Morfi, for example, not only speaks frequently of the convenience or necessity of establishing pueblos on the haciendas, but he also tells us of some concrete attempts, such as that of a group of renters on one of the haciendas confiscated from the Jesuits, on the shores of the unsettled Bolsón de Mapimí "who presented themselves in Parras at the time of the Temporal Junta in that district, asking for title to these lands under obligation of settling upon them sixty-five families who would undertake to pay an evaluation and assessment of 7,000 pesos." [20] Far to the north, near Santa Rosa, we encounter a soldier "offering to the king his ranch, San Ildefonso, for the erection of a village, with the obligation of settling it entirely with his own children and grandchildren." [21] But we do not know if these plans were really carried out.

We do have evidence of the resistance of certain large landholders who feared for their lands. Thus, on many haciendas such as that of the Conde del Valle de Súchil, the peons and renters were allowed to form their villages, "but no one opposed this more than their masters, fearful that if their servants should constitute themselves a community with such domestic conveniences, they would be called to the village and despoiled of their title to their possessions." In fact, the Conde de San Pedro del Alamo expelled the soldiers of the presidio from his haciendas near Cuencamé, "fearful that they would present themselves with a petition to establish a community." [22]

We need to find out if the viceregal authorities managed to impose their will, for example in the intendency of Durango, or if the triumph went to the opposition of some of the great landholders (others may have been more understanding and perhaps even in favor of settlement). At least, it is interesting to note these antecedents of agrarianism in the minds of these men of the Enlightenment, and also the aspirations of certain groups of settlers.

After Independence these ideas continued to take root, although slowly, among the thinkers and economists, while one notes a certain pressure on the part of the inhabitants of the haciendas. For the first time we note sure cases of the actual establishment of such municipalities—although further investigation will probably discover earlier examples.

Thus, on March 28, 1827, a congressional decree gave the title of "Villa de Cos" to a congregation of San Cosme located within the limits of the hacienda of Bañón, north of Zacatecas, in recompense of the services of its curate, José María Cos, to the cause of the insurgents. But the decree stipulated that the concession would only go into effect when the *ayuntamiento* should have legally acquired the lands, a condition which was not fulfilled until 1845, because of disputes regarding the price with the *hacendado*, D. Lorenzo de la Canal. Later the community was able to augment considerably its commons and its lands with the transfer of title in its favor of hacienda lands suitable for large livestock, which was divided among 155 of its citizens. [23]

Thus from one hacienda a new municipality had been erected, possessing ample lands, inasmuch as the later acquisitions alone represented some 4,375 hectares, though in dry lands, to be sure. Another case in the same region is that of the vast hacienda of Valparaíso, whose inhabitants founded their first *ayuntamiento* in 1829 under the presidency of the administrator and which attained the status of a "village" in 1845. This operation had been favored by the embargo placed upon the hacienda by the creditors of the proprietor. In the end the renters themselves were able to scrape together enough money to buy the hacienda in default, dividing about 1,000 lots among urban proprietors and from 250 to 300 large parcels among rural proprietors, the parcels consisting of "from half an acre to a square mile." The best lands were held in common, the main house of the hacienda was used as the *ayuntamiento* and school, while the church and manse also passed into the hands of the community.[24]

One notes, then, in this creation of free villages a marked interest on the part of certain groups of peons and renters from the haciendas; but probably no one would have favored them more than D. Francisco García, governor of the extensive state of Zacatecas from 1829 to 1835. This intelligent and energetic man arranged for the state to buy many haciendas in order to transform them into pueblos of small proprietors or in order to distribute the lands among neighboring villages which lacked them. Three haciendas near Sombrerete in 1832–1833; two ranches of the same region leased to "a company of military colonists" in 1834; the hacienda of La Quemada divided among two similar companies in 1832; two other haciendas in the region of Jerez, to which should be added a congregation advanced to status of a municipality in 1820, and a few years later metamorphosed into the Village of Escobedo, in possession of the lands of the hacienda of Santa Teresa, also purchased by the state.[25]

What happened in other states remains to be studied. In Guanajuato, for example, we observe several congregations which are made pueblos, and particularly in the north of the state the attempt of the inhabitants of the hacienda of Jaral, in a decree of 1857. Pending indemnization or arrangement with the proprietor, the new pueblo, called "Mina," would remain in the center of a square league and would have "two alcaldes from the people, proprietors both, a substitute and a *síndico procurador*." Its jurisdiction must have been much greater. Nevertheless, in 1880 this decree for the creation of the pueblo in Jaral is rescinded.[26]

In truth, opposition to these steps continued to be very strong, as various decrees show, whether or not they were rescinded later on, such as the decree of Santa Anna in 1853, "prohibiting the creation of towns without the consent of the local proprietor."[27] True it is that three years later, in 1856, this decree "prohibiting the congregations of families living on the haciendas to be erected into pueblos without the consent of the local proprietor was declared void." The Congreso Constituyente commented as follows on the matter: "Laws favorable to the masses . . . are those which have permitted the inhabitants of an hacienda, when they reach a considerable number, . . . to establish their municipal rights and obligations, and, finally, to remove themselves from the patriarchal tutorship of the landholders, which so resembles slavery; then the unfortunate workers have the right to comply with certain formalities and constitute themselves a pueblo in order to attain some form of government other than the caprice of master, heretofore the arbiter of their fate." It is added that if approved—as it was—this proposition "will leave the congregations of families in the neighborhood of the haciendas in the enjoyment of their ancient rights."[28]

We may conclude, awaiting further studies, that there seem to have been many attempts and certain interesting achievements in the way of founding independent pueblos on the haciendas during the nineteenth century. But there is no doubt that the opposition was significant; several times it managed to impede these agrarian impulses, and drowned them out completely, it would seem, during the long dominion of Porfirio Díaz. The ultimate triumph of the small proprietor was nevertheless to be definitive with the Revolution initiated in 1910.

FOOTNOTES

1. *La formation des grands domaines du Mexique. Terre et société aux XVI–XVII S* (Paris, 1952, trad, into Spanish in *Problemas agrícolas e industriales de Mexico,* VII, No. 1, 1956).

2. Fray Juan Agustín de Morfi, *Viaje de Indios y diario del Nuevo México,* intro. and notes by Vito Alessio Robles (México, 1935), p. 184.

3. Manual Payno, *Los bandidos de Río Frío,* ed. Castro Leal (México, 1945), II, 376.

4. Morfi, *op. cit.,* pp. 253–427.

5. *Ibid.,* pp. 93, 165, 364, 393.

6. *Informe particular del Intendente de Durango Don Felipe Díaz de*

Ortega (1787, Archivo General de la Nación, Civil Vol. 1363198, etc.). This document was kindly sent to me by Dn. Luis Chávez Orozco.

7. *Padrón de la Ciudad de Durango* (1778, publ. Atanasio Saravia in *Memorias de la Academia Mex. de la Hist.*), II, 1958. Many examples pp. 133–145, 159–160, etc.

8. Morfi, *op. cit.*, pp. 89, 188, 363, 375.

9. *Memoria presentada por el C. Gabriel García, Gobernador del Estado de Zacatecas, 16 de Sept., 1874* (Zacatecas, 1874), p. 91.

10. *Op. cit.*, II, 362, 381.

11. Morfi, *op. cit.*, pp. 47, 345.

12. Payno, *op. cit.*, II, 381–385.

13. Morfi, *op. cit.*, pp. 62–63, 71, 351, 356–357. Abandoned haciendas: *Informe del Intendente de Durango, op. cit.*, p. 206.

14. Morfi, *op. cit.*, pp. 52, 348.

15. *Memoria presentada por el C. Gabriel García*, p. 91.

16. An extreme case is that of Payno's Conde del Sauz, in *op. cit.*, II, 359, 361–362, 398; III, 218, etc.

17. Morfi, *op. cit.*, pp. 46–50, 344–345, etc.

18. *Ibid.*, pp. 149–150, 387–388.

19. *Informe del Intendente de Durango Don Felipe Díaz de Ortega*, 178, Secs. 21–41, Secs. 62, *et seq.*, Secs. 80, *et seq.*, Secs. 90, *et seq.*, Secs. 101, *et seq.*, Sec. 177, Secs. 198–200, particularly Sec. 199 for phrase cited, Sec. 203, etc., particularly Sec. 309 (government of the newly erected communities), Sec. 216 (the dispossessed in unsettled lands), etc. Follows: The Answer of the Viceroy, etc. All in: Archivo General de la Nación, Civil Vol. 1363. This document was brought to my attention through the kindness of D. Luis Chávez Orozco.

20. Morfi, *op. cit.*, pp. 122–123, 376 (Hacienda of Hornos). See also p. 370 (Mapimí), p. 392 (Coahuila), p. 405.

21. *Ibid.*, pp. 251, 426.

22. *Ibid.*, pp. 67–69, 354–397, 366.

23. *Memoria presentada por el C. Gabriel García*, pp. 80–81.

24. *Ibid.*, pp. 67–70.

25. *Memorias presentadas por el C. Francisco García, Gobernador del Estado de Zacatecas . . . en los añas 1829 a 1834* (reprinted by Gabriel García, Zacatecas, n.d. [partial copy]), pp. 19, 29, 38, 40–41. This work was brought to my attention through the kindness of D. Luis Chávez Orozco. We will study the labors of the governor in more detail in a work now in hand concerning the origins of the Mexican small proprietor.

26. *Colección de leyes, reglamentos y circulares sobre municipios* (Guanajuato, 1878), pp. 313, 662. Cf. also pp. 178, 463, 478, 612.

27. *Ibid.*, p. 215.

28. *Sesión del 19 de mayo de 1856 del Congreso Constituyente.* (Document kindly sent to me by D. Luis Chávez Orozco.)

The Texas Ranch

BY J. C. DYKES
United States Soil Conservation Service

SUCH OLD BRANDS as the XIT, Turkey Track, Hashknife, JA, Four Sixes, SMS, and 3D's; such old ranch names as Matador, King, Spur, Pitchfork, Taft, and League; such old range giants as John Chisum, Charles Goodnight, Thomas Bugbee, Oliver Loving, Shanghai Pierce, Barbecue Campbell, Luke Brite and George Littlefield; and such Texas ranch families as produced not one but several outstanding cowmen as the Swensons, the Klebergs, the Mitchells, the Slaughters, the Kokernots, the Reynolds, the Matthews, and the Waggoners call to mind a past era in the range history of Texas. This was the day of the open range, followed by huge fenced spreads; of the great trail drives of beef to rails' end in Kansas and Nebraska; of carousing cowboys in Dodge, Hayes, or Abilene at the end of the trail; of drives of cows to stock the northern Plains just wrested from the hard-fighting Plains Indians; of Indian raids on isolated ranches; of the roundup; and of foreign capital invested in Texas lands and Texas cattle.

I could easily spend my allotted time in acknowledging our indebtedness to our friends from south of the Rio Grande and thanking them for the gifts of cattle and the "know-how" of handling them. For well over two centuries cattle have been of tremendous economic significance in Texas and even now two-thirds of the land area of the state is devoted to grazing. The trail drives, following the Civil War, hastened the economic recovery of Texas by pouring an estimated two hundred million dollars into its business arteries. It would be easy to dwell, nostalgically, on this age of range romance about which I heard so much as a boy. Some of the old brands and some of the old ranch names are still in use and, while the range giants are all gone, many of the great ranch families are still in the cattle business, having made—even taken the lead in—the adjustment to the modern way of ranching.

It is impossible in a paper of this length to trace properly the evolutionary changes from the old to the new—the influence of barbed wire, windmills, railroads, highways, new and improved grasses, new and improved breeds, rural electricity, and the application of soil- and water-conservation principles to range lands.

The Texan ranch of today is small by the old open-range standards, although James C. Tanner, writing recently in the *Wall Street Journal*, stated that there are more than a hundred ranches of more than 100,000 acres in the state today. The modern Texan ranch is fenced and cross-fenced to permit rotation grazing. It has adequate water (at least, in nondrouth years) from living streams, stock ponds, and wells. There are electric lights in the ranch house and in the barns and electric pumps on part of the wells. The ranch is near a paved road and a bus takes the ranch children to a modern school. There are some farming tools on hand and most of the supplemental feed needed to carry the cattle through the winter without loss of weight is produced on the ranch. The ranch family eats its own beef, carefully aged in its own deep freezer. The ranch owner is a cooperator with (and often a supervisor of) the locally organized and managed soil conservation district and is actively engaged in practicing soil and water conservation to assure the maximal production of a grass crop for harvest by his cattle.

Are there cowboys on these modern Texan ranches? you may well ask. Yes—some. But the cowboy is no longer the historic "Hired Man on Horseback" who was willing to do anything so long as it could be done from the topside of a horse. I learned this lesson the hard way nearly forty years ago when I was a Kansas cowboy for a summer—I spent considerably more time on a Fordson tractor seat than I did in the saddle and about twenty times as many hours putting up hay as I did working cattle. The cowboy of today is likely to be as expert in the handling of a jeep as a horse. My good friend and fellow Texan in exile (in Maryland), Dr. Frank Goodwyn, in his book *Lone Star Land* (New York, 1955) shows a photo of a helicopter in use on a roundup on the Waggoner Ranch in Wilbarger County. I am not suggesting that a present-day cowboy must be a flyer, although a goodly number of Texas cowmen are members of the "Flying Ranchers" and pilot their own planes. Skill in operating and repairing machinery is as highly prized in present-day cowboys as skill in handling cattle.

Texas cattle, more than 8,000,000 in number, are still dominated by the Herefords. However, Texans are particularly proud of the Santa Gertrudis cattle, the only breed developed in America, which are a product of the great King Ranch. As I understand it, the ranch sold only Santa Gertrudis bulls for some years. Now that there are females available, a number of South Texas cowmen are changing to Santa Gertrudis. The use of Brahman bulls on grade cows has been a common practice in South Texas for many years and there are a good many ranches stocked with registered Brahmans (red or gray) to supply this bull demand. There are Angus and Short-horn enthusiasts but the Whitefaces remain the favorite with the Texas cowman.

Conservation Ranchers

In describing the Texan ranch of today in general terms, I have pointed out the use of soil- and water-conservation practices on the range. The Texas ranchman of today is a "conservation rancher," a term applied to Charles Pettit, the owner of Flat Top Ranch at Walnut Springs, Texas, by the late Louis Bromfield, noted novelist and conservationist of Malabar Farm, Ohio. I will have quite a lot to say about Charlie Pettit and his ranch, but for fear you will think he is unique I want to mention several other outstanding Texas conservation ranchers.

Dolph Briscoe has root-plowed and reseeded most of his Catarina Ranch near Uvalde. He systematically rests his pastures to maintain grass vigor and now has a Santa Gertrudis breeding herd. He has tripled his carrying capacity (twenty acres per cow instead of sixty acres per cow), using the conservation system.

Horace K. Fawcett of Del Rio has been a staunch advocate of conservation since the beginning of the modern movement. He was a member of the first State Soil Conservation Board and has been following a conservation ranching system on his land for about twenty years. He says that despite seven years of drouth recently the grass is now better than it has been at any time since the ranch went under fence.

Clayton Puckett of Fort Stockton is a former soil conservation district supervisor and president of the Association of Texas Soil Conservation Districts. He also had his troubles with drouth during the early 1950's but he materially improved his ranch by reduced stocking, resting pastures, pitting for moisture conservation, controlling mesquite and cedar, and reseeding. He received some returns on his investment even during the worst of the drouth years.

Joe Boyd of San Angelo is a cooperator with the Upper Clear Fork Soil Conservation District. Water development, deferred grazing, and control of cedar, plus some reseeding, have paid off for Boyd. He is now extending the conservation program to other ranches that he owns.

W. B. Osborn of Rio Grande City started spraying mesquite in 1948 and has since reduced his stocking rate, chopped the smaller brush, and done some reseeding. He produces 450-pound calves now and markets more beef from a smaller number of cows than he ran before starting his conservation program. He feels that the day of 350-pound calves on his ranch are gone forever (and for those interested, the deer are bigger and fatter now).

Joseph Vander Stucken of Sonora is a pioneer in the control of brush on his range. His system consists first of chaining, then of using goats to control the sprouts, and finally of alternate grazing and resting. He drastically reduced stock numbers during the recent drouth and when the rains came last year the range readily absorbed moisture and has made an excellent recovery. Livestock and deer come from neighboring ranges to this ranch because of the quality and quantity of the Vander Stucken grass.

Waters S. Davis of League City is a grandson of J. C. League, a sea captain, who like Captain King saw a future in Texas grass and cattle. Waters is a past president of the Texas Association and of the National Association of Soil Conservation Districts. In addition to improving the drainage and to reseeding the home place at League City, he is actively cooperating with the other districts in Texas and Louisiana wherever he owns farm and ranch lands.

And I mention with some pride that two of my very close friends and former associates in the Soil Conservation Service, Louis Merrill and W. H. (Bill) DuPuy, are doing quite well, thank you, as conservation ranchers. Merrill's Running M brand, registered by his father in 1872 in Somervell County, is now used on the Ellis County ranch near Midlothian. DuPuy is taking advantage of the additional moisture, common to East Texas, to operate successfully in Anderson County.

No. Charlie Pettit is not the only conservation rancher in Texas—there are literally hundreds of them and the tribe increases daily as a result of the examples set by such pioneers in the movement as those I have mentioned. However, I want to use Flat Top as a specific example of how sound conservation practices can be used to reclaim eroded, gullied, and abused land and of how, with astute management, it can be made to pay. I offer no apologies for using Flat Top as my example—it happens to be the Texan ranch that I know the most about now. There is also a certain amount of sentiment involved in the choice, since my own father ran cows on a part of the present Flat Top range back in the eighties.

Pettit Buys a "Lemon"

Charlie Pettit grew up on a ranch in Archer County and he never got over it. He taught school (one of his pupils was Dr. Walter Prescott Webb), ran a country store, and finally made a considerable amount of money in the oil business. But the desire to own a ranch was ever with him and in 1936, feeling that he could spare some time to ranching, he started looking for a suitable piece of land to buy. In 1938 he bought the seven thousand acres of brush-infested and overgrazed, nearly worn-out range known as Flat Top Ranch. Roy Bedichek, Texas naturalist and educator, who headed the Texas Interscholastic League when I was a young high school teacher and coach many years ago, called this piece of range "heartbreak land."

Frank Reeves, long-time ranch editor of the Fort Worth *Star Telegram*, saw the ranch shortly after Pettit bought it. His interest in the place had been whetted by a remark made by Bob Coody, an experienced West Texas rancher who had the place leased prior to the time of its purchase. Coody had asked Frank if he knew the man who had purchased Flat Top Ranch and on being told that Frank did not, said, "I am sorry for that man Pettit. He certainly bought a lemon, and it will not take him long to find it out. I moved most of my cattle off the place before my lease was out to keep them from starving. If you had the feed, it would not be a good place to keep them." Frank reported that the place looked "shabby, worn and depressing—the open places were bare of grass and the ugly signs of erosion caught and held the eye—brush was so thick in many places there was very little room for grass to grow." It is most fortunate for all of us that Frank Reeves saw the ranch before the conservation practices were installed. He is one of the keenest observers of range and livestock operations in the Southwest.

Far from discouraged with his purchase, Charlie Pettit decided to buy more land to add to his original seven thousand acres. Over the years, he has succeeded in buying many of the eroded, cropped-out farms adjoining the ranch, and Flat Top now consists of seventeen thousand acres. He was aware that this new land of his was in the native bluestem belt. The bluestem belt, the most productive native grassland of the primeval American continent, according to my associate B. W. (Bill) Allred, lay in the area extending from Lake Winnipeg, Canada, to the Gulf of Mexico. It was bounded on the east by the hardwood forest and on the west by the Great Plains (short-grass country). The important native grasses in this huge belt are big bluestem, little bluestem, Indian grass, switch grass, side-oats grama, and the wild ryes. I am sure from many talks with him that Charlie Pettit could see with his mind's eye, even in 1938, the bluestem belt restored in all its glory on his range—why not? This was its own, its native land. Charlie Pettit recognized another asset that Bob Coody had failed to see—the East Bosque and its tributaries, Rough Creek and Flag Branch, and a tributary of the main Bosque, Tough Creek, and he was already seeing the acres of water that he would one day impound.

The cowman's trinity—good *grass*, an abundance of clean *water*, and well-bred *cattle*—were well known to the Flat Top owner. But he knew that he had to have the grass and water before he got the cattle and that grass was highly important in controlling runoff and in capturing and storing the water. While some water-conservation measures were started almost immediately, the first real project on the new ranch was the improvement of the grass.

Grass

About a fourth of Pettit's land was covered with suffocating stands of trees and shrubs, and he immediately tackled the job of reducing this cover to give the grasses a chance. A good many different ways of ridding the ranch of the unwanted woody vegetation were tried over the years but the cheapest and most effective proved to be hand cutting followed by spraying with 2,4,5-T. All brush under four inches in diameter was cut off and the stumps were sprayed. Tree trunks were girdled and the cut space was sprayed. Only about ten per cent resprouted and required a second spraying. A considerable acreage was infested with cactus when the new owner took over. Hand grubbing, due care being taken to remove the "potato" (a tuber at the base of the plant usually several inches underground), was found to be the most satisfactory way of eradicating cactus at Flat Top. The grubbers assisted in reestablishing the grass by dropping a few grass seed into the soil disturbed by the removal of each cactus plant and by stepping on them. The native grasses, given a chance by the elimination of competition, began to increase almost immediately.

There was another grave problem to be solved in restoring the bluestems—the reclamation of seriously eroded land. Of the 3,400 acres cultivated by the various previous owners, about 2,400 acres should never have been plowed. These had to be reseeded. This land was badly eroded, infertile, and often caked as hard as flint. Native grass-seed supplies were inadequate. Water-conservation and water-control measures plus the use of heavy crust-breaking tools and nurse crops of small grain got the grass started and a deferment of one to three years in the grazing program resulted in the restoration of the bluestem range. On much of the rest of the ranch the bluestems needed only a chance to grow and a program of deferred grazing gave them that chance.

The management of the restored range is a fetish at Flat Top—the policy is to leave almost half of the annual grass production on the ground for conservation and improvement. You may wonder how a cow can tell when she has eaten her 50 or 60 per cent. She can't, of course, but managers can, and there is where the real gift of management counts. This policy has paid off handsomely for Charlie Pettit. His "heartbreak land" was carrying 2,500 purebred Herefords before the drouth started in December, 1950. This was a cow to each five acres—need I say more?

This management principle resulted in the progressive reduction of livestock numbers through the drouth years of 1951–1956. In July 1956 the herd numbered only a thousand head. Charlie Pettit had practiced what he had preached (often a difficult thing to do) and disposed of fifteen hundred registered Herefords, but he had not overgrazed or destroyed his grass cover.

Water

Along with the grass-improvement program the water system was gradually developed. At the present time there are twenty-four wells and forty-three impounding dams of all sizes on the ranch. The ranch is divided into about one hundred enclosures, ranging from small traps to a pasture containing about one thousand acres. Nearly all the enclosures are grazed sometime during the year and this means water must be available in each. For the most part the wells are located on high points on the ranch and water flows by gravity from substantial rock and cement or concrete storage tanks, located at each well, through pipes to concrete water troughs in the various pastures served by the particular well. There are wind-mills over eighteen of the wells and electric pumps on the other six.

While all the forty-three dams that impound water are an important part of the ranch-improvement program, those constructed on the East Bosque (five) and on its tributaries, Rough Creek (six) and Flag Branch (six), are making the greatest contributions. Water backs up in the stream channels along the gentle valleys from one dam to the downstream toe of the dam above it in the series. This has restored the water table in the valleys where formerly flash runoff from the denuded uplands had cut deep trenches through which the streams flowed. After the flood runoff passed, the deeply entrenched channels served as drains which lowered the water table. Approximately two hundred acres of land will eventually be subirrigated by the restored water table in these valleys. Well over one hundred acres have already been reclaimed. As these fertile valleys have been cleared of scrub trees and brush, the tall native grasses have taken over. Now these valley meadows, if not cut, could hide a cow herd in summer.

Charlie Pettit has a real affection for his impounded water. He puts it this way, "An acre of water is worth much more to me than an acre of land." This is his way of saying that an acre of land will produce only its quota of grass, hay, or feed, while a surface acre of water (usually several acre-feet) can be used to irrigate or sub-irrigate several acres, with much greater production the result.

The reservoirs back of the dams will impound well over three thousand acre-feet of water in normal years. This will permit the irrigation of about eight hundred acres of bottom and benchland along the streams in addition to the two hundred acres which will be subirrigated. The feed, hay, and grazing produced by this thousand acres, with the help of added water as needed, may approach the total of the forage produced on the rest of the ranch. The owner states, "I consider the thousand acres of irrigated and subirrigated land to be equal in value to the sixteen thousand acres of grazing land on the ranch."

Grass is the basic feed on the ranch the year round but there are periods in Bosque County when most of the grasses are dry and low in feeding value. Supplemental feeds are used when the native grasses are dormant, and the croplands are grazed for short periods during the growing season to permit the deferment and improvement of the range. Sudan, alfalfa, oats, Madrid sweet clover, and button clover are the only cultivated crops raised on the ranch. While some land is still dry-farmed, the supplemental feed program is tied closely to the one thousand acres that can be irrigated or subirrigated.

There are five stream miles of the East Bosque on the ranch and in July 1956, after five and one-half years of short rainfall, there was no water coming onto the ranch in its channel as it entered from the north. However, it became a living stream not long after crossing the boundary.

In July 1956, one of Mr. Pettit's neighbors, living below Flat Top on the East Bosque, came to him to say, "I was pretty sore when you started building dams on the East Bosque, but, by God, you've made it into a flowing stream the year round. It always went dry during the summer when we had drouths before." While there was no reason to doubt this good neighbor, this was something that had to be seen. On July 14, 1956, Mr. Pettit and this writer drove to the lower of the five dams on the East Bosque. We left the car, left the ranch by climbing through the fence, and some hundred yards or so below the dam, found a place where we could descend the rather steep bank to the bed of the stream. There was flowing water where we reached the stream bed, and as we followed it downstream the flow seemed to increase. Finally it was too wet for us to walk and we turned back.

The changing of the East Bosque from a dry to a flowing stream as it crosses the ranch from the northwest to the southeast is not a miracle or even a mystery. Flat Top *grass* and Flat Top *dams* are responsible. They are also responsible for making Rough Creek and Flag Branch year-long flowing streams.

Flat Top grass is the most important factor in the changed water situation. Charles Pettit says, "Water is the thing that the ranching country runs short of too often. But there is one sure way to make the best use of the rain we get and that is get the ground coated with a heavy grass sod so that the water can quickly soak into the soil."

Together, runoff and evaporation used to get most of the water that fell on the ranch, but now rains soak into the ground to grow grass, and a considerable amount seeps slowly into underground channels, and part of it eventually reaches the natural drains (the stream beds) or breaks out as springs. Protective plant cover reduces evaporation losses to a minimum; growing vegetation gets the use of a large part of the total rain because it soaks deeply into the soil reservoir, where it is recovered by plants as needed.

Flat Top *grass* and *dams* were ready when the excessive rains fell in the spring of 1957 and again in 1958. The forty-three ponds and lakes, created by the dams, were at low-water level when the heavier rains started. Big Lake, a part of the East Bosque system, with a drainage area of nearly thirteen thousand acres and a hundred acres of water surface, filled slowly and it was not until April 29, 1957, after 20.7 inches of rain in the year that the water reached spillway height. It flowed over the spillway into the channel below for weeks as the springs and seeps continued to pour clear water into the lake. During the wet spring of 1957, and again in 1958, the East Bosque was never over about half bank full while neighboring streams flooded the bottoms, not once but several times.

Permit me to quote directly from *Flat Top Ranch* (Norman, Oklahoma, 1957) and the chapter I wrote on "Flat Top Water at Work" in the summer of 1956 after five and one-half years of drought: "Perhaps the greatest unearned increment will accrue to those farmers and ranchers who live downstream on the East Bosque. For some distance they are going to have almost complete protection from floodwater damage to their bottomland fields and improvements. Until tributaries of sufficient size and number to put water over the banks enter the creek below the Flat Top boundary, there will be no floods." The statement I made with such finality in the dry year 1956 has been confirmed in the very wet years of 1957 and 1958 by the performance of Flat Top *grass* and *dams*.

Cattle

Mr. Pettit is a Hereford enthusiast, not because the cherry red cattle with the white faces look good on his green grass (and that, they do) but because he sincerely believes in the superior beef-making qualities of the breed. This opinion is widely supported by his fellow cowmen, since about 80 per cent of the beef cattle today are Herefords.

Mr. Pettit started with polled Herefords but soon added some horned Herefords. He spent a lot of time in the pastures with his cattle and as soon as he had determined to his own satisfaction that the horned cattle outweighed and outgained the polled, he sold the muleys. He has been in the forefront in the American Hereford Association in fighting the trend to the smaller compact type, which was in demand to compete with other breeds for honors at livestock shows. His early experiences with his father on the home ranch in Archer County convinced him that the roomier cows and bulls were the ones that paid the bills. So the big ones stayed, to the delight of the ranch's commercial bull customers who stayed "old-fashioned" almost to the man.

W. B. (Bill) Roberts, an excellent Hereford judge and cattle-breeding expert, has been the resident manager of the ranch since 1941. Mr. Pettit and Bill Roberts are a real team—they agreed shortly after Bill came on the job that they were in the registered Hereford business to provide bulls which would improve the commercial herds of beef cattle of their customers. Bill puts it this way: "The goal is to produce a calf that will look good and weigh heavy at weaning time—the same calf to develop and look good and still weigh heavy at approximately eighteen months to two years."

The term *a Flat Top Bull* has come to have a special meaning in Hereford circles—big—with ample bone, strong hindquarters, masculine head, and the inherent quality to do well on the range. This is because the motto of the ranch—"Dedicated to the Improvement of Herefords"—applies to the herd as a whole and not to just a few show cattle.

Some of the best Herefords in America are to be found at Flat Top and despite the predominant attention to the business of providing bulls for commercial herds the ranch has had its share of show-ring winners.

During the short time that the ranch had some commercial (grade) Herefords, two carloads of steers were fitted and shown at the Houston Fat Stock Show. Both won grand championships. Flat Top won the grand champion carload of bulls at the 1942 Fort Worth Fat Stock Show. CP Tone, the first great herd sire at Flat Top, was the grand champion at Fort Worth in 1942. There have been other winners at the country's top shows but I believe that both Charlie Pettit and Bill Roberts get a bigger kick out of a telephone call from a Texas cowman ordering a half-dozen bulls (to be picked by Bill) than they do from winning a blue, or even a purple, at a show. Bill regards showing cattle as a necessary evil, because it is one of the best forms of advertising. He likes better the repeat orders that follow his choice of bulls shipped to a customer unseen. This is the real pay-off—it shows the esteem in which Bill and his employer, Charlie Pettit, are held in Hereford circles.

Ranch Improvements

The first thing that Charlie Pettit did when he bought the ranch was to sell all the houses, barns, fences, and other improvements to one of his neighbors for $500 with the proviso that they be removed in six weeks. The old shabby improvements were replaced by substantial, but by no means fancy, ones. Rock, plentiful on the ranch, was the main structural material used in the new improvements. Concrete, corrugated iron, and iron pipe have been combined with the native stone to construct feed barns, hay barns, loading ramps, shelters, and corrals that are, for all practical purposes, permanent and that blend into the landscape. These improvements were planned for efficient and constant use, with "labor saving" the watchword.

The fences and cattle guards match the other improvements. After a considerable period in which various types of fences were tried, a staggered seven-wire fence, with four strands on one side of the post and three on the other, became the standard. This type of fence keeps the animals where they are supposed to stay and at the same time discourages young bulls from fighting through the fence. There are forty-five cattle guards on the fences dividing the various traps and pastures. The cattle guards, like all other improvements, are built to stay, being constructed with concrete, steel I-beams, and two-inch pipes on six-inch centers.

The one hundred different enclosures on the ranch are connected by about one hundred and fifty miles of graded, ditched, graveled, and carefully maintained roads. Permanent bridges or concrete crossings are used over all streams of any appreciable size. Two cowboys using a two-horse trailer pulled by a car or pickup look after Flat Top cattle. The good roads and the cattle guards (they don't have to stop to open gates) make it possible for them to do the work that would ordinarily require ten or more cowboys, stationed at various places on the ranch. The roads and cattle guards save time and labor in the winter, when it is necessary to put out feed to livestock in the pastures. The feed troughs are of concrete with heavy pipe dividers and are practically indestructible. Their weight minimizes the chances of their being tipped over and they are set on sloping ground (on south slopes or other protected spots), with a drain hole in the lower end for the escape of rain water. I have already mentioned the water system, which was planned and established with the same objectives in mind—permanency, minimal expenditure of time and material for maintenance, and the greatest efficiency of operations.

Wildlife

Soil and water conservation measures applied on farm and range lands are often of great incidental value to wildlife. Food, cover, and clean water are the fundamentals of a satisfactory wildlife habitat. The conservation treatment of the range has provided these essentials to an increasing wildlife population at Flat Top but there is nothing incidental about the wildlife program on the ranch. The original conservation plan developed for the ranch by Mr. Pettit, in cooperation with the Bosque County Soil Conservation District, provided for the improvement of 2,300 acres for wildlife. As other land was added, additional wildlife-habitat improvements were included in their conservation treatment.

My Uncle Jack Bradley, a Confederate veteran, who was my fishing companion when I was a boy, and my own father both lived within sight of Flat Top Mountain in the eighties. Their tales of the abundance of game in Bosque County were enough to send me on a number of hunting trips along the East Bosque when I lived in neighboring Erath County in 1921–1926. I sighted Flat Top Mountain more than once but very few doves or quail. When Mr. Pettit bought the ranch he estimated that there were no more than six coveys of quail on the seven thousand acres and no large game, although a few predators were still around.

Today the white-tailed deer herd is estimated at between five hundred and a thousand animals. This herd has resulted from forty-nine animals released on the ranch in 1946 by the Texas Game, Fish, and Oyster Commission, although there is some indication that deer released on neighboring ranches at about the same time found Flat Top grass and water more to their liking and moved in. One of the real thrills on a visit to the ranch is a drive along the ranch roads in the East Bosque bottom at dusk to see numerous deer grazing the alfalfa and irrigated grasses.

The Commission released ten antelope does and six bucks on the ranch in 1941 and by 1945 there was a herd of eighty. But by 1953 there were only three does left—twenty-five does escaped through a water gap; the bucks fought among themselves, with many dying from infections to their wounds; and the herd refused feed offered them. Two bucks were added in 1953 and by 1956 the herd had grown to fifteen animals. Antelope cannot jump the Flat Top fences (although deer can) and with their known migratory habits even the largest pasture (about a thousand acres) may not be a suitable habitat for them. Small antelope gaps are planned in some division fences and in the boundary fence between Flat Top and Rough Creek Ranch (owned by Mr. Pettit's daughter and son-in-law) to improve the antelope habitat.

It is estimated that the ranch population of wild turkeys has reached the one-thousand mark. No turkeys may be shot on the ranch but Mr. Pettit feels that they earn their keep by eating huge quantities of grasshoppers.

Bobwhite quail are now found in abundance on the ranch and hunting is available for a fee, with a guaranteed limit of birds. This is made possible by the quail enterprise on the ranch—like all others, a paying proposition. About ten thousand quail are raised a year and the ranch sells fertile eggs, dressed birds, or live birds for release. The hunter who fails to reach the bag limit has the difference made up to him in dressed birds.

One of the real disappointments to date has been the failure of the famed Texas prairie chicken to reestablish themselves on the ranch. Two trials, 1951 and 1953, were made with the help of the Commission but both failed, for no known reason. They were there once in great numbers and with the almost complete recovery of the grassland there seems to be every reason to believe that they can and will find Flat Top a suitable habitat in the not too distant future. They belong there.

Mourning doves, although migratory, are at Flat Top the year round in great numbers. The "summer" doves fly south in the fall and are replaced by birds from the north and this process is reversed in the spring—the doves that wintered to the southward come home to the ranch to nest.

Prior to the construction of the Flat Top dams, migratory waterfowl passed the ranch up. Now three to five thousand ducks winter on the ranch each year. Duck hunting is permitted on part of the ranch but usually not over a hundred birds are killed a year. When the first ducks arrive in September, feed is put out on the shore of House Lake—the one close to the ranch house where no hunting is ever permitted. There is a great flight in to the lake each evening when the feed is scattered. The annual cost is about $500 for corn but Mr. Pettit says it is worth it to watch the evening flights.

Flat Top water, in addition to attracting migratory waterfowl, is stocked with fish—bluegills, redears, crappies, channel cats, and bass. The ranch staff and their families, plus a few friends, do most of the fishing at Flat Top although an area of about one thousand acres, with some fishing water, is leased for $2,500 a year to a group of businessmen who have formed a hunting club. The total cash take from hunting and fishing on the ranch probably averages $10,000 a year. And the value of game and fish used by ranch families is certainly considerable. However, the impact on the game population is negligible—one hundred ducks out of three to five thousand; seventy-five deer out of possibly a thousand; only half as many quail as are released annually from the breeding pens; and the doves are there in such abundance that those killed aren't missed. No antelope or turkey may be killed and the lakes and streams are really overstocked and need to be fished more than they are.

The story of Flat Top wildlife does not end with game—every kind of native or migratory bird or small animal common to Central Texas has found its way to the ranch. The scissor-tailed flycatchers and the roadrunners are among Mr. Pettit's favorites of the nongame birds. No attempt has been made to restore the so-called "balance of nature" on the ranch—some of the former wild creatures that were natives are frankly unwanted on a range now used primarily for the production of high-value Herefords. In this unwanted group are bear, buffalo, panther, wolves, coyotes, and bobcats. Their presence would simply not be in harmony with the grazing of fine Hereford cattle. The wildlife that is compatible with the main business of the ranch is wanted and provided for—food, cover, and clean water are there in abundance. Charlie Pettit says, "Whatever I do on the ranch, I would like for there to be a little profit in it"— Flat Top wildlife pays in cash, in insects and rodents destroyed, and in the pure pleasure of the ranch owner, his friends, and the Flat Top families.

Ranch Romance

If I have given you the impression that the Texan ranch of today is just another place to make a living, it is unintentional. It is true that many of the ways of ranch life of yesteryear considered to be of great romantic interest by the Western fiction writers are gone. The range war, the bucking horse, the brush-popper, the horsebreaker, the linerider, and the roundup rep are no more on most modern Texan ranches. The chuck wagon, if there is one at all, is used only when there are important visitors. Herd bulls no longer walk a thousand miles to their new home in Wyoming—they go by air, or if the distance is short, by truck. Few Texas cattle are herded today and most of the fence riding is done in a jeep. The fence riders with their line camp and the lone cowboys who used to guard the outposts of the range are gone, too. The cowboys no longer ride to town in groups on Saturday for a night of wine, women, and song—most of them are married and their families wouldn't stand for such. The fast gunman is for the movies and the shoot-outs are few and far between these days.

Yes, it is another day in another age, and these modern Texas conservation ranchers get their "kicks" in other ways—by changing spring floodways and summer dry streams into year-round living water; by restoring the native range to its former composition and vigor; by introducing new grasses and legumes; by turning back the invading cedar, mesquite, and cactus; by producing more beef from fewer cows; and by community action through their soil-conservation districts in preventing floods. These modern conservation ranchers regard wildlife as an economic asset, and they have time to hunt and fish—and they do. They go on ranch tours and listen to a little bragging about a bull, a cow, the grass, or all three, and learn something they can take home and use on the home ranch. There are ranch libraries; radio is almost universal and TV is becoming common. Paved roads and automobiles put the pleasures of their city cousins only minutes away in most cases. The "kicks" are different but they are there and who is to say, for sure, which ranch era offered the most?

As a professional conservationist I am in a position to appraise the impact of this new breed of rancher on Texas land. They are good for it and they are helping to preserve the bragging rights of future generations of Texans. The Charlie Pettits, the Dolph Briscoes and the hundreds of other modern conservation ranchers are showing the way by restoring the productive capacity of some of the best native grassland known to man, which was overgrazed by another generation. When the grass competition was removed the mesquite, cedar, and cactus moved in, gullies formed, and the streams dried up in the summer when the need for water was the greatest. The damage that older generations permitted has made the job of the modern rancher a lot tougher but he is meeting the challenge.

Frank Reeves in writing of Flat Top puts it this way: "I probably have seen as many ranches and as many beef animals in the past quarter century as any man in America. My job has made this not only possible but necessary. One of the great rewards of my job as a range reporter and livestock editor is the regular opportunity to observe the continuing improvement of certain ranches. In no case that I can recall has the improvement of the range, the hay meadows, the water system, the houses, barns, fences, and the cattle been so constant as at Flat Top." I am in agreement with Frank's statement, but I know that there are others who are close on Charlie Pettit's heels. The closer they get, the better I like it, for then I know we have the leadership so essential to matching the safe and sound production of red meat to our ever increasing population.

READING LIST
Texas Ranches
CALLAGHAN
    Wellman, Paul, *The Callaghan*, Encinal, Texas, 1945.
FLAT TOP
    Allred, B. W. and J. C. Dykes, eds., *Flat Top Ranch*, Norman, Oklahoma, 1957.

JA
  Burton, Harley True, *A History of the JA Ranch*, Austin, Texas, 1928.
KING
  Goodwin, Frank, *Life on the King Ranch*, New York, 1951.
  Lea, Tom, *The King Ranch*, 2 vols., Boston, 1957.
  Rowe, James, and others, *King Ranch:100 Years of Ranching*, Corpus Christi, Texas, 1953.
MATADOR
  Campbell, Harry H., *The Early History of Motley County*, San Antonio, Texas, 1958.
  Pearce, William M., *The Establishment and Early Development of the Ranch, 1882–1890*, Abilene, Texas, 1951.
  Warren, John and Colquet, *The Matadors*, Dickens, Texas, 1952.
SMS
  Hastings, Frank S., *A Ranchman's Recollections*, Chicago, 1921.
  Swenson, W. G., *SMS Ranches*, Stamford, Texas, 1956.
SPUR
  Elliot, W. J., *The Spurs*, Spur, Texas, 1939.
  Holden, William Curry, *The Spur Ranch*, Boston, 1934.
TAFT
  Watson, May M. Green, and Alex Lillico, *Taft Ranch*, n.p., n.d.
  North, Gene, *The Tafts Went to Texas*, Cincinnati, 1957.
XIT
  Haley, J. Evetts, *The XIT Ranch of Texas*, Chicago, 1929.
  Nordyke, Lewis, *Cattle Empire*, New York, 1949.
GENERAL
  Evans, Will F., *Border Skylines*, Dallas, 1940.
  Hamner, Laura V., *Short Grass & Longhorns*, Norman, Oklahoma, 1942.
  Harper, Minnie Timms, and George Dewey, *Old Ranches*, Dallas, 1936.
  Williams, J. W., *The Big Ranch Country*, Wichita Falls, Texas, 1954.
  Willis, W. S., *A Story of the Big Western Ranches*, Comanche, Texas, 1955.

Texas Ranchmen
Anderson, August, *Hyphenated*, n.p., 1916 (Swenson).
Dobie, J. Frank, *A Vaquero of the Brush Country*, Dallas, 1929.
Douglass, C. L., *Cattle Kings of Texas*, Dallas, 1939 (King, Kenedy, Chisum, Slaughter, Loving, etc.).
Emmett, Chris, *Shanghai Pierce*, Norman, Oklahoma, 1953.
Haley, J. Evetts, *Charles Goodnight, Cowman & Plainsman*, Boston; New York, 1936.
———, *George W. Littlefield, Texan*, Norman, Oklahoma, 1943.
Hammer, Laura V., *The No Gun Man of Texas*, Amarillo, Texas, 1935 (Goodnight).
Holden, William Curry, *Rollie Burns*, Dallas, 1932.
Keith, Noel L., *The Brites of Capote*, Ft. Worth, 1950.
Kupper, Winifred, *The Golden Hoof*, New York, 1945.
———, ed., *Texas Sheepman*, Austin, 1951.

Jones, J. O., A *Cowman's Memoirs*, Ft. Worth, 1953.

Matthews, Sallie Reynolds, *Interwoven*, Houston, 1936, and El Paso, Texas, 1958 (Matthews, Reynolds).

Siringo, Charles A., A *Texas Cowboy*, Chicago, 1885, and New York, 1950.

Sonnichsen, C. L., *Cowboys and Cattle Kings*, Norman, Oklahoma, 1950 (Swensons, Evans, Kokernots, etc.).

Wallis, George A., *The Cattle Kings of the Staked Plains*, Dallas, 1957 (Slaughters, Chisum, Goodnight, Littlefield, etc.).

Texas Cattle and Range Life

Adams, Andy, *The Log of a Cowboy*, Boston, 1903.

Adams, Ramon F., *Cowboy Lingo*, Boston, 1936.

Cox, James, *The Cattle Industry of Texas and Adjacent Territory*, St. Louis, 1895.

Dobie, J. Frank, *The Longhorns*, Boston, 1941.

————, *The Mustangs*, Boston, 1952.

————, *On the Open Range*, Dallas, 1931.

Haley, J. Evetts, *Life on the Texas Range*, Austin, Texas, 1952.

Kleberg, Robert J., Jr., *The Santa Gertrudis Breed of Beef Cattle*, Kingsville, Texas, n.d., and El Paso, Texas, 1954.

Ridings, Sam P., *The Chisholm Trail*, Guthrie, Oklahoma, 1936.

Webb, Walter Prescott, *The Great Plains*, Boston, 1931.

Comment: Fallacies in the Turner Thesis

BY WILLIAM R. HOGAN
Tulane University

FREDERICK JACKSON TURNER frequently expressed the hope of every true scholar-
teacher: "I hope to propagate inquiry, not
to produce disciples." But his disciples
became a priesthood, his frontier interpretation hardened into their
orthodox gospel, and the frontier thesis became the predominant
United States view of its own past. Although certain critics of a later
generation have built reputations upon chipping away parts of
the Turner thesis, the frontier is still a favorite explanation for an
astounding variety of alleged cultural phenomena. For example,
Arthur M. Schlesinger, Jr., in a vein reminiscent of the 1920's, writes
in a popular magazine: "Whether because of Puritanism or the
frontier, there has been something immature in the traditional male
attitude toward women—a sense of alarm at times amounting to
panic." [1]

Ray Allen Billington, whose highly respected publications include
a textbook that "attempts to follow the pattern that Frederick Jackson Turner might have used," [2] here presents a paper that is less
Turnerian than some of his previous publications but is still well
within the framework of the master. There is less emphasis upon
frontier optimism, self-reliance, individualism, and inventiveness.
There remains the isolationist search for the "truly American part of
our history," the limitless opportunity to exploit "the Western wilds,
from the Alleghanies to the Pacific, . . . the richest free gift that
was ever spread out before civilized man," the temporary regression
to primitivism, and the relative neglect of the southern half of the
United States.

In the light of modern criticism, recent research, and certain findings of the behavioral sciences, Professor Billington undertakes to
restate at least part of the Turner doctrine, with especial attention
to the region that fits it best. His analysis provokes certain questions
and comments:

It is doubtful that the early Virginia settlers, described by Gerald
W. Johnson as being "The Expendables," were unusually well
equipped to establish their beachheads. One can argue, moreover,
that England, as well as Spain and France, began New World settlements within at least a framework of mercantilism. Some of "the
hallmarks of an advancing capitalism" mentioned in this paper are
in fact elements of the internal mercantilism, however altered from
the ideal by colonial conditions, described by Richard B. Morris in
his *Government and Labor in Early America.*

Underlying all of Professor Billington's remarks about New Spain
is the agrarian assumption that the highest virtue for an exploiter
resides in the yeoman farmer. Yet the cultural achievements of the
"civilization" partly created by the numerous large-scale entrepre-
neurs in colonial Latin America compared more than favorably with
those of the Yankee frontier of a later period.

In addition to the comparative shortage of arable land and the
more formidable geographical barriers in Latin America, the Spanish
frontiers were also marked by these differences: the comparative
ineffectuality of the resistance of the sedentary Latin American Indians in the richest regions to virtual enslavement, the coexistence
and partial amalgamation of three races without near extermination
of any of them, and the rich cultural heritage transmitted by the
Catholic Church.

In his summary of "differences" between frontiers, Professor Billington apparently paraphrases a part of a recent statement by Max
Lerner, which deserves to be quoted more fully: "Along with the
ferment of a moving frontier there was the ferment of democrati-
zation and industrial development in the area of early settlement.
What Russia, Australia, and the other instances of frontier settlement lacked, and the American instance had, was a major industrial
and capitalist revolution taking place at the same time as the frontier settlement and linked with it, and an extension of the democratic idea linked with both. . . . The sense of renewal of the
frontiersmen came not only from facing a natural environment with
directness but from never losing contact with the sources of me-

chanical and governmental transformation that gave Americans their commanding control over the environment as a whole." [3] An obvious example of this mechanization taking command is the complex of new facilities involved in the nineteenth-century Transportation Revolution, which the perceptive Irish actor Tyrone Power called "the true wonders of this country." These facilities accelerated and changed the nature of the westward movement in the United States, resulted in the Pacific Coast being closer to the East than to much of the interior, made Western standards and mores more heavily felt in the East, perhaps enabled us to survive as a single democratic nation, and later played a central role in transforming the unknown number of frontiersmen who moved *several times* into "The Moving American" of the twentieth century.

In Professor Billington's textbook, "the frontiersmen . . . relied on the immediate social group far more than Easterners." He here speaks of Ohio Valley "forces of nature" that stripped "the lone settler" of "the sense of social interdependence normal in areas where men lived through cooperative enterprise." These same forces of nature were so strong that they caused "a regression to primitivism" that "altered the social order to a remarkable degree." No historian should be chided for changing his mind, but "the regression to primitivism" theme as applied to the farming frontier can be overdone. Certainly there was violence on any frontier. But let us take "gouging" as an example of possible exaggeration. For all of R. Carlyle Buley's researches on the entire Old Northwest, cited by Professor Billington, he documented his page on this subject with one 1905 account of social life in early central Illinois.[4] Everett Dick's *Dixie Frontier* discussion is half based on the account of an English traveler who also described ferocious mosquitoes that bit through tough shoe leather, a particle of information that cannot be doubted because he gave as his source of information that well-known exponent of the truth, George Washington.[5] In a number of years of research on two Southern frontier areas not notably averse to violence, I found very few credible descriptions of gouging, and my experience has been shared by others who have labored even longer in the same records. I doubt that gouging on any frontier was much more prevalent than cannibalism, which of course was not unknown. If gouging was a frequent practice, where are the descriptions of the men without eyeballs in the years after they had been deprived of sight?

This paper further supports the theory of certain literary historians that the Ohio Valley frontier embraced a paradox—a deepseated anti-intellectualism and a strong but conservative desire for literary culture. The evidence for anti-intellectualism is the less impressive of the two. And if the geographical base of the paper had been extended, it would have had to account for the birth of American realism in the folk literature of the humorous newspaper sketches and oral tales of the Southwest. This boisterous, often satirical writing developed its own tradition, and, as Henry Nash Smith declares, "its own striking symbols . . . that were destined to survive the Civil War and to have important consequences for American literature." [6]

Despite the well-known aversion of the Primitive Baptists to education, the Presbyterian teacher-preacher and the circuit rider often constituted major cultural ties with the East. At the same time, church history may yet demonstrate that the development of altered religious patterns has been a major product of the frontier process.

Professor Billington deserves credit for attempting to analyze the ways in which the migrating process altered the migrants, but caution should be exercised in a facile application to the frontier scene of the findings of two sociologists who made a study of the comparative admission rates of movers and nonmovers to New York state mental hospitals in 1939–1941.[7] The sociologists themselves are fully aware of the limitations imposed on generalizing their conclusions. Migrants to unsettled frontiers may turn out to have had decidedly different population characteristics from migrants in an age of urbanization.

Finally, this provocative paper suggests that some of the darker aspects of the westward movement are becoming a part of the New Turner Doctrine. Perhaps this will be completely evident when the historical millenium arrives and mechanical sorting techniques assist in furnishing the answers to those frequently asked and rarely answered questions: Who actually secured, *retained title to, and occupied* dependable units of high-quality land and other resources? How many frontier democrats adhered to the favorite aphorism of Captain Simon Suggs: "It is good to be shifty in a new country." How much fraud was involved in both small and large acquisitions? Who made or lost large fortunes out of these transactions? Was the "limitless opportunity" of the western garden the great delusion for a substantial number of Anglo-Americans? [8]

FOOTNOTES

1. Arthur M. Schlesinger, Jr., The Crisis of American Masculinity, *Esquire,* November 1958, p. 64.

2. Ray Allen Billington, *Westward Expansion: A History of the American Frontier* (New York, 1949), vii.

3. Max Lerner, *America as a Civilization* (New York, 1957), p. 37.

4. R. C. Buley, *The Old Northwest: Pioneer Period, 1815–1840* (2 vols., Indianapolis, 1950), I, 318.

5. Everett N. Dick, *The Dixie Frontier* (New York, 1948), p. 140; Allan Nevins (ed.), *America Through British Eyes* (New York, 1948), pp. 21–22.

6. Henry Nash Smith, *The Virgin Land* (Cambridge, Massachusetts, 1950), p. 152. See also Franklin J. Meine, in Foreword to W. Stanley Hoole, *Alias Simon Suggs* (University, Alabama, 1952), xiv–xvi.

7. Benjamin Malzberg and Everett S. Lee, *Migration and Mental Disease: A Study of First Admissions to Hospitals for Mental Disease, New York, 1939–1941* (New York, 1956).

8. Thomas Le Duc asks these questions about the Trans-Mississippi Plains. *Agricultural History,* XXIV (October 1950), 199–204. These and related questions about other regions need to be asked and answered.

Part Four

THE GREAT FRONTIER CONCEPT

The section on the "Great Frontier" concept of Walter Prescott Webb is of particular interest because none of those who present papers or comment is a historian of the United States or of Mexico. Here the reader will note a dialogue which expresses a considerable difference of opinion. Sir Keith Hancock, a historian of Australia and of the British Empire, reveals that he finds considerable merit in the concept of the Great Frontier. Professor Lower, a Canadian, who is sensitive to the differences which exist between the experience of Canada and that of the United States, is, on the other hand, sharply critical. So is Professor Rodrigues, who brings to the discussion a knowledge of Brazil's vast interior, which probably still represents a frontier in the American sense of the word. Then from the perspective of medieval and modern Britain and Europe, Professor Barraclough strongly disagrees with Professor Lower and, by implication, with Professor Rodrigues, and finds the Great Frontier concept of seminal importance to those who would understand modern history. Here is play and interplay in the historical dialogue at its best.

The Moving Metropolis

BY SIR KEITH HANCOCK
The Australian National University

WE ARE MET TOGETHER in Texas from
many countries near and far to honour
Walter Prescott Webb and to discuss his
book, *The Great Frontier: An Interpre-
tation of World History since Columbus.* I love the splendour of this
title. Splendour, span, audacity—these qualities are out of favour
nowadays amongst the scribes and pharisees of our profession. "His-
tory-writing today," says Sir Steven Runciman, "has passed into an
Alexandrian age, where criticism has overpowered creation. Faced
by the mountainous heap of knowledge and by the watchful severity
of his colleagues, the modern historian often takes refuge in learned
articles or narrowly specialised dissertations, small fortresses that
are easy to defend from attack. . . . I believe that the supreme duty
of the historian is to write history, that is to say, to attempt to
record in one sweeping sequence the greater events and movements
that have swayed the destiny of man." [1] In Webb's work, I have
observed various "fortresses" which might be captured by local as-
sault; but such small-scale operations do not interest me today. The
"sweeping significance" of *The Great Frontier* will be my theme.

Let me, at the outset, confront Webb's view of the frontier with
Turner's. Turner proclaimed the significance of the frontier in
American history; Webb proclaims its significance in world history.
To Turner the American frontier was a unique thing; to Webb it is
one of a class. Turner emphasised its separateness from the European homelands; Webb links together Great Frontier and Metropolis
within the complex interplay of shared historical experience.

It would be foolish to judge one of these views true and the other false, for each view has illuminated different aspects of truth. Still, here are two hypotheses; and the historian must decide which of the two will be the more fruitful for his inquiries. His answer is likely to vary with the varying circumstances of time and places. Let me illustrate some of the possibilities.

Afrikaner historians of the dominant school would certainly plump for Turner. For example, J. P. van der Merwe of Stellenbosch has written in true Turner vein three substantial volumes on the theme of *trek*—not merely or chiefly that dramatic cataclysm called the Great Trek, but the whole "sweeping sequence" of pastoral expansion which carried the Boers right up to and even beyond the political boundaries of present-day South Africa.[2] Van der Merwe's trekkers are the very image—possibly the exaggerated image—of Turner's frontiersmen. In their relations with each other they are individualistic, independent, democratic; in their relations with the other groups and tribes of South Africa they are the master race. The economic ties which bind them to the metropolis, and even to the areas of old settlement around Cape Town, are of the slightest. As they move ever deeper into the African hinterland they discard piece by piece their European *impedimenta*—saving always their firearms and their Bibles, those indispensable titles of their dominion over land and people. They discard even the memory of Europe. They call themselves Afrikaners.

The above is a highly simplified epitome of a complicated story. Moreover, as van der Merwe and other critical historians very well realise, trekking is not by any means the whole of South African, nor even of Afrikaner, history. Nevertheless, it dominates the nationalist propaganda which too often passes for history. The epic of the trekkers' frontier is appropriated by the politicians of *apartheid*. Did any similar alliance ever arise in America between frontier historiography of the pre-Webb era and the politics of isolationism?

In Australia, such an alliance could not possibly arise. Australians are constrained by the facts of economic geography and history to view their frontier through Webb's eyes rather than through Turner's. Their hinterland did not grant them the American boon of plentiful quarter-sections in rich homesteading country; but neither did it inflict upon them the South African bane of economic isolation. Paradoxically, the squatting wave which swept westward from Sydney was running *towards* its markets. Wool tethered the squatters to the world.

"When the clipper fleet comes over
When the scent is on the clover,
And the scarlet streaks the blue;
When the Western sheds are ringing
And the Western men are singing
  As their rolling teams come through,
  Then it's ho, ho—Wool ho!
For the busy shears are clipping, and a stir
  is in the shipping,
  And it's yo, ho—Wool ho!"

E. J. Brady's ballad paints a romantic picture of the Australian grasslands, which never had the scent of clover in them until these latter decades of pasture improvement; but it paints a realistic picture of transport and trade. The squatter's frontier, like every other Australian frontier that followed it, was from the very beginning linked indissolubly with the European metropolis.

The same is true of the Canadian frontiers. In this gathering on North American soil I feel moved to express my admiration for one of the truly great historians of this continent, the late Harold Adams Innis. Consider his first large study of the Canadian staples, *The Fur Trade in Canada*. The wealth that can be mined from this book is truly astonishing—elucidations so penetrating of the economics of transport and of commercial organisation that they have remained for nearly thirty years the starting point of new research: interpretations of the technological and social interplay between Red Indian and European society which are of equal illumination to the historian and the social anthropologist: a vision of the making of Canada, not in spite of geography (as historians used to say) but along the massive geographical grain of the rivers and lakes, portages, trails, and passes of the Dominion. Innis saw the axis of Canadian nation-building run east to west across the North American continent; but he saw it also running west to east across the Atlantic, back to the European homelands. It was the demand in European markets for beaver hats that set the fur-traders on the trail of the beavers and the Indians in their retreat westwards. So it was with the whole procession of Canadian staples—furs and fish, lumber, wheat, and metals: it was the demand of metropolitan markets that set the frontiers moving.

So far I have been performing one of the exercises which Webb proposed for non-American historians; I have been mobilising evidence from various countries of the New World in order to test his hypothesis—that part of the hypothesis, at least, which emphasises the interdependence of Great Frontier and Metropolis. But what about the metropolitan evidence? Webb insists upon the two-way interaction of influences. He ascribes to the Great Frontier a decisive role in breaking down the hierarchies and corporate institutions of European society. He insists still more upon the dominant part it played in promoting that great "boom" of economic expansion which continued from the time of Columbus right up to the present century.

I must confess that I find it difficult to bring these theories to a precise test. On the social and political side I see, for example, no way of measuring the degree of American influence upon the French Revolution, or upon the "revolution from above" which Stein and Hardenburg carried through in Prussia, or upon the widespread revolutionary ferment of the 1840's. The evidence is, in the nature of things, predominantly literary and subjective—for example, the impressions of sensitive observers like Tocqueville, who discovered in democratic America the shape of things to come in Europe.

The economic evidence, on the other hand, lends itself more easily to weighing and measuring. It does not, however, invariably favour the illustrations with which Webb supports his argument. For example, he makes a great deal of "windfalls." No doubt they fell easily into the lap of some fortunate first-comers; but, in the half dozen or more trades which I have studied, the average rate of return upon capital was never sensational. Admittedly my first-hand studies fall altogether within the nineteenth and twentieth centuries; for the earlier periods I have to rely on secondary sources. Still, the impression I gain from Innis is that the fur trade required a very heavy investment of capital, and I believe that the slave trade— "the lottery of Liverpool," as it came to be called—was constantly afflicted by a high rate of bankruptcy. Certainly, there were no "gifts from the gods" in any of the African trades—palm oil and kernels, cocoa, cotton, groundnuts—which fall within my own period of study: even on the fabulous goldfields of the Witwatersrand the average return upon capital amounted in the period 1887–1932 to a bare 4.1 per cent.[3] Does Webb imagine that the Great Frontier offered to the Metropolis a surplus not only of land but also of capital?[4] How then could one explain the net import of capital which developing countries usually show in their international accounts? Australia, to take the example which I know best, remains to this day a capital-importing country. Throughout the nineteenth century her development depended almost as much upon the British investor as it did upon the British immigrant.

Webb ought to feel pleased if some of the controversial detail in his book suggests new research tasks for economic historians, for it has been his purpose "to open a subject, not to close it." [5] However, I doubt whether many people will feel moved to controvert his central theme. After all, the boom hypothesis is essentially a restatement, in more moderate terms, of Adam Smith's resounding generalisation: "The discovery of America and that of a passage to the East Indies by the Cape of Good Hope, are the greatest and most important events recorded in the history of mankind. . . . By uniting, in some measure, the most distant parts of the world, by enabling them to relieve one another's enjoyments, and to encourage one another's industry, their general tendency would seem to be beneficial." [6]

So far from being too expansive, Webb is more restrictive than Adam Smith in his view of the oceanic discoveries and their economic consequences. He excludes Asia and Tropical Africa. Every historian, of course, is free to choose his own field of study and to define it in words which he finds convenient: Webb's Great Frontier is "an empty land, a vacancy inviting occupancy." [7] On the other hand, the historian of metropolitan activities such as shipping, banking, and investment is bound to include not only the "vacant" but also the populous countries. The process of economic expansion and the sum total of its results cannot be fully envisaged from the metropolitan point of view if countries such as India, China, and West Africa are omitted from the inquiry. For this reason I felt myself constrained, in researches which I was pursuing twenty years ago, to choose the more comprehensive framework of Adam Smith.[8] At the same time, I found it convenient in exposition to borrow and perhaps to embellish Turner's metaphor of moving frontiers: the settlers' frontier led me into South Africa; the traders' and planters' frontier led me into Tropical Africa; the missionaries' frontier was with me all the time in both regions.

The missionaries' frontier? Here is a complicated theme which I have no time to pursue, beyond stating my belief that the Metropolis is not merely an economic system but also a system of ideas. One consequence of its expansionist energies has been an intermingling of civilisations and cultures on a scale unknown to humanity since Hellenistic and Roman times. Here is a fascinating field of study for historians and other students of mankind.

If you protest that such explorations are remote from those of Turner and Webb I can only state my belief that they are linked within a system of ideas. If you think that I am misusing the Turner-Webb phraseology I am ready to discard it and use a different one.[9] For it is the ideas, not the phrases, that matter most.

Today I am coining a phrase of my own, *"The Moving Metropolis."* [10] I do not take the phrase too seriously and I shall not be cast down if nobody ever uses it again. It does suggest, however, an idea which I should like to see discussed. Let me recall the economic functions of the Metropolis: it is a provider of markets, of population, and of capital. Now let me recall the cattle ranchers in Webb's book, *The Great Plains*. These men are Americans. So far as I can see, their capital is home-supplied. They drive their cattle to market in Abilene, Kansas. Surely their Metropolis is upon American soil?

Webb's Great Frontier is empty land—"a vacancy." What takes the place of the vacancy as it becomes filled? Turner's moving frontier is a "procession." What happens after the procession has passed by? Let me suggest the answer by an Australian illustration. Half a century ago, some relatives of mine moved into the heavily forested mountain country of southern Victoria. They lived hard—assailed the tall timber with axe and fire, ploughed the land, and sowed the grain between the smoking stumps of the devastated forest. Here was the American drama of the frontier, reenacted in another continent and in another century. Today, these Victorian hills are bare of timber and as velvety as the rolling grasslands of the English west country. Thriving townships serve the needs of prosperous dairy farmers. A motor journey of an hour and a half along the South Gippsland Highway brings the farmers and their produce to Melbourne, a commercial and manufacturing city of one and a half million people, the main centre of business expansion throughout Australia. The frontier has passed by. The state of Victoria, with its great city and encircling countryside, has become metropolitan.

I do not think of The Metropolis as an inert slab of geography—unchanging Europe confronting the unchanging New World. I think of it as a function—mobile, flexible, and increasingly dispersed throughout the whole western world, in Europe, in Australia; above all, in America, that great powerhouse of metropolitan energies. Following the moving metropolis is a game that one might play in other societies than our own. Might not we follow it from Rome eastwards to Byzantium, to Moscow—even to Peking?

NOTES

1. Steven Runciman, *History of the Crusades* (3 vols., Cambridge, England, 1951–1954), I, xiii.

2. For the work of van der Merwe and some other Afrikaner historians see the review article "Trek," by the present writer, in *Economic History Review,* X (1958), 331–339.

3. See S. H. Frankel, *Capital Investment in Africa* (London and New York, 1938), p. 91.

4. Walter P. Webb, *The Great Frontier* (Boston, 1951), p. 12.

5. *Ibid.,* p. 409.

6. Adam Smith, . . . *The Wealth of Nations,* ed. by Edwin Cannan (5th ed., 2 vols., London, 1904), II, 125.

7. Webb, *op. cit.,* p. 284.

8. W. K. Hancock, *Survey of British Commonwealth Affairs,* II (London and New York, 1940 and 1942).

9. Turner would have tolerated frontiers in the plural but Webb says (*op. cit.,* p. 284): "There is no plural for the frontier."

10. I thought that there was some novelty not only in my phrase but in my idea until, after writing this paper, I read "Frontiers, Metropolitanism and Canadian History," by J. M. S. Careless, *Canadian Historical Review,* XXXV (March, 1954), 1–21. To Professor Careless and other Canadian historians the Metropolis is frequently a "chain," with links both in the New World and in the Old. These historians are not system-builders, but are carrying further a method and point of view whose great utility was demonstrated by Innis.

Professor Webb and "The Great Frontier" Thesis

BY ARTHUR R. M. LOWER
Queen's University, Ontario

IT IS NOT GIVEN to many historians to become the centre of a cult. For one at least that honour, however, has been reserved—for the man whose spirit may be assumed to hover over the gatherings of his disciples, Frederick Jackson Turner. He being dead, yet speaketh. Nor does he lack a priesthood to expound his message.

Turner had the good luck to put into a few words ideas that had been latent right from the days of the discoveries. Like a lesser Darwin, he reduced the innumerable descriptions and observations made before him to a few simple sentences. A short, precise essay gave him the reward of the man who hits upon a synthesis—not only a place among historians but a place in history. It is not the object of the present paper merely to fill another prescription to the original formula, but, insofar as the insight of its writer permits, to raise some basic questions, and in particular to look at the latest set of variations upon the original theme, that of Professor Webb's in his *Great Frontier*.

In the dim past, as an undergraduate in a not undistinguished Canadian school of history, the present writer never heard of Turner. It was not until he got to the Harvard Graduate School that the name of the god began to beat upon his ears. Not everyone there was a worshipper at the shrine, then some thirty years old. But there was little hostility, nor did I hear any fundamental criticism. Some years later, at a meeting of the American Historical Association, a session was devoted to the elucidation of Turnerism. Again I can recall no basic criticism. Since those days Mr. Webb has become the leading exponent of the Turner thesis, and now in his *Great Frontier* he tries for a new and greater synthesis, which shall carry forward and complete the work of the master.

How successful has he been? How successful, for that matter, was his master? I can only give my personal reflections. They may be useful as coming from a Canadian, a being who is at once within and without the American scene; far enough in to understand it pretty well, and far enough out to be cold-blooded in his evaluation of it. I remember distinctly my first reaction to Turner. "How interesting this is!" I thought, "what a light it casts over our own historical experience as well as that of the United States. How much it tells me about myself, especially about myself in the presence of those twin magnificences, Oxonians and Harvard men." As a humble product of the frontier, I was complimented by Turner on my excellence and in my turn I complimented him upon his.

Turner's limitations, however, soon began to make themselves apparent. I framed a topic for debate in our graduate history club: "Social inheritance or physiographical environment, which shall we rate the more powerful?" I thought then and I still think that the question goes to the root of the matter. I put my views in an article published in the Canadian Historical Association's *Annual Report*, and based my thesis upon a comparison of English and French Canada. I claimed, and I would still claim, that the severest indictment of Turner is that he never worked his position out into some such general terms. He apparently was a man who saw clearly but saw narrowly. He did not get beyond the American frontier. He never made of his synthesis a grand, sociological doctrine such as Darwin made out of his data for biology. Professor Webb, his disciple, now essays to supply the missing elements and to frame them all into one intellectual concept, Metropolis (Europe) and Frontier (New World). Is his work sound? What criticisms shall we offer of it? Are there alternatives? (That is, can the writer of this paper do any better?)

Like Professor Webb, I knew the frontier at first hand, a very different frontier from his, however, that of the northern Canadian forest. I did not grow up in it, but I spent several formative seasons there. And I did grow up in an environment not far removed from the forest frontier. Moreover, as a Canadian I was familiar through politics, books, and accumulating personal experience with another pioneer people as different from mine as well could be, my French-speaking fellow citizens. I therefore may have had certain advantages over many American students of the frontier.

Turner, it seems to me, under an exterior of objectivity, had a good deal of the romantic about him: he was romantic, or nostalgic, for the familiar environment which he had left forever and which had left him forever. In consequence, did he not overplay his hand, or, rather, as dealer did he not throw all the best cards to his favourite—the new land as compared with the old? Here, on the edge, in the bush, is simple honesty and manly vigour, here is native courtesy and a native sense of equality: here, in short, are all the rude and commendable qualities of the Forest of Arden. Here is Thomas Jefferson in the shape of Jaques, and here is Rousseau masquerading as—who else could it be—Touchstone! We do not hear overmuch from him about what a recent Canadian writer terms "the harshness of necessity, the stultifying effects of hard labour, the bigotry bred of illiteracy."

Virtually the whole of Turner's thesis, and much of Webb's, can be put in two words: geographic determinism. Put Frenchmen and Germans down alongside each other in the same habitat for long enough and they become the same people. Well, they have been alongside each other for a great many centuries in various parts of the Rhine valley, and are they the same people? French-speaking Canadians and English-speaking New Englanders have been alongside each other in similar habitats for three and a half centuries. Are they the same people? English-speaking Canadians and English-speaking Americans have been alongside of each other and mixed up with each other for several generations. Are the two peoples identical? Remarkably similar, I grant, but rather owing to similar traditions than to a similar habitat.

It is my invidious duty, in this place and on this occasion, to pour some critical acid on Professor Webb's work. It is not my task here, I take it, to criticize his book, but his thesis. Nevertheless, since the two cannot be completely separated, I feel compelled to observe that I detect in the book the same ground swell of nostalgic romanticism which seems to me present in Turner. More seriously, I detect limitations of interest and limitations of knowledge. Webb speaks of *The Frontier* in the abstract but his leading illustrations are drawn from the United States and most of them from a book with which historians have been familiar for some years, to wit, *The Great Plains*—whatever may be the point of departure for his study, it tends to end up in western Texas. I must use, as I would use for Turner, the harsh word *parochial*. If this paper could be of ample enough length, I would cite examples. I must say, also harshly, that to me, his acquaintance with the history of the rest of the world seems limited and cold. There are a dozen references to the medieval world which seem to indicate lack of sympathy, lack of knowledge, and lack of insight. Every reference he makes to my own country, Canada, is either smudged or else downright wrong. These are not good qualifications for a man who presents a thesis which he tells us may well revolutionize the art of writing modern history.

I come now to the thesis itself. As stated many times in the text, it is (unless my stupidity is hiding something from me) simply that the great discoveries were collectively the most important event in human history and that they have greatly affected the Europe from which the discoverers set out. Well, if there is any reputable historian alive in the Western world who will contest the general truth of such a thesis, he must be a queer specimen. Mr. Webb quotes Adam Smith in support of his thesis. Rather he should quote himself in support of Adam Smith's thesis, for it is hard to see how he has done more with it than dotted a few "i's": he has given some lively and readable descriptions of episodes or developments that have not perhaps before been put into consecutive sequence. His description, for example, of the eighteenth-century "Bubbles" is perhaps one of these, but it cannot claim originality. Similarly, his chapter on "The Parabola of Individualism" is useful, but the subject has been discussed a dozen times. Laski attempted to make the same point in *The Rise of European Liberalism* (which it is evident he would have preferred to call *The Fall of European Liberalism*). George Soule, I think it was, during the Depression talked about American liberty as consisting of two centuries of hardwood lands and one century of open plain. Barbara Ward appears to see these centuries since the Reformation as temporary aberrations on the part of the children of Mother Church, who sits patiently waiting for their return to the fold. Aldous Huxley in his *Brave New World* and George Orwell in *1984* have imaginatively pictured the fate that awaits the sons of liberty when free lands are no more. Professor Webb tells us about it once again, in the language of the scholar but with more than a shade of the accent of Karl Marx on the one hand and of Mother Church on the other. We Westerners are to be scourged with a lash having many thongs.

It may be that now, with the free lands of the world occupied, individualism and freedom will disappear and the ant-heap society replace them. The assumption, both in Webb's book and in various others, seems to be that man broke out of some such society at the end of the Middle Ages, kept out of it for a few centuries while floating along on the "boom" which accompanied the successful conquest and occupation by western Europe of the outlying world, and is now lapsing back into it because migration, that is, the availability of new land, has to come to an end, or, in other words, because there is no more frontier. It is a large assumption. From status to contract back to status. But were there any individuals among the Crusaders? Was there any freedom in an England that forced out of the various kings the great monuments of our parliamentary and legal institutions?

If a society is "closed" it may well be that the effect is to make people fight all the more vigorously for their rights. Someone has characterized the frontier as a region marked by "the philosophy of retreat." If you don't like it here, you get out and try somewhere else. If the wrong kind of people begin buying up houses on your street, you sell yours and move. You don't stand and fight. Some Puritans left England because conditions were not to their liking. Others stayed behind and fought it out, incidentally laying many courses in the wall of English liberties. The thesis could be argued that the frontier, for the English-speaking peoples, stifled as much freedom as it created.

"Democracy," which is supposed to be the major product of the frontier, especially of the American frontier, is a large and loose term. The American conception of it lays more emphasis upon social equality than does the British, and rather more than does the Canadian. By "democracy," the British seem to mean little more than parliamentary government and the rule of law; they still accept a hierarchical society without much demur. We in Canada do not accept such a society, though we do accept the monarchy. Undoubtedly the new world has made for social equality. But there is a very important point here, the one I made years ago in the ancient article to which I have referred, and that is, that every new country, whatever the shape of the society of its motherland, makes for a degree of social equality and a corresponding sense of freedom. Every difficult environment, old or new, does the same thing:

"Two voices are there; one is of the sea,
One of the mountains; each a mighty Voice!
In both from age to age thou didst rejoice,
They were thy chosen music, Liberty!"

In French Canada, daughter of absolutism in church and state, the new free environment of the forest turned French feudalism right round and made it work in favour of the *habitant*; all the French writers of the eighteenth century agreed that the Canadian peasantry was without sense of social distinction and far too independent for the liking of superior persons like themselves. But there was nothing more likely than that the twin absolutisms brought across the water would have regained their hold as society became more fixed: year by year, as escape to the bush became more difficult, their bonds would have tightened until New France approximated to Old. What saved the political freedom of the new world French was the English conquest: they were conquered into the freedom of English political institutions. Their religious freedom was not saved—the church did reassert itself, and for freedom from it, a French Canadian would either have had to oppose himself to his own society or to return to the post-Revolutionary mother country. For New France an infinite frontier of free land would not have eventually meant either freedom or democracy.

I yield to no one in my estimate of the place in human history of the addition of a new world to an old. Of course it was the most important thing that could have happened to man! How could it possibly be otherwise? But does not this constitute a basic criticism of *The Great Frontier*? Is it not one prolonged labouring of the obvious?

Dropping down a level, I cannot accept the author's low view of western Europe at the end of the fifteenth century, nor does it seem necessary to his thesis. Of course man secured a new world, a second chance, a free field, but that hardly means that he had his back to the wall. I doubt if a Renaissance Italian, if he could return, would feel that he owed much to the new world. More probably he would feel that the new world owed a good deal to him.

The preceding sentence brings us to the second term in the Webb thesis, metropolitanism. This term has intrigued me for years and I have elsewhere written a good deal about it. I can find little similarity in my views on the subject and those of Mr. Webb.

It does not seem to me that the concept of the Metropolis can properly be applied to an area as large and varied and amorphous as Europe. But the frontier concept can be applied to much of that area. Baltic forests for some centuries had been contributing those same "wind-falls" of capital, to use Professor Webb's happy term, that the forests of the outer world were later—mainly in the nineteenth and twentieth centuries—to augment. There are many other examples—Baltic and North Sea herring, and at a later date, for the indirect harvests, that northern staple wheat: wheat, so important to metropolitan Great Britain in the nineteenth century, whether it came from Prussia, Roumania, Kansas, or the Ukraine.

Incidentally, his discussion of windfalls may entangle Professor Webb, as windfalls should. On p. 184 of *The Great Frontier,* to show enormous gains easily reached, he quotes the experience of the Hudson's Bay Company from 1670 to 1720. A share of stock, he states, purchased at £100 in 1670, brought its owner in the following fifty years declared dividends of 343 per cent and in addition an undivided profit of £800, a total of 1143 per cent on the original investment, slightly less than 23 per cent annually. Now the interest tables inform us that one dollar, or one pound, or one anything, compounded semi-annually at 6 per cent will in fifty years become 19.22 dollars, pounds, etc. Six per cent does not seem an unreasonably high rate for the period 1670–1720. At seven, one dollar becomes $31.19. Webb's $11.43 for both reserves and dividends represents slightly less than 5 per cent, a very low return, it would seem to me, for the times and the risks. Windfalls probably seldom were as lucrative as Webb's simple arithmetic works them out to be. The so-called "Great Frontier" was a good deal harder nut to crack than a person otherwise uninformed would gain from this book. It has remained a hard nut to crack, not only in dollars but in blood.

The frontier, that is, the outer world, always will be a hard nut for any metropolitan centre, or power, to crack, simply because before the cracking has gone to its logical limits, internal resistance to it sets in. The North American Indians constitute almost the only example of a native people easily swept aside. The Africans and Arabs cannot be swept aside. The East Indians, both of the peninsula and of the islands, were not swept away, though for generations their countries were greater sources of wealth than was North America. The Chinese, towards whom gestures of sweeping were made, may end up by sweeping us away: their historians could then write about the trans-Pacific frontier, as I suppose Gothic, Mongolian, and Turkish historians, had they existed, would have written about "the South West" and as Arab historians actually did write about "The West"—the Moghreb.

The idea of the new land, "the land out there," new frontiers, is surely as old as man. How many Naples—Newtowns—have been founded since man set out on his upward road! Naples, Neapolis, Neuvilles, Neustadts, Novgorads, Nijni-Nofgorads—they must exist all over the world. A history of the idea "frontier" would be a history of civilization itself and a sound sociology of the same.

Evidently, the idea of the frontier, as originally announced and often since assumed, needs vast enlargement.

In like manner, the idea of the metropolis, which is antecedent to that of frontier, or hinterland, requires exploration on many fronts. It must include not only conquest, colonization, imperialism, but also all the countless factors that make for growth. And these are not only outward and physical but inward and cultural. What made some cities into metropolitan centres with almost limitless powers of growth? What is the role of politics, what of the staple trade, of geography? It does not help elucidation of the idea "metropolis" merely to equate it to "Europe," a large enough term in itself.

The historian may well ask himself how much of this tremendous burden legitimately rests on his shoulders.

The so-called metropolis "Europe" has contained both metropolis and frontier. With or without the new world, it is apparent that for a couple of thousand years or so now it has had considerable powers of growth. The Middle Ages, far from being ages of stagnation, as *The Great Frontier* seems to regard them, were themselves witnesses of development in many directions. There was the *Drang nach Osten,* carried out, as the late J. W. Thompson showed, in much the same spirit and with much the same results, if on a smaller scale, as the later conquest of the outer world. The fourteenth-century German newspaper editor, if he had existed, could well have said to the rising generation, "Go east, young man, go east." "There," he could have continued, "you can get free lands and cheap labour, merely for the taking. The lesser beings from whom you take them you can sell in the markets of the west as [what Europe soon came to call them] Slavs, or slaves. With the Slavs or slaves you retain, you can work your land and rise to baronial rank."

The idea has never died in Germany: it was revived forcefully under Hitler. Hitler had promised, according to one writer, that warriors who had attained certain honours "would be given estates in conquered countries." One of the Nazi air aces, Von Werra, "thought he would see what Poland had to offer in the way of estates." He took his bride there on their honeymoon. She writes: ". . . we drove around but could not make up our minds whether we wanted to breed cattle or fish. I wanted a lake and streams with fish, and also a house that had a tower. He wanted land and facilities for breeding horses."[1] That sounds very much like the men who believed they had a right to singe the king of Spain's beard, or their successors who acted on the maxim that the only good Indian was a dead Indian. No one would deny that the scale was vastly enlarged when the outer world was opened but the psychology was much the same and probably the unsettling effects on institutions not dissimilar.

It is ridiculous to believe, and surely no serious historian does believe, that without the new world Europe would have lain stagnant. The old continent had already built a brilliant civilization and made many of the fundamental inventions (one need only mention the clock and printing) and no doubt would have gone on to make many more, new world or no new world. It got a powerful "assist" from the new resources made available by the discoveries (especially the psychical resources), and possibly this is all that Professor Webb is claiming.

At any rate, European metropolitanism had risen to considerable heights well before the discoveries. Venice, Genoa, the Hanse cities, Antwerp—these and others could properly be considered metropolitan. To explain their growth would be to write their history. Pirenne tells us that Italian metropolitanism germinated from the reopening of the trade routes to Constantinople after they had been cut by the Arab thrust west. He says that free trade made Antwerp after the older Flemish cities such as Bruges and Ghent had wound themselves up in the restrictions of the various guilds. But these are merely large, impressionistic strokes. What is germane to our purpose here is that in the prediscovery period a large, though naturally not a world, scale of growth was evident.

I agree—who would not?—that we can probably give the largest share of the credit—or discredit—for what has happened since to the opening of the outer world. Might I dare to be personal and say that for years I have taught that the Industrial Revolution was "made in America," proceeding from the seller's market set up by colonization, a market which for many reasons impinged with greatest force upon England? To "made in America," I should add "made in India." I am sure, however, that the complex structure we call "growth" cannot be explained on the basis of any one factor, however impressive. "When we begin to search for the causes of the economic growth of a country . . . our embarrassment is not of poverty but of riches. We are swamped by explanations," says J. K. Galbraith (*Queen's Quarterly*, Summer, 1958).[2] Mr. Galbraith goes on to examine a number of the more prominent explanations of growth, such as population increase, capital formation, natural resources, and various others. He comes to the conclusion that, while all are significant, they operate with varying intensity at various times and places, and no one of them is dominant. He thinks growth can go on today, if I understand him, without what have always been regarded as its prime necessities, new resources. His argument is probably too abstract to suit most historians, but if historians persist in searching for causes, they would do well to be familiar with lines of thought that are evidently not far from commonplace to the economists.

It seems to me that "the frontier" in the hard terms of economic development (which possibly drags in in its wake, political and cultural development) must consist in usable resources. The frontier as a way of life is another matter: I love a lodge in some vast wilderness or a life on the ocean wave as well as any man, but that is another story. So the hard-headed economists probably must have their way, for they are at least logical, and "frontier" must be equated to "usable resources."

When we avail ourselves of what is a mile down under earth and sea, the additional resources result in growth just as surely as additional land. Oil a mile underground may create a community on top of it which will go through all the stages of social growth and manifest most of the frontier phenomena in the process. If it is American or Canadian oil, with a sense of self-government in its molecules, there will be easy informality among the new arrivals in the field, meetings will be held and committees formed. Later on, if the field holds out, the familiar signs of class differentiation will become visible—and just as much on the basis of oil as of land. If it is Arab oil, with polygamy in its chemistry, then, of course, the social evolution which slides along on it will be different.

But, again, one must always be careful to add that no one would deny the overwhelming scale of the land frontier experience of North America and the consequent interest and conspicuous nature of the social phenomena based on it.

Americans have rejoiced in their new society and until yesterday most of them were glad to believe that they had turned their backs on the old world. Their Revolution has influenced their thinking on this matter of the frontier, as on all others. Canadians did not make the same sharp break with the past; as a result, they have been ready to give weight, perhaps undue weight, to tradition. While Americans with names like Smith and Brown have been busy proving to themselves that they have long since ceased to be Englishmen, Canadians with names like Brown and Smith have been apt to congratulate themselves on how English—or, rather, how British—they still were. Both may have gone too far. To me, an English Canadian, my American friends seem to have just as many English traits as I have, and in some directions more. If new societies are to get clear views of themselves, they will have to try to give true weight to both tradition and environment.

American students of the frontier have been apt to stress how much the new environment changed their institutions. Canadians have been apt to emphasize the continuity of theirs. As in all historic situations "there is much to be said on both sides." The great institutions which the English-speaking world shares, such as representative government and the common law, were not worked out after the American Revolution but before it. They were not worked out in the modern period but in the medieval. If the new world had never been discovered, the English presumably would have gone on developing their free institutions nevertheless. We owe much of our freedom today to medieval Englishmen, and that is what I was taught as a boy in a little town close to the edge of settlement when we had to memorize the thirty-ninth section of Magna Carta. We in Canada have no bill of rights of our own and we have never made a declaration of independence. But we believe pretty generally, I think, that "no freeman should be captured or imprisoned or disseized or outlawed or exiled or in any way destroyed . . . except by the lawful judgement of his peers or by the law of the land."

Yet nothing is clearer than that a new environment changes institutions in detail. Professor Webb thinks that some of them are too big and hard to go through the frontier sieve: he instances the Catholic Church. I agree, except in that I imagine the Catholic Church itself has also been changed in detail by new environments: I doubt if Chinese Catholicism is quite the same as the Catholicism of French Canada. The latter, for example, is kept in fighting trim by the Protestant world around it. Would this be true of Catholicism in, say, Bolivia. There is a field here for much further work.

I wish that to Catholicism, as more or less frontier-proof, Professor Webb would add English parliamentary government. I also wish that students of the frontier would exercise their skill in attempting to refine the word *democracy*. A glance at non-English frontiers would be enlightening to them in this respect, for, as I have already said, every frontier brings forth the same phenomena of adaptability, energy, and a rough kind of equalitarianism.

As opposed to the loose social democracy of the frontier, which is transient unless supported with well-established institutions, I put weight on the medieval inheritance. But the medieval inheritance was badly disrupted during the earlier phases of colonization, and as a result a gulf was flung across Europe and the western world which has never closed—the gulf of the Reformation. The Reformation cannot be well understood unless it is viewed as a revolution—the first of the great revolutions that have made the modern world. It was a revolution which touched every nook and cranny of life. If we must have a single explanation for things, and I hope we must not, I would prefer the Reformation to the frontier. It goes wider and it goes deeper. It is not a matter of mere economic determination. It changes the nature of man.

If ones makes a journey from Ottawa to London, to Melbourne and Auckland, and thence to San Francisco, Washington, and back to Ottawa, he will have gone round the world, a long way. If, however, he walks a few hundred feet from west to east along Sherbrooke Street in Montreal, he will have gone further in fifteen minutes than he did on his journey round the world. If he walks ten yards or so across the Mexican border from California, as I did recently, he will have gone further still. If you go round the world on the route I have mentioned, you remain within the encompassing mantle of English speech and English institutions. You note many local differences in detail but they are small as compared with the similarities. Then you take your walk along Sherbrooke Street, or across the border at Tijuana, and immediately—you are in another world! You have crossed cultural frontiers that are of greater dimensions than land frontiers and infinitely more stubborn. The approximate coincidence of these frontiers with the success or failure of the Reformation is sufficiently obvious.

The occupation of the lands now forming the United States was a vast and mighty episode in human history, and no one will belittle the bulk of it, its colour, and the innumerable consequences that have flowed from it. But it was not the whole story of man's dispersal throughout the world. And its characteristics did not arise solely from the process of expansion. They were not by any means all made on the spot.

Coming from a country that still has a frontier and that, in the unconquerable north, must always have one, I am just far enough outside American frontier studies to feel that while they have given rise to admirable new historical insights, they have also been marked by a certian parochialism and some of the lack of objectivity that goes with romanticism. I would hope that as they go on, they will gain that catholicity of knowledge and outlook which is a distinguishing and distinguished aspect of the general edifice of American historiography.

NOTES

1. Kendal Burt and James Leasor, *The One that Got Away* (New York, 1956), p. 218.

2. John Kenneth Galbraith, "The Causes of Economic Growth," *Queen's Quarterly*, LXV (Summer, 1958), p. 169.

Webb's *Great Frontier* and the Interpretation of Modern History

BY JOSÉ HONÓRIO RODRIGUES

Arquivo Nacional, Rio de Janeiro

THE RISE, growth, and meaning of the modern world have inspired many interpretations and attempts at historical understanding. Again and again men have tried to fix the limits of historical periods and to search for the motives that have led to their formation, the forces that have contributed to their development, and the reasons for their decline. Karl Marx was probably inspired by the observation of Adam Smith that the discovery of America and of the passage to the East Indies by the Cape of Good Hope were the two major facts in the history of mankind, when he affirmed that world commerce and a world market were responsible in the sixteenth century for the rise of capitalism, a new product resulting from the dissolution of the feudal form of society and the rise of new forces of production.[1] The truth, according to John Nef, is that since Marx the distinction between modern and contemporary civilizations and the older ones is based on the notion of capitalism.[2] Capitalism has thus become the fundamental fact that differentiates the medieval from the modern world.

Later studies developing the Marxist thesis or reacting to it have laid still greater emphasis on the central theme of the formation of capitalism (great commerce and navigation, huge capital, the moral freedom to charge and receive interest, the founding of the stock exchange and of the banks, the price revolution) and its political, social, and religious repercussions (the Reformation, the growth of the idea of nationality, the elaboration of the idea of democracy, the secularization of politics, the transformation of international relations between the East and the West, and the new man). The Economic Revolution that accompanies the geographical revolution broadens the limits of Christianity and marks the beginning of the Europeanization of the world, a process now coming to an end as a result of the change from European predominance to non-European predominance, as Professor Barraclough has said.[3]

There are many factors that explain the rise and fall of this historical process from Marx to our day, some isolated and some connected with each other. Some theories are born from facts; others take the facts as a means of building up generalizations. Some theories consider the facts as a complex of circumstances; others see only the isolated facts. Marx offers us a part of the truth, and so does Max Weber, when he formulates as an antithesis the possibility of the reaction of spiritual factors. The studies of Hamilton, those of Braudel, Renouard, and Chaunu, which continued those of Pirenne, Hauser, and Sée, as well as those of Sombart, Brentano, Troeltsch, and Tawney, all the result of extended research, offer us invaluable data for the understanding of the motives of the opening of "The Great Frontier" and of its economic, social, and political repercussions.

Webb's thesis gives us one more explanation of the historical period 1500 to 1900. It not only sets the limits of the historical frontier of one period, but represents an attempt to discover the structure of a historical epoch, with its transformations and effective nexuses, its dominant and antagonistic tendencies, its values and aims, its tensions and sufferings, its limitations and beauties. Its significance lies, to my mind, in a new contribution to the understanding of the modern world as a fact and in the fixing of its limits as a period. Webb isolated himself from all previous explanations, and he ignored, voluntarily or involuntarily, the traditional lines of European historical bibliography on the formation of the modern world. The literature he used is more North American than Anglo-American; of all the studies on the formation of capitalism he is especially familiar with those of Earl J. Hamilton. It also seems that the concept of "capitalism" in the sense of a period of economic history is repugnant to him, since we do not find any connection between his concept of the Great Frontier and the concept of capitalism, which has been so prevalent in the historical bibliography of this last century. Although Webb's thesis is born of factual

observations of North American history and is based on very restricted bibliographical information, it does not confine itself to the
limits of the North American historical scene: it grows until it comes
to an abstraction, i.e., a general theory of the historical period 1500–
1900, or a general scheme of the history of the modern world.

Viewed from this angle we must applaud it, for it tries to express
a part of universal historical truth. After the United States attained
world power and became one of the giants of the world of today it
abandoned isolationism and became immersed in the ocean of universal thought. It is therefore as a world contribution that Webb's
thesis merits the most careful scrutiny on the part of all historians,
no matter what their origin or intellectual formation.

We have already said that Webb did not know or has deliberately
ignored, perhaps in order to pursue his argument more freely, the
historical bibliography on capitalism, the fundamental characteristic
of the period of the Great Frontier. Nor has he even shown the
connection between these two factors: the frontier and capitalism.
Quoting Hermann Heimpel we can say that all historical knowledge
is the "understanding of factual connections" (*das begreifen von
Sachzusammenhängen*).[4] Professor Webb tried to establish many
connections among many facts in order to formulate a general concept, the Great Frontier. But the Great Frontier fact itself was not
clearly established, and many times certain possible connections
such as, for instance, Lutheranism and democracy, are put side by
side with facts like the Texas Rangers. It doesn't make sense to
oppose the facts to the connections or the connections to the facts.
To take another example: capitalism and Protestantism form a connection and the price revolution is a fact. It will add little to our
understanding of the limits of this historical period to talk of capitalism and Protestantism and of the price revolution without first
interrelating them in an integrated synthesis. We can only conceive
of unity by taking as a point of departure a whole, more or less
hypothetical. That is why it seems inadequate to us to say that
"Europe mothered mercantilism, commercialism, capitalism, and in-
dustrialism, but the frontier mothered democracy" (*The Great Frontier*, p. 30). Professor Lower criticized this point and I agree with
him ("Professor Webb and 'The Great Frontier' Thesis"). One may
say that the connections established between the various social,
political, and economic facts, which became apparent after the
opening of the Great Frontier, would have been much more numer-

ous and important if Professor Webb had not confined himself to examples taken almost exclusively from North American history. Again we agree with Professor Lower: "Whatever may be the point of departure for his study, it ends up in western Texas." Webb's thesis sometimes appears to be a Texan conception of modern world history because of his insistence on universalizing facts that are peculiar to or characteristic of the North American frontier. In the words of Professor Lower, there is not a single dominant factor that explains "the complex structure we call growth." And there is no single frontier, for the frontier presents many varieties, as does the European Metropolis. As an abstract concept, the Great Frontier of the fifteenth-to-sixteenth centuries presents many different aspects, which act and react according to the specific and peculiar conditions of each aspect. As pointed out by Professor Hancock, "Turner would have tolerated frontiers in the plural, but Webb says: There is no plural for the frontier." ("The Moving Metropolis.")

Let us admit that there was in the beginning of the period one world frontier (the Great Frontier), but there was not one Metropolis. If we look, not at the similarities but at the differences that distinguish Portugal from Spain, we will also see the differences that distinguish Luso-Brazilian America and Spanish America, and we shall observe in America the national unity of the world of Portuguese origin and the national diversity of the world of Spanish origin. One can note many variations in American frontiers when one takes as a basis of comparison the examples given by Professor Webb on the various effects of the frontier in the United States. If the "American way of life" is a product of the frontier, it is also true the frontier has not always produced the same results. None of the characteristics of love of work, desire for efficiency, belief in *laissez faire*, in profit, in competition, in the machines, and in corporations was characteristic of Brazil, or, I think, of Spanish America; they did not belong to the creed of the Metropolis and the frontier did not suggest or impose them.

The frontier has not suggested to the Brazilians the rejection of the past, of the old world of Portugal, as it did to the Americans and the "Afrikaners" (Hancock). As in the case of the Canadians (Lower), the Brazilians are always conscious of their past. A French traveler (Pierre Denis) observed in 1908 that the Brazilians love to say that their country is young. But he says that the European who has traveled in other American countries, such as Argentina or the United States, would feel less strange in Brazil since he would not experience the same sensation of surprise or fear that he did in those countries, in which there is no hierarchy and, indeed, a certain rootlessness, and where the lives of the people are directed chiefly toward individual independence and acquisition of money. These characteristics are only recently to be noticed in Brazil. Recent also in Brazil are the ideas of the acceleration of the historical process (fifty years in five years was the slogan that led President Juscelino Kubitscheck to victory in his presidential campaign) and of the valorization of economic activity (commercial and industrial).[6] The Iberian peoples conceive economic activity as a negative of leisure (*negotium* = *negócio*) instead of an affirmation of activity as business (from busy). The best things of life were not in business (*negócio*) but in leisure (*ócio*). The frontier in the Ibero-American world has neither engendered the dynamic character it did in the United States (Webb, *op. cit.*, p. 150), nor exaggerated individualism or favored competition and profit.

If these Brazilian examples are adequate to test Professor Webb's thesis, then we must consider that the frontier in itself was not a general determining factor in the history of modern civilization, as he claimed (Webb, *op. cit.*, p. 1). One must look for the action of other factors in order to see, according to Max Weber, how material and spiritual conditions are functionally interrelated. The new ingredient—the Great Frontier (Webb, *op. cit.*, p. 10)—may have a *general* influence on the opening of the World Frontier, offering, as Keynes said, an exceptional opportunity to the business man, the speculator, and the profiteer (Webb, *op. cit.*, p. 177), as well as a *particular* influence, peculiar to each frontier itself. In the first case it is connected with the rise of capitalism ("in these golden years modern capitalism was born"), which has also undergone the most varied transformations, advances, retrogressions and lags. Even today there are countries of the Great Frontier belonging to the Have and Have-Not classification of Simonds and Emeny. So the Great Frontier thesis should take more account of the studies and the bibliography on capitalism which reveal the factors that have stimulated or delayed the advance of capitalism. And it is necessary not to forget that the boom does not begin with Christopher Columbus, whose travels proved to be a disappointment from the economic point of view, but with Vasco da Gama, who put an end to the economic predominance of the Italian merchant men.[7] In the second case, Webb's thesis must be broadened in order to include the study of the varieties of national frontiers, and to find out how far this aspect can be isolated or to what extent it acts in conjunction with certain specific and local conditions.

The opening of the Great Frontier is a new factor connected with the already known factors that have given birth to the modern world: the discovery of America, the discovery of the passage to the East Indies by the Cape of Good Hope, the price revolution, capitalism, and the Reformation. The last three events have excited the imagination of scholars in the same way that Vasco da Gama's voyage excited the imagination of the Europeans. I think that Webb's thesis may perhaps provoke great interest and stimulate an important bibliography all over the world. If it is to do this, however, it must free itself of certain naïve ideas, like that of the "right-hand side of the road" (p. 46) which has nothing to do with the frontier, since both the Old World and the New use it; or the Texan examples of the "Texan Rangers and the Revolver" (pp. 241–245), the "New System of Cattle Culture" (pp. 245–247), "The Invention of a Fence" (pp. 247–250), "The Methods of Farming" (pp. 250–254), "A Revolution in the Law of Water" (pp. 254–259), and so on, which rather belong to the Little than to the Great Frontier. In Brazil, and I don't think there was any North American influence there (p. 268), the abolition of the entail was passed by a law of October 6, 1835, and the democratic evolution was already accentuated in the Imperial Constitution of 1824.

Some generalizations, like that of the position of the Church in the Great Frontier (Webb, pp. 86–96), also deserve critical comment since they correspond to a revival of old explanations today out of date. Professor Webb believes that the divided Protestantism was in harmony with the frontier man and favored democracy, whereas the Catholic Church, predominant in Latin America, was the natural companion of the Absolute State. "It is not strange, therefore," he says, "that in the Latin American or Catholic frontier the temporal governments have alternated between efforts at democracy and efforts at dictatorship" (p. 87). It is an affirmation full of vagueness and the same can be said of Professor Lower's phrase: "If we must have a single explanation for things, and I hope we must not, I would prefer the Reformation to the frontier" (p. 15).

I see in both affirmations the reopening of the old controversy on the relations of the historical process and religion. Henri Pirenne, in his *Histoire de Belgique*,[8] recalled in this connection a medal engraved in 1587 with an inscription that represented the progress of the Reformed states and the misery of the Catholic nations of the Western World, as a punishment of God to unbelievers and as a reward to believers. During the nineteenth century Weyrich, Flammarion, and Lavelleye[9] studied the economic inferiority of the Catholic nations and the prosperity of the Protestant countries without being able to understand the connection between the economic and moral factors. Max Weber was the first to discover the spiritual, ethical, and philosophical conditions that made possible the formation of the spirit of capitalism. Professor Webb attributed no significance to the Calvinist ethic that has prepared the soil for the growth of the spirit and the system of capitalism. On the contrary, he emphasizes the role of Luther, whose doctrine produced no major social and economic consequences,[10] whereas Calvinism, according to Max Weber, encouraged everything that Webb cited as a psychological fruit of the frontier (p. 32). If the "psychical resources" made available by the discoveries to which Professor Lower refers are the same as those that Max Weber and his followers or commentators, like Tawney, emphasized as the spiritual fruits of Calvinism, why not examine them in the light of Weber's ideas, instead of speaking simply of the Reformation, a general term full of implications as to its spirit, teaching, and influence? And why not dispel the vague suspicions of ethnic or religious discriminations, as Max Weber did? Those cultural frontiers to which Professor Lower refers, if they have not the material values of the world, if they are subdeveloped frontiers, still they possess moral, ethnic-democratic, and pacifist values that represent a great deal in the history of the modern world devastated by European wars in pursuit of political and economic hegemony. Protestant and Catholic Europe became rich on the profits of a brutal colonialism that created its Great Powers at the cost of the work and efforts of populations subordinated to strange and alien interests. The "epochal" change of 1945, which puts an end to the European domination of enormous areas of the world and to the agony of a process of historical development, does not close the frontier in the sense of enterprise, optimism, hope, and the opportunities offered to millions of human beings living in the frontiers of subdeveloped areas. This is so true that Professor Webb (pp. 285 and 416–417) speaks of the

new kinds of frontiers rejected by the pioneers of the eighteenth
and nineteenth centuries and affirms that if the United States would
be willing to spend the amount of money it is now spending in
Europe and Asia, in the development of areas like Amazonia, they
"would recreate the boom of the old frontier on a small scale, and
[this] would result in a net gain to the wealth of the Western
World." It is necessary to note that in Brazil, which occupies half
of South America (8,500,000 sq. km. against 8,700,000 sq. km.), the
so-called Amazonia (comprising the States of Amazonas, Pará, the
western part of Maranhão, the northern part of Mato Grosso, Goiás,
and the Territories of Acre, Rondonia, Rio Branco, and Amapá)
represents two-thirds of the Brazilian territory, i.e., five and a half
million square kilometers. This region is not a torrid one, as Professor Webb thinks (p. 285), and its climate has, so to speak, been
rehabilitated by Professor Charles Wagley, who also spoke of its
possibilities.[11] It is a frontier that has been occupied since 1616 by
the Brazilians, who have tried to develop it without major results.

Finally, I do not believe that Professor Webb's thesis can be sum-
marized in two words—geographical determinism, as Professor
Lower maintains, for the simple reason that Professor Webb always
gives first place to man and not to geographical conditions. Quoting Professor Webb's words: "Thus frontier man became the only
active agent on the scene, and his acts were unrestrained by other
men" (p. 32), and the "management of land" is one of the examples of his thesis.[12] I don't think either that Professor Webb's
thesis is "one prolonged labouring of the obvious" (Lower). It is
parochial in the illustrations and examples but not in the general
idea, which seems to me an original contribution, although its
validity is threatened by the limited examples of the regional frontiers, especially that of North America. Even if the Great Frontier
may not be the sum of the different regional frontiers, it is necessary
to broaden the research and try to conduct it more accurately in
order to attain a basic concept through the integration of the various frontiers. If this will not explain all the troubles of modern
western history, it may perhaps lead to the definition of one of the
aspects of the adversities and successes of adaptation to the New
World, to the explanation of the tremendous opportunities offered
to the Old World, and to the formulation of interesting hypotheses.
The truth is that neither has he established the facts that exemplify

the Great Frontier nor has he indicated their connection with the other great facts of the epoch.

A vision of the world, according to Anderle,[13] consists not only of a quantitative sum of isolated knowledge but of a qualitative choice in order to achieve an integrated synthesis. The integrated synthesis has not been made. I remember Collingwood's criticism of Toynbee and I wonder if it is applicable or not to Professor Webb's thesis: "His whole scheme is really a scheme of pigeon-holes elaborately arranged and labelled, into which ready-made historical facts can be put." [14]

I think that Professor Webb had great insight when he conceived the concept of the Great Frontier. But the Great Frontier is divided into little frontiers, which had different destinies and exercised different influences. Professor Webb lacked the specific knowledge of these little frontiers and he defined the Great Frontier using the facts pertinent to the little frontier of the United States. It is to be desired that his concept may inspire special studies that will contribute the elements for the future definition of the Great Frontier. Nevertheless, even so it will be necessary to establish the connection among the various facts of the little frontiers in order to attain the definition of the concept of the Great Frontier. The knowledge of the facts and the practical connections, chiefly between the frontier and capitalism, have not yet been sufficiently established in order to make possible a better definition of the Great Frontier. Capitalism was at first a concept that defined a fact; the Great Frontier up to now is still a concept that has expressed a fact only in an insufficient manner.

Only when a historiography becomes mature does it begin to think and express itself in universal terms. Professor Webb's thesis represents, on the whole, one more attempt at a definition of a universal historical period.

NOTES

1. Karl Marx, *A Contribution to the Critique of Political Economy* (Chicago, 1904), p. 267.

2. John U. Nef, "Essence de la civilisation industrielle," in *Eventail de l'Histoire Vivante* (Paris, 1953), I, 62.

3. "History, Morals and Politics," *International Affairs*, XXXIV, No. 1 (January 1958), 11.

4. H. Heimpel, "Geschichte und Geschichtswissenschaft," in 23 *Versammlung deutscher Historiker in Ulm* (Stuttgart, 1957), p. 30.

5. José Honório Rodrigues, "Conhecimento dos paises hispano-americanos no Brasil," in *Conocimiento y desconocimiento de América* (Washington, 1958), pp. 64–92.

6. The delayed development and the valorization of the liberal professions were the characteristics of the colonial and imperial phases in Brazil.

7. Yves Renouard, *Les hommes d'affaires italiens du Moyen Age* (Paris, 1949).

8. Henri Pirenne, *Histoire de Belgique* (7 vols., Bruxelles, 1900–1932), II, 407.

9. J. B. Weyrich, "Inferiorité économique des nations catholiques," *Revue Sociale Catholique*, 3e année (No. 7, 1er Mai, 1899; No. 8, 1er Juin, 1899), pp. 214–219, 225–234; A. Flamérion, *De la prospérité comparée des nations catholiques et des nations protestantes, au point de vue économique, morale, sociale* (Paris, 1899); E. Lavelleye, *Protestantism and Catholicism in Their Bearing upon the Liberty and Prosperity of Nations* (London, 1875).

10. E. Troeltsch, *The Social Teaching of the Christian Churches* (2 vols., London, 1949).

11. Charles Wagley, *Amazon Town: A Study of Man in the Tropics* (New York, 1953).

12. Walter P. Webb, "The Western World Frontier," *The Frontier in Perspective,* ed. by Clifton B. Kroeber and Walker D. Wyman (Madison, 1957), p. 117.

13. Othman F. Anderle, "Theoretische Geschichte," *Historische Zeitschrift,* Vol. 185, No. 1 (Feb., 1958), 10.

14. R. G. Collingwood, *The Idea of History* (Oxford, 1946), p. 163.

Comment: The Seminal Character of Webb's Frontier Thesis

BY GEOFFREY BARRACLOUGH
*The Royal Institute of
International Affairs*

THE TWO PAPERS upon which I have been
asked to comment seem to me to illustrate
the seminal character of Walter Prescott
Webb's frontier thesis. They are critical,
and many of the criticisms have substance; but do they invalidate
the theory? In the short space available I can only pick out a few
of the central questions; and I propose to comment rather than to
reply point by point to the criticisms. Of the two critics Professor
Lower is the more radical; and for that reason I shall concentrate
more upon what he has to say than upon Professor Hancock's more
sympathetic amplifications.

There is no doubt, in the first place, that the idea of the frontier
is capable, as Professor Lower says, of vast enlargement. I have
already pointed out the significance of the story of the Russian
frontier.[1] An earlier session of this Congress, and Spanish historians
working independently, have explored the medieval Iberian frontier.[2] Professor Lower himself has referred to the familiar example
of the German *Drang nach Osten,* and we can all think of other
examples. I myself would refer to the little-known but illuminating
example of the County Palatine of Chester, on the confines of England and Wales, where political and social institutions were pro-
foundly modified over five centuries by frontier conditions.[3] There
is, therefore, no sharp division between the periods before and after
the Great Discoveries; and we may agree with Professor Lower that
a full history of the idea "frontier" would amount to little less than
"a history of civilization itself." Nevertheless, the impact of the dis-

covery of the New World—though perhaps slower than Webb admits, a phenomenon of the seventeenth rather than of the fifteenth century—was so incomparably greater that the difference, most of us will agree, was qualitative rather than quantitative. It is significant that Professor Lower himself repeatedly admits this fact. "We can," he agrees, "probably give the largest share of the credit— or discredit—for what has happened since to the opening of the outer world." Is not this an affirmation of Webb's thesis?

To treat the frontier as the only factor in "the complex structure we call growth" would, of course, be a gross simplification.[4] In Professor Lower's view, "social inheritance" was, and is, more powerful than "physiographical environment." This is a question which cannot be decided by any objective test; it is one of those things which, as Professor Hancock says, there is "no way of measuring." But we may, I think, admit that Professor Lower's argument is important insofar as it points to the fact that the impact of the frontier was not uniform. Undoubtedly the reaction to the frontier was different, for example, in Spanish America and in North America, and "social inheritance" was no doubt one reason for this difference. It was not necessarily the only one. In addition, frontier conditions were varied in the extreme, and their variety doubtless called forth different responses. That is why it is important, as Professor Hancock indicates, to supplement Webb's work by studying the different impacts of frontier conditions in Australia, Canada, South Africa, etc. Here again, however, it is a question of giving greater flexibility to Webb's thesis rather than of controverting it. Professor Lower makes great play with the example of French Canada; but the very fact that he admits that frontier conditions there "turned French feudalism right round" and produced a society "without sense of social distinction" seems to me to tell in favour of, rather than against Webb. Is not that the essence of Webb's frontier theory? If Webb preached a doctrine of "geographic determinism," as Professor Lower suggests, his views would be rightly suspect; but, in fact, frontier conditions left room for a wide range of different reactions, and the next step, it seems to me, lies with comparative history, which can clarify what is unique or specific and what is common or general.

For Webb the opening of the frontier lands of the Western Hemisphere to a static European society in 1492 was the beginning of a new epoch in the story of mankind. The thesis is not new; as both

Professor Lower and Professor Hancock point out, it goes back to Adam Smith. And without doubt we may also query the word "static." In Professor Lower's view, it would be "ridiculous to believe . . . that without the New World, Europe would have lain stagnant." The answer, it seems to me, is that we simply do not know. But it is hard to think that the new impetus or "propelling force" of the Great Discoveries failed to induce a vast increase in tempo. "If the new world had never been discovered," Professor Lower argues, "the English would presumably have gone on developing their free institutions nevertheless." I wonder. The argument, it may be, underestimates the role of the new wealth of the English mercantile classes in enabling them to resist the crown during the constitutional conflicts of the seventeenth century. If Professor Lower argues this way, it is evidently because he places greater emphasis on the Reformation than on the expanding frontier as a factor in the rise of the modern world. It is, of course, a return to the conventional point of view which makes the Renaissance and the Reformation the starting points of modern history. Yet, as I pointed out some years ago: "There had been other renaissances, a long series reaching back to the time of Charlemagne; there had been reformers without number before Luther. But the earlier reforms had withered, the earlier renaissances had failed to produce a turning point in the human mind. Why was it that the sixteenth century registered a permanent advance where other centuries had experienced only a transient stimulus?"[5] Was it not, perhaps, that a new factor—as Webb suggests—so "enlarged the field in which the human mind could operate" that the decisive leap into the future which had baffled earlier generations became suddenly feasible?

Professor Lower, if I understand him aright, emphasizes the significance of the Reformation because he believes that the features of modern history which Webb identifies with the frontier are in reality a product of English Protestant conditions. I confess that, on both counts, it is an argument I find difficult to follow. The argument that the Reformation changed "the nature of man" is one which modern historical scholarship has increasingly left behind; the emphasis today is rather on continuity and the persistence—at least in Europe—of old ways of thought.[6] The identification (for such I take it to be) between Protestantism and representative institutions recalls the old sterile controversy over the alleged connexion between the Reformation and the rise of Capitalism. When Professor

Lower contrasts ideas and institutions along an axis running through Ottawa—London—Melbourne—Auckland—and back to Ottawa with those "across the Mexican border from California," he provokes the retort that we in England feel closer affinity with Burgundy or Catalonia or Umbria than with the "frontier" environment of Canada or South Africa or Australia. An Englishman and a Spaniard, both participants in the Graeco-Roman cultural tradition of the Old World, share the same terms of reference; an Englishman and a Canadian, divided by the totally different conditions of the frontier, do not. Admittedly this is a subjective reaction; but it is (I submit) no more subjective and no less legitimate than Professor Lower's contention. All I would emphasize, however, is that for me the difference between a "frontier" environment and a European environment is more real than that between Protestant and Catholic or between Latin and Anglo-Saxon. For this reason—but not for this reason alone—Webb's thesis is more persuasive to me than Professor Lower's.

Webb's frontier thesis reminds me in many ways of Pirenne's famous theory about the economic and cultural consequences of the Arab invasions. Like Pirenne's theory, the frontier thesis is bound to be hotly debated; opinion will swing first one way, then another. But, like Pirenne's theory, it is an interpretation which cannot fail to fructify historical work, and, like Pirenne's theory, it cannot be ignored or dismissed out of hand. Even those who, like the present commentator, are sceptical of certain aspects, will salute, with Professor Hancock, its "splendour, span, audacity." It provides new intuitions, new avenues of research, interpretations to stimulate historians of all periods and countries. We shall never prove or disprove it in its totality; but in examining it, our knowledge of historical processes will be widened and deepened, our understanding made more secure.

NOTES

1. G. Barraclough, *History in a Changing World* (Norman, Oklahoma, 1956), pp. 145–149.

2. Cf. *La reconquista española y la repoblación del país* (Instituto de Estudios Pirenáicos, Zaragoza, 1951).

3. Cf. G. Barraclough, *The Earldom and County Palatine of Chester* (Oxford, 1953).

4. Since Professor Lower appears to suggest that this is what Webb does, it is perhaps important to emphasize that he does not maintain "that the frontier originated ideas or institutions, but only that it altered them"; it was not, in short, the only factor, but it was the formative factor which provided the impetus otherwise lacking. Cf. Walter P. Webb, *The Great Frontier* (Boston, 1951), pp. 15, 101, 143, 173, 174, 239, 258.

5. Barraclough, *History in a Changing World*, p. 139.

6. Cf. Otto Brunner, *Adeliges Landleben and europäischer Geist* (Salzburg, 1949). Professor I. M. W. Tillyard, *The Elizabethan World-Picture* (London, 1943) showed how much that was specifically pre-Reformation continued to exist in the outlook of the Elizabethan Englishman.

Part Five

THE HISTORIAN'S TASK FROM MEXICAN AND UNITED STATES VIEWPOINTS

The Historian's Task: The Mexican Perspective .
. . . . Luis Villoro

The Historian's Task: A United States Historian's View
. . . . Arthur P. Whitaker

Comment: Freedom for the Historian . . .
. . . . France V. Scholes

Comment: Classical or Ontological History . .
. . . . . . Edmundo O'Gorman

*Comment: The "Mestizo" Quality of Current
Historiography* . Guillermo Céspedes del Castillo

This final set of papers and comments also reveals contrasting attitudes. The contributions of Professor Villoro and Professor Whitaker seem to show how differently Latin American historians and those of the United States tend to view the historical past. Professor Villoro of Mexico is in the great Spanish tradition, which sees history as one of the humanities, closely linked to philosophy. Professor Whitaker, on the other hand, has a very different emphasis. He appears to believe, as perhaps most historians in the United States do, that history's closest links are with the social sciences; thus his thought has a certain pragmatic essence.

The comments on these views are equally interesting. That of Professor Scholes is a balancing effort, an attempt to find a common ground between the two positions. That of Professor O'Gorman is sharp and incisive, revealing his own well-known and strong preference for history viewed in the light of reasoned philosophical thought. The final comment is perhaps the most surprising of all. In surveying this basic disagreement, Professor Céspedes del Castillo, one of Spain's leading younger historians, seems to agree with Professor Whitaker, viewing history as more allied to the social sciences than to the humanities and philosophy. Thus, in this case, Spain casts its vote for Sancho Panza and against Don Quixote.

The Historian's Task: The Mexican Perspective

BY Luis Villoro
Universidad Nacional
Autónoma de México

The historian's task varies according to his idea of historiography. To ask ourselves about the historian's task from the present perspective of Mexican historiography is equivalent to posing this other, more disconcerting, question: What is the Mexican idea of history? And I say "disconcerting" because there are no few indications that, for decades now, the idea of historiography has been going through a period of crisis. A crisis not of the instruments and techniques used, nor of the wealth of scientific works published—a crisis, rather, of the *principles* on which historiographical labor is based and its *human function*. We can say that a discipline enters into a state of crisis when it begins questioning the fundamental concepts it took for granted and the problems it considered already solved. And for any impartial observer, the present moment in Mexican historiography shows profound signs of such a situation. We can agree or not with the ideas that animate the historians of the crisis; it is incumbent on us now only to try to situate them and understand them. To do this, it will be necessary to look back to the beginnings of American historiography.

II

In Mexico historiography was not born as the fruit of a merely contemplative action. The first works of real American history were the response to a decisive deed that radically altered the life of its protagonists: the discovery and conquest of the New World. This was a crucial happening that upset habitual concepts and revealed an unsuspected dimension in the life of the men who participated in it. For them this great event was no matter for erudite studies: it was a situation for action, and they spent themselves, their very lives, in discovering its meaning. On the one hand, the conquerors had to enter their deeds in the history of Christianity, integrate them into the scheme of historical categories that they knew and mastered; the official chroniclers had to place them with relation to the interests and ends of the state; the jurists had to determine by the light of their principles unforeseen situations. To accomplish this, one and all had to present the meaning of the New World, that is, show *what its significance was* for the Spanish state and for the general history of Christianity (which they identified with the universal history of man). On the other hand, missionaries and theologians saw themselves obliged to clarify the nature and supernatural condition of the Indian and his society, *to point out his meaning* for the divine economy; that is, to manifest the true being of those peoples by the light of Providence. Only after that operation could they know what to rely on amid such strange realities. American historiography shares in the general perplexity resulting from the sudden realization of the existence of something that did not easily fit into the world as known up to that time; it consisted of the job of transforming the unaccustomed into the understandable, of turning the inhospitable and strange into the familiar. For man was incapable of resisting the naked presence of a reality of whose human nature and significance he was ignorant, and he saw himself obliged to provide for it immediately a meaning within his world.

Thus, historiography was presented in America invested with two basic traits. First, it consisted not only of the description of things never before seen and of the narration of epic deeds, though it *also* consisted of those things. Second, it was principally an attempt to *reveal* the natural and supernatural *meaning* of such things and deeds: to reveal their meaning in a double sense of the word—to grant them a meaning within the world at that time and to indicate the future world that they augered and indicated. The conquest and the discovery were not merely deeds among other similar ones; they were a decisive overturning that indicated what all previous deeds truly consisted of and what future ones were to be like; they were events that placed all deeds in a true light, that manifested the authentic nature of all happenings. Thus, as the conversion to a new faith or a new state of life throws a distinct light on earlier and later stages, so that the convert only then discovers what his life really consisted of and what the real meaning of his acts was, so also the encounter with a new world manifested the true essence and meaning of the peoples they confronted. American historiography surged forth to acquire an awareness of it. It will suffice to recall three outstanding examples.

From the time of the letters of Cortés, in the work of many conquerors and chroniclers it is clear that the conquest of America showed the ecumenical destiny of Spain, and at the same time, gave birth to a new land, welcoming it for the first time into the course of Christian history. The historian wished to broaden the significance of actions; he began to understand the past only at the moment in which the gest became integrated into a process directed toward universal ends and the New World showed the value it held for Christianity. In Sahagún, as in other evangelists, the discovery permitted the American reality, concealed by divine will for so many centuries, to be exposed finally with its true face; it offered then the figure of a fallen and demoniac world. The word of the Scripture made patent the new reality and pointed out its role in the divine designs. Nor were the deeds themselves as important here as the sign, holy or infamous. In Las Casas, finally, the conquest showed in Spain an instrument of Providence and the tide of a singular mission; on the other hand, the destruction of the Indies sealed the future fate of the same treacherous people that Providence had assigned it. In all cases, the historian sought to give to the deeds an intentional structure, when he interpreted their meaning.

Second: A significant structure is not closed and consumed; on the contrary, it encompasses the present moment of the historian and his people, so decisively that the present life becomes transformed by its impact. The past is not seen as distant and split away (from the present); it constitutes a dimension that affects present life. Because the direction we discover in it gives a proper value and consistency to our lives and places a *decision* before us. If the past were reduced to unadorned, "objective" events, stripped of vital significance for the present, our liberty would move in nothingness; *events* that have taken place, as soon as they have taken place, do not at all affect other events that are in the process of happening, for between them no physical causality fits. Only if deeds have a *significant* dimension by which they announce, postulate, demand something that has not been realized in them yet, only then does the past aspire to fulfill itself in us; only then does it convert itself into life that obliges affirmation or rejection. We must answer for it; our own life is bound up in it. That explains the *practical* character of the first American historiography. It tried to transform, to solve, to convince in order to force a decision. From Gómara to Bernal Díaz, the chroniclers were animated by "selfish" objectives; the past they spoke of concerned them personally for it pointed out to each his rights and deserts. The indigenous writers sought in the past noble titles that might grant some worth to their lives and permit them to place themselves in the conqueror's society. The missionaries wrote only to detect where sin and grace were found, with the object of transforming souls. Las Casas, as a good prophet, took up his pen to break through hard hearts and oblige them to be converted. The historian had to fulfill a practical mission. Not because he conceived history as a propaganda organ at the service of the changing objectives of the moment; no. What happened was that, when the *sense* of the past was clarified, former times did not appear as a gathering together of things that "were," but as a still unfinished human structure that demanded our decisions in order to be fulfilled.

Thus history was born in America as a vital knowledge. It had a precise role in the community: it was the revealer of life's meaning, the director of action, the announcer of ends. Thanks to it, the daily happenings of the people were illumined. The historian's task is not a thing of archives or museums; it is the business of life itself.

III

This idea seems to have permanently stamped later historiography in Mexico. Well into the eighteenth century its task continues to be the demonstration of the meaning of the past in order to clarify present life. It is not surprising that a Clavijero, for example, should search in the remote indigenous past for a classical tradition to oppose to that of Europe, in order to emancipate us from our spiritual subjection; nor that he should write with the purpose of attaining a new attitude for the *criollo* (creole) face to face with himself. Clavijero gives importance to the past, dresses it up with the finery of tradition and exemplary qualities in order to kindle better the *criollo's* pride and awaken his confidence in his own possibilities.

With the political historians of the first half of the nineteenth century the practical character of history is revived. Conservatives and liberals incite their readers to take up an attitude. They see how the past changes according to one's design. The historical attitude that one has will explain the particular meaning that is given to the past. Given the attitude of the liberals, the past urges a radical conversion; its significance consists in leading to the moment of emancipation, in approaching a decision which the people determine freely. It reveals a negative being: it is there to be rejected and to permit the appearance of the act of liberty. But, though denied, that past integrates our own life, for it poses the demand of a liberating conversion. In the conservatives' attitude, on the other hand, the sense of the past consists of a slow vegetal transformation. Little by little the new society is being formed, without conversions or violence. The conservative historian also poses the necessity of a decision: that of being faithful to the evolutionary rhythm of history. In both cases, the past is not an accumulation of "objective" facts that we may contemplate impartially; it is, on the contrary, a call to each "type" to accede to a particular attitude. In both cases, the historian reveals the meaning and direction of human life and demands, therefore, a personal decision.

IV

But if the historian's task consists of showing, from his unique perspective, the significance that events have for life; if this depends on the attitude of the historian; if, in short, our present situation obliges us to emphasize one or another meaning of the past, will not the facts of the past result as dependent on the perspective of the one considering them and will not history in its entirety be dependent on the historian's subjectivity? Will not events lose their character of *invariable* facts and, therefore, their "objectivity"? To answer those and other similar questions, scientific positivist historiography was born, as is well known. In our country it was dominant beginning with the era of positivism and still exists in numerous writers.

The positivist historian thought that he could let the facts talk for themselves, eliminate all personal perspective and reduce all judgments to asseverations that were verifiable; in this way only, he thought, would history accede to the objectivity proper to all positive science. With it he succeeded, undoubtedly, in setting aside the discord of the different historical considerations, born of the circumstantial choices of the historian, and in purging—forever, we hope—scientific history of the capricious play of our subjective whims. Its fight against the arbitrary interjection of the spectator in its object, its demand for objectivity and rigor in historical method will remain as definitive gains; we cannot do without these if we are to constitute historiography as a science.

But, at the same time, converted into a mere object like natural objects, the past definitely seemed remote from present life. Facts, lined up and classified, became as alien and indifferent to present human life as a physical phenomenon. Because we can see in an event only something that concerns us, if we awaken in it a significance that transcends it and points to the present. Mere "objective" facts lack, as such, significant structures; the historian's activity is necessary to give them life. The positivist historian gave to the past a quality of invariability, forgetting its most essential characteristic: that historical facts are but the substratum of *human meanings,* which are not facts but rather intentions that bind the facts together. By considering the object of history to be mere objective verification of data, as physical objectivity is constituted, the positivist historian subtracted his own dimension of meaning from history. At the same time he realized the most radical divorce between his science and his life. The historian no longer had a vital function in which it was incumbent on him to give directives to present life or to clarify its significance.

V

Now, the present moment in Mexican historiography gives signs that the idea of history is in full crisis. The symptoms are many and known to most of you. I shall only point out some of them with the purpose of emphasizing the task that the present situation of the discipline of history imposes upon the American historian.

The first who forcefully pointed to the fundamental crisis of historiography was, among us, an historian whose work deserves, we believe, more attention than it has been given—Edmundo O'Gorman. His criticism led him to reject, as unauthentic, the attempt to convert historiography into a science of bare events, "objectives" after the fashion of the facts of nature. The historian's task would consist, on the contrary, in the creation of the intelligibility of human happenings, using the raw material of facts as a point of departure; a task in which man gives existence to the past and converts it into his own past. In his works is posed the question of the existence of a historical process, America, which would not predate historiographic labor, but would be, in a certain way, its result.[1]

Another symptomatic current is the one usually called in Mexico, with a name that is too restrictive, "the history of ideas," in which the work of Leopoldo Zea is prominent. This type of history had its birth in a question apparently alien to the field of historiography: "What is the Mexican?" that is to say: "What are the traits of our circumstances that, setting us apart, might point out to us our own task?" This question, though born of a philosophic reflection, could only be answered by referring to the process in which our circumstances are formed. The question becomes authentically historic because it asks about a temporal structure animated with meaning: the living circumstances. Here the historian's task would consist of pointing out spiritual directions, collective projects and ideas which order according to purposes the historical process of a nation and admit our moment into an event directed rationally. The historian thus converts yesterday into a rational structure capable of explaining the present.[2]

For our part, in connection with the trends mentioned, we have essayed in a couple of works the application of a new criterion and historiographic method. In accord with them the object of historiography would not be properly the series of "objective" events, but the collective human attitudes that, at each moment, grant them a meaning. While the task of the natural scientist begins by stripping the object of all the "human" notes that cover it, the historian's task begins precisely when he manifests the human meanings that animate the facts; his labor consists of recuperating the human, "interior" dimension of his object.[3]

However different may be the ideas that inspire the trends described above, however greatly they may diverge from each other, they seem to coincide on the two following points: they attempt new ways of access to the past in order to discover in it what constitutes one's own object of historical knowledge; and they share the conviction that the historian's task should be the clarification of significant structures that transcend the sum of the bare facts.

But not only in these trends can symptoms of crisis be observed. Also among the historians who maintain with the greatest vigor the "scientific objective" character of their knowledge, with the legitimate anxiety of not wanting to compromise the universal value of their discoveries, we find signs of a certain concern for recovering the vital dimension of the historical task. José Miranda has expounded in lectures the need for historiography as a help in the solution of theoretical problems in specialized knowledge and has upheld the idea that history should respond always to the practical requirements that community life poses. The historical task would have a social function, present at all times. And in the most ambitious and promising attempt of recent years, *The Modern History of Mexico*,[4] undertaken by a group of historians directed by Daniel Cosío Villegas, we seem to perceive a certain ambiguity: on one side, the expressed attempt to maintain the "impartiality" of history, radically eliminating the historian's subjectivity, reducing his labor to the rational classification and orderly relation of facts; on the other, an implicit attempt to utilize those facts as practical teaching. Questions are asked about those "responsible" for a situation, human causes of failure are sought, with the objective, perhaps, of establishing a diagnosis of the immediate past that might clarify the significance of the present moment. If this is what they are aiming at, under a layer of dispassionate objectivity, it would again point out the vital and practical roots of history. But *The Modern History of Mexico* is not yet concluded and we must still reserve judgment.

VI

The symptoms described above tell us something of the crisis of historiography, and more still of its perpetual dignity. For the crisis comes from the fact that the historian does not resign himself to forget the distinguished human range of his science. Indeed, history possesses a unique dignity among all the "spiritual sciences." While all the others have to do with some kind of human *products* or some region of culture considered objectively, history should not stop at any cultural product, but rather ask about the very *producing activity*. It should not treat properly of all the things left by men, but rather of human life and of its component process in the world. Therefore one must not consider cultural documents and remains as finished things, whose sense would be contained completely in themselves, but rather as vestiges, as indices of the creative life of the spirit. The documents that man leaves in his passage, the testimonies of his external deeds, the sum of his products, should be only signs to be interpreted, ciphers that give to active life its meaning.

But its dignity does not stop there. The historian must respond to the question that man poses to himself about his temporal condition. His science permits him to say a great deal about the human condition and its fugitive destiny. When he unveils the past the historian must discover characteristic attitudes and processes in which we participate by the mere fact of being men. When he asks himself about the meaning of life that extends ours toward the past, he must manifest the intentional vectors and indices of processes that are fulfilled in us. Thus, history teaches us, not because we ingenuously ask for remedies for the solution of our present problems, but because, in regaining the human meanings of the past, it clarifies a dimension of our own situation and grants a new significance to each one of our actions. Because of it, historiography cannot be a theoretical science in the same sense that other sciences are; it has, essentially, a practical function to fulfill, which derives directly from its theoretical labor.

But to fulfill that task, it is necessary to have a clear idea of its object and its methods of work. If present historiography seems to us, often, divorced from life, occupied as it is in the hunting for data whose deep dimension it pretends to be unaware of; if at times we fear that it has sold its humanist range for "objective verification," it is doubtless because it has become confused about the true object.

Dilthey and his school on one side, Windelband and Rickert on the other, pointed out with precision the difference between the object and method of history and the object and method of the natural sciences. To continue to confuse these categories, as many historians in America do, without having at times a full awareness of that confusion, results in historiography moving away from its vital and human function. We cannot renounce, of course, the scientific character of history, nor do without, therefore, the invariability and transcendence of its objects, nor the rigor of its methods. But all science must adapt its methods to the specific character of the object it treats. If that of historiography consists of human meanings, which animate the past without being confused with it, the methods leading to its knowledge should be procedures destined to show, by the vestiges of that past, the activity giving it meaning, and cannot be at all like the methods of the positivist natural sciences.

We believe that American historians need to consider more seriously the problem of the object and methods of their science. We do not ask them to write philosophy. Whoever thinks this shows that he has a poor idea of the historian, reducing him to the role of simple technician or ingenuous narrator. The historian must reflect on the human bases and ends of his science. Only he can formulate new hypotheses of work and apply them in concrete procedures; until this is done all the philosophic theories about history are empty speculations. Therefore, the great reforms of historiography were never the result of the philosophers of history as such, but of the historians. Only if the historian acquires a complete awareness of the specific character of his object and rediscovers in it the creative life of man in all its richness, only if he considers the dignity of its human function, will he regain the leading role in society which was his of yore.

NOTES

1. See especially Edmundo O'Gorman, *Crisis y porvenir de la ciencia histórica* (México, 1947) and *La invención de América* (México, 1958) [published in English as *The Invention of America: An Inquiry into the Historical Nature of the New World and the Meaning of Its History* (Bloomington, Indiana, 1961)].

2. See particularly Leopoldo Zea, *Dos etapas del pensamiento en Hispanoamérica: del romanticismo al positivismo* (México, 1949); *América como conciencia* (México, 1953); *América en la historia* (México, 1957).

3. See especially Luis Villoro, *La revolución de independencia: ensayo de interpretación histórico* (México, 1953).

4. Daniel Cosío Villegas, gen. ed., *Historia moderna de México* (5 vols., México-Buenos Aires, 1955–1960).

The Historian's Task: A United States Historian's View

BY Arthur P. Whitaker
University of Pennsylvania

IDEALLY the historian's task is manifold and enormous. Anyone who lived up to all the job specifications would have to be a combination of universal genius and perpetual-motion machine. I speak advisedly, in the light of both my own observation and my own experience, which cover more years than I like to remember, and also the testimony of others, many of whom will be named below.

To be sure, there is no universally accepted statement of the job specifications (to me, that is one of the more attractive features of our attractive profession), but I believe there is in this country a kind of consensus on certain matters, and these alone are more than enough to fill an active man's life. Reduced to their simplest terms, they are set forth in the criteria recently adopted by the Council of the American Historical Association for election to honorary membership in that body, to-wit, distinction in writing history, in teaching it, and in promoting national and international historical activities.

Even J. Franklin Jameson, one of the outstanding American historians of his generation, had to make a choice among these three areas of activity. He taught only briefly; he wrote little, though well; and he owed his merited leadership among historians to his long and highly successful labors as editor of the *American Historical Review* and as organizer and promoter of historical and archival projects at home and abroad. That Jameson made the right choice has been strongly affirmed by another distinguished scholar, Waldo G. Leland, who in 1955 described Jameson's "services to American historical studies" as "far more useful and far-reaching over the long period than the historical works of highest merit which he would have produced." Whether this was intended as a judgment on Jameson's potentialities as a writer or on the relative merits of historical writing and historical statesmanship, it is an unequivocal recognition of the latter as one of the major components of the historian's task.

But our census of the task's many facets has hardly begun, for either in connection with those already mentioned, or in addition to them, a host of obligations has been laid upon the historian. While some of them date from antiquity, fresh ones are added by almost every presidential address at the annual meetings of the American Historical Association. Sometimes the new requirements oust one or more of the oldsters, but more often they settle down to a peaceful, however strange, coexistence with them, which means for the historian a net accretion to his task. For example, many of us still believe with Thucydides that it is the historian's obligation to present "an exact knowledge of the past as an aid to the interpretation of the future." And while Bolingbroke's typically eighteenth-century apothegm that "history is philosophy teaching by example" went out of fashion long ago, I suspect that in its core meaning it commands today a wider following than is professed or perhaps even realized. Of course, philosophy is not the same today that it was in Bolingbroke's time, but it is fashionable once more—according to some, it is *de rigueur*—for historians to have a philosophy; and having one, they not unnaturally find history full of examples of it.

To be sure, there is an element of truth in Trevor-Roper's assertion that the study of history has recently changed in this respect. "In the old days," he writes, "history . . . was designed—if it had any purpose beyond mere entertainment—to offer noble examples for imitation, or perhaps to illustrate the triumph of an idea: Christianity or liberalism or democracy. But nowadays . . . we seek in history not wisdom or morals or a message but immediate explanation . . . In a hasty, practical world . . . we want to be briefed, not taught; and history, today, is our briefing."

Insofar as this is true, it is true of the consumers of history—that portion of the public, all too restricted, that reads the works produced by historians. It is not entirely true even of the consumers, not in the United States at any rate; else why the extraordinary vogue currently enjoyed by Civil War books, which are surely read mainly for entertainment? And I do not think it is at all true of the producers, the professional historians. On the contrary, I believe that today the latter are pushing their quest for wisdom (or, if you prefer, for understanding) with a seriousness unexcelled in the history of historical writing. An illustration of my point is provided by Trevor-Roper himself in the article (a book review) from which the foregoing quotation comes, for while he admits that the book under review provides excellent "briefing," he expresses keen disappointment that it fails to grapple with ideas or even to suggest that unsolved problems exist. In other words, he does not belong to the school of historical study that he describes as predominant today.

He has a great deal of company in the United States. As witnesses we may call several presidents of the American Historical Association in the past decade to repeat the testimony contained in their presidential addresses.

Conyers Read is "inclined to think that the first prerequisite of a historian is a sound social philosophy," since he "follows the evolution of society with constant reference to" his "concept of what is socially desirable" and "by implication, the curve which he plots for the past inevitably projects itself into the future."

According to Samuel Eliot Morison the historian's main task is to describe events "simply as they happened," then to "*understand* the motives and objects of individuals and groups," to "answer some of the questions that contemporary society asks of the past," and finally to point out any "unmistakable lesson of the past" he may think he has learned, with a view to "influencing the future."

Louis Gottschalk charitably holds that in a "society inquisitive about its past" there is "room for all kinds of historians," including the "mere practitioner of a descriptive science," but he also believes that every man is "his own philosopher of history" and that historians should "reach for some tiny fragment of the wisdom so sorely needed" and should respond to "the anxious demands for guidance."

Merle Curti's message is an exhortation to American historians to combat anti-intellectualism and demagoguery, to defend "freedom of thought and expression in its widest scope," since this is "the chief value to which historical scholarship, all scholarship, is committed," and not to "fail our country in time of great crisis, as the German intellectuals failed theirs."

Finally, William L. Langer, while finding it "difficult to envisage much further horizontal expansion of the area of [historical] investigation," sees ample scope and urgent need for the "deepening of our historical understanding" with the aid of "dynamic" or "depth psychology." What is more, after a reference to the International Geophysical Year, he concludes: "We may, for all we know, be on the threshold of a new era when the historian will have to think in ever larger, perhaps even cosmic, terms."

I hope you will by this time agree that I did not exaggerate when I described the historian's task as manifold and enormous. Most if not all of you may have agreed with me at the outset, but even so I believe my elaboration of the point will serve two useful purposes: first, by identifying some of the major features of the landscape that would have to be examined in a complete survey of the historian's task; and second, by getting you into a mood to accept willingly—nay, with glad relief—the announcement that I have no intention of trying to cover this whole vast area in the time allotted me, nor of exceeding the limit.

To begin with, I am going to exclude two of the three aspects of the historian's task mentioned at the outset. The first to go is the teaching of history, which, though highly important, could be discussed more profitably in a gathering expressly designed for that purpose, as the present one, judging from its program, was not. The other aspect to be excluded is the historian as organizer and supervisor and promoter of historical activities. This aspect, too, is highly important, and I personally have spent quite a bit of time taking a modest part in it. But since I must be selective, I have decided, though with regret, to leave this subject with a reminder of Waldo Leland's implied tribute to it in his encomium on J. Franklin Jameson quoted above.

There remains then, the third aspect of the historian's task, historical writing, and even within this selected area I am going to confine my remarks to, first, some general considerations about the task of the historian as writer, and second, to certain specific problems of the historian-as-writer which happen to interest me as well as others.

Even when reduced to the mere writing of history, the historian's task has become so overwhelming to most of us that perhaps some interest may attach to the following modest proposals for lightening and simplifying the task and discharging it with becoming dignity.

With a view to lightening it, we could do much worse than begin with Alfred North Whitehead's more-than-half-serious suggestion that half of modern history should be, as he says, "handed over to the mathematicians." By mathematicians he evidently means statisticians and social scientists, for he explains that this half of history would be that based on "quantitative estimates of the forces which are moulding modern society." "Without such estimates," he continues, "modern history . . . is a meaningless tangle," but conventional historians ("our classical colleagues," he calls them) are "not very fitted by their mental equipment" to handle such estimates; hence the "mathematicians" must be called in.

Whitehead's suggestion could draw support from sage observations made by Robert M. Hutchins and Charles A. Beard. Hutchins remarked that there is no such thing as history in the abstract, but only a history of something—of politics, religion, civilization, or what not. From this it follows that we are not historians in an all-embracing sense but historians of some particular kind, so that our obligations and liabilities are not unlimited but are defined by the particular function in each case.

Similar relief may be found, perhaps unexpectedly, in Beard's dictum that history is central to all the social sciences, since it provides them with the data on which all their conclusions, principles, and laws are based. At first sight this assertion, which has the air of an imperialist pronunciamento, would seem to aggravate the historian's burden. On reflection, however, it is seen to have the opposite effect since, to use an analogy from politics, it makes of history a kind of federal system in which all the subdivisions are bound together by the historical method and its product, but in which each of them is autonomous and has its own responsibilities as well as powers. In other words, we are brought back to the essence of Hutchins' comforting thought that we are not historians in general but historians of something in particular, with the limitation of liability that this differentiation implies.

Also, if you sorrow over the prospect opened up by Langer that we may soon have to write history in cosmic terms, you may derive surcease from Carl Becker's statement that "We write history from the human rather than from the cosmic point of view." We do so, Becker explains, because "however indifferent the doings of man may be to the cosmic force of which they are the result, they are vastly interesting *to us*." The point to be stressed here is not so much the assurance that the proper historical study of mankind is man—opinion about that could change—as the proposition that our criterion of selection among the enormous mass of materials available to us historians is simply their interest *to us*. To be sure, as Becker and many others have pointed out, the historian who wishes to have an audience and leave a trace will be guided in his choice by the interest of others and not merely by his own personal preferences: the historian should not be a solipsist. But even so, Becker's proposition reminds him that his occupation has flexible requirements, and that he has rights as well as duties. In the proper exercise of his rights he can reduce his responsibilities within manageable limits.

He can also simplify his task. One way is to remember that from the point of view of the writer's intent all historical writing falls into one of three categories: it is either for something, or against something, or it is neutralist. To give some extreme examples, we have in the first category Orosius' *Historia Adversum Paganos* (how much of all historical writing has been "against the pagans"!); in the second category George Bancroft's *History of the United States;* and in the third, most doctoral dissertations in history written a generation or two ago, when facts were permitted a freedom of speech to which we now agree they are not entitled. It has been at least a generation since historians thought they could let the facts "speak for themselves."

The existence of these categories is certainly no new discovery, but it might well be more often remembered and the choice among them more deliberately made and followed up to the hilt. The choice would best be for one of the first two—pro or con—for there is nothing like a good fight to give tone to the participants and pique the interest of others. For the sake of humanity and history, however, let the target of an attack be an idea or a problem or a hypothesis rather than a person or a nation.

If there is one part of the historian's task from which he cannot escape, it is the duty to integrate data from all relevant sources. This is indeed the most distinctive as well as the most exacting feature of his profession. Accordingly, dignity as well as efficiency requires him to maintain his autonomy with reference to the social sciences on the one hand and the humanities on the other. He operates in both fields but belongs to neither. Of course this may not always be so, and some day he may become a mere auxiliary to one or the other, for historical writing is itself a part of the historical process of change that it records; but I do not think that day is at hand or approaching.

One of our most distinguished Latin Americanists in the United States, Irving A. Leonard, calls himself a mestizo because he is a specialist both in history and in Romance languages and literature. In this sense all historians are mestizos. Precisely because their major interest is in change and the concrete, they share the social scientist's preoccupation with social patterns and uniformities or laws, for without these fixed points of reference the variations that concern the historian are meaningless. On the other hand he partakes in the concern of the humanities with the aesthetic component of the life of mankind. As Becker said, "History is an art . . . (a) story, in aim always a true story . . . that employs all the devices of literary art (statement and generalization, narration and description, comparison and comment and analogy) . . ." And many of us believe with Sir Richard Livingstone that while science gives us the tools of civilization, it is from the humanities, if at all, that we learn how to use these tools.

Because of the spectacular expansion of the social sciences in the past half century, the impression seems to be gaining ground that this mestizo character of history is something new. From this alleged fact it is sometimes further assumed that history is in a transition stage on its way to becoming pure social science, purged of the dross of the humanities and cleansed of the original sin of entertainment in which it was conceived. The fact is that the mestization of history took place a very long time ago. While this is not the place to review the many convolutions in the history of historical writing, I may point out that Thucydides made as good use of the social science approach as the feebler light of his age permitted, and that so also did Gregory of Tours a thousand years later and still more than thirteen centuries ago. Of Gregory, my colleague Professor William McDermott has written that he left no phase of history untouched, whether social and economic or political and ecclesiastical. "Without developing a conscious theory of history," says McDermott, "[Gregory] approached the modern idea that political action cannot be studied in a vacuum."

While not in the least endorsing the exploded notion that the human mestizo, as such and of biological necessity, has a split personality, let me note briefly my recognition of the fact (which I take it to be) that the mestizo character of history has produced in it certain schizophrenic symptoms and that these seem to be increasing as a result of the sharpening conflict in the present century between history's social science id and its humanistic superego. An interesting contribution to the resolution of this conflict has been made by another of my colleagues, Professor Paul Schrecker, of the Philosophy Department, in his book *Work and History: An Essay on the Structure of Civilization* (1948). While reproaching historians with their failure to keep up with the progress of scientific thought since Descartes, Schrecker admits that "all fields of civilization are susceptible of being approached" along the path of history as well as that of science. He also admits that these two paths are equally valid and yet, apparently, mutually exclusive. His book was written in an effort to reconcile these two aspects and to prove them complementary. How he does so cannot be told within the limits of this paper, but some of his judgments on particular points will be noted below, and I strongly recommend his book to your attention in case you have not already had the pleasure of reading it.

In fact, I shall cite Schrecker in connection with the first of the particular problems to which the rest of my paper will be devoted. This is the problem of the proper role of political history in history. That it was once assigned far too prominent a role has long been a common complaint. That the complaint was once justified no one is likely to deny: who does not know that Freeman's dictum, "History is past politics," was two and three generations ago not only the motto of the influential Johns Hopkins group but also the countersign of the American historical fraternity at large?

Schrecker repeats and deepens the familiar complaint. He regards the overemphasis on political history that began with Hegel as one of the major reasons for the "unsatisfactory state of philosophy of civilization and history," since "many a problem traditionally obsessing philosophers of history can originate only in the political sphere and becomes . . . meaningless as soon as transferred to another province of civilization." For example, the overemphasis on politics has made objectivity a "centerpiece" of the theory of history, and yet this problem hardly exists in other provinces, such as the history of languages. Likewise, the question of "the parts played by great men and the masses in history hardly makes sense," he insists, "if raised in the field of economy or, again, of language."

The complaint is moving; indeed, as long since raised by others, it has been heeded. Yet I venture to say that the reaction against politics, while once overdue, was then overdone. I cannot think of civilization and history without thinking of particular civilizations and histories. Considered in this light, the role to be assigned politics depends on the area and period one is discussing (as well as, of course, on one's conception of political history). Its role is obviously very important in the history of Western Europe and America since about 1500, when first the rise of the nation-state and then the rise of national imperialism were dominant themes a large part of the time. And can anyone who has had half an ear for the nationalist clamor of the so-called underdeveloped countries in other parts of the world in recent years doubt that politics is a major theme in the history of those countries in the present century?

I would be among the last to deny that the political-minded nineteenth century overstressed the political factor, and that the bias still lingers in certain quarters, for, in a paper presented to the International Congress of Historical Sciences held in Rome in 1955, I went to some pains to show how it has distorted the history of the Enlightenment. Nevertheless, I think the efforts at correction have led to overcompensation. To give no more recent example, let us take the multivolume *History of American Life,* edited in the 1920's and 1930's by Dixon Ryan Fox and Arthur M. Schlesinger, Sr., which covered almost every aspect of life in the United States except politics. On the whole, within its chosen scope it was an excellent series, but many of us agreed with Becker's observation, in a review of the whole series, that a history of the United States without politics was like Hamlet without the Prince of Denmark.

What is needed, I think, and what is now being provided, is a balanced, integrated treatment which presents political history as a major theme made up of the convergence of many forces, a compound of many ingredients in addition to straight politics (or crooked politics, as the case may be).

My second problem, national character, is related to the first but represents an even wider convergence of forces and an even higher proportion of the nonpolitical as compared with the political. For a time, about a generation ago, the idea of national character fell into rather bad repute, but today it is being studied again by quite respectable scholars in various fields. Interestingly enough, its rehabilitation seems to have been due in considerable measure to events of World War II and the immediate postwar period, and perhaps most of all to an experience with Japan. Briefly, the experience was this: a debate in Washington at the close of the war over whether to keep the Japanese emperor or get rid of him was settled in favor of keeping him by a scholarly national-character study of the Japanese people, and the decision turned out to be pragmatically the right one; *ergo*, national character is a reality and scholars have the tools and the brains to identify it. I wish all our historical problems could be settled that easily.

The problem of national character has not in fact been settled to the satisfaction of all scholars. The Social Science Research Council's report of 1954 on *The Social Sciences in Historical Study* is not enthusiastic about it. After noting that "national character" and other essentially synonymous terms such as "basic personality structure," "modal personality," and "social character" are used to designate "the underlying features of personality organization common to or most frequent among the members of a social group," the report observes that the "considerable research" already done in this field has brought knowledge "closer to the level of clinical insight than of systematic validation" and that "standards of rigor have not been very high in this field." The research referred to in this report was conducted by psychologists, psychoanalysts, and cultural anthropologists; historians in the United States such as Carlton Hayes, Hans Kohn, and Boyd Shafer have made penetrating studies of the subject, but the report does not cite anything historians have had to say about it.

Writing from a philosopher's point of view, Schrecker gives the concept of national character a highly qualified approval but is more than dubious about the value of anything psychologists may have to say on the subject. "Any attempt to account for the phenomenon of the national differentiation of civilization on psychological or pathological grounds," he writes, "will be as inevitably misleading as the racial chimera," for it it were sound, "a nation reputed to be more intelligent, aesthetic, religious, greedy, or legalistic than others would be expected to show a hypertrophy of the respective aspirations," but that has never happened. Rather, he insists, the phenomenon should be conceived of as "a structural particularity of the systems of patterns actually uniting the passing individuals composing a nation." In other words, "the many national civilizations or characters represent as many diverse disturbances of the equilibrium between the vying provinces or fundamental aspirations," all of which are found in some degree in all civilizations. From this point of view, he concludes, each national character is a distortion, a national caricature, of civilization.

Undeterred by the doubts of social scientists on the one hand and philosophers on the other, historians go on blithely employing the concept of national character, often without defining it and sometimes quite possibly without being aware that they are using it. Outstanding examples of studies made with a full awareness of its presence are the histories of Spain by three distinguished Spanish scholars: Claudio Sánchez-Albornoz, Américo Castro, and Salvador de Madariaga.

As regards the United States, a recent example is David M. Potter's *People of Plenty: Economic Abundance and the American Character* (1954). This book presents the results of a study in which Potter drew on the behavioral sciences to explain the formation of the American national character in terms of the interrelation between the human environment and personality on the basis of the distinctive American trait of abundance. In reviewing this book Boyd Shafer, himself an authority on national character and nationalism, praised it warmly but raised some questions that seem to me highly pertinent. "Can even the changing national character be explained in terms of one condition, one concept, abundance?" asks Shafer. "Are not the answers pluralistic? Perhaps history is not a science and historians cannot in Newtonian fashion find one causal factor. Perhaps it is here that history may temper the new behavioral sciences." Quite likely it is. I think pluralistic explanations must be sought for and that Schrecker's approach can be used to good advantage in the quest.

In this connection two other problems arise which I can only mention briefly. One is that of leadership. This seems to me much more than a mere political question. Its wide ramifications were suggested many years ago by José Ortega y Gasset in his brilliant essay *España invertebrada*. Answering the then current complaint that Spain no longer had any real leaders, Ortega replied in effect: "No leaders? Spain has as good leaders today as she has had in many a day. The trouble is, the leaders have no followers." Underlying this quip was a theory of leadership as a product of a state of society—a theory that I find attractive and regard as potentially very useful to historians.

The other problem that I can only bow to in passing is that of universal characteristics, which social scientists today are apparently finding it easier to believe in than in national character. For example, we are assured on high authority that there are "moral values universal in all cultures." Perhaps this is a fact, but I think that belief in it is a sign of the times we live in. At any rate, it suggests the way of looking at things which found expression in the Middle Ages in *"semper, ubique, et ab omnibus,"* and later in the Heavenly City of the Eighteenth-Century Philosophers.

This in turn brings up a problem of which I should like to speak a little less cursorily, namely, the double-barrelled and highly important problem of facts and value judgments. On this subject I find myself in disagreement with the later-phase Charles A. Beard as represented by his American Historical Association presidential address, "History as an Act of Faith," and in warm agreement with Morison's presidential reply. I do not think the case has been better stated anywhere than by Bertrand Russell in his protest against "the rejection of 'fact' as a fundamental concept in defining 'truth'":

"We find ourselves in a universe of a certain sort," writes Russell, "and we find out what sort of universe it is by observation, not by self-assertion. . . . To forget that we are hemmed in by facts which are for the most part independent of our desires is a form of insane megalomania [which has] grown up as a result of the triumph of scientific technique. . . . The pragmatic theory of truth is inherently connected with the appeal to force. If there is a non-human truth, which one man may know while another does not, there is a standard outside the disputants to which, we may urge, the dispute ought to be submitted; hence a pacific and judicial settlement of disputes is at least theoretically possible. If, on the contrary, the only way of discovering which of the disputants is in the right is to wait and see which of them is successful, there is no longer any principle except force by which the issue can be decided."

The historian is properly very much concerned with values as facts of history, and this concern is, in my opinion, the mainspring of that important aspect of history, the history of ideas, which is the last of the problems which I shall discuss. As Schrecker says: "To investigate what is or is not in itself a vital [economic] need is not the concern of historians or students of economy; just as the historian of science does not necessarily have to decide, once and for all, what truth is, nor the historian of art what beauty is, nor the historian of religion what salvation is. What does concern them is to report what, at each point in time, was believed to satisfy the human desire for knowledge, beauty, or salvation, and what norms determined human work aiming at this satisfaction."

I take pleasure in noting evidences of a growing interest in the history of ideas among historians of the Americas, as well as across the Atlantic. A recent item of very special interest to us is the spirited dialogue on conceptions of the history of ideas between two leading authorities on the subject, Marcel Bataillon of France and Edmundo O'Gorman of Mexico. Another noted Mexican historian, Leopoldo Zea, heads a Committee on the History of Ideas, of the Pan-American Commission on History, which has begun to publish country-by-country studies in this field. Zea's committee is aided in each country by a national committee; in the United States the national committee is under the capable chairmanship of Max Savelle.

There is also much activity in the special field of historiography. This subject is included in the program of the same Commission on History, ably led by Silvio Zavala, and Lewis Hanke's *Hispanic American Historical Review* has in an advanced stage of preparation a series of articles on the historiography of the national period of Latin American history. To give only one more example, Gottschalk devoted a large part of his recent presidential address to historiography.

All this is highly gratifying, but I think it is important to stress the fact that historiography is a branch of the history of ideas, not of bibliography—a distinction which a good many historians find it difficult to maintain or even to perceive. Properly understood, the subject ought to be of interest to all historians, whatever their field of specialization. It will provide them with the clearest view of their highly variegated profession and will suggest how they may become more perceptive, more articulate, and at the same time more modest and more sure of themselves.

In conclusion, let me state my position on some important aspects of the historian's task that I have not had time to discuss. We historians may be one of the last remnants of a pluralistic society in which there was elbowroom for the individual craftsman, but so long as the privilege is vouchsafed us, let us make the most of it and try to safeguard it for others. This means, among other things, that the historian still functions best as an individual—as the "lonely scholar," in Carl Sauer's phrase. Let us by all means get together with one another, as we are doing here, and with social scientists and humanists and others, in the hope of benefiting by cross-fertilization while avoiding the peril of cross-sterilization; but, in the end, a worthy product is more likely to come from an individual than from a committee, a team, or any other group.

Profiting by Gottschalk's timely reminder that there is still room for all kinds of historians, let each of us follow the path of his own choice rather than one designated for him by a public or private authority in Washington, New York, Mexico City, or anywhere else. But in making the choice, let us remember that even the greatest historian can't do everything; that for instance, as Becker pointed out, the ideal of combining a "synthesis of social forces" with the "evolution of society"—an ideal dear to the "Newer Historians" of his day and not forgotten even now—presents the "fundamental and unsolvable" difficulty that while generalization spreads out in space, the wretched thing will not move forward in time.

Finally, while I agree with much that Morison said in his presidential address, I think that in one respect his standard for the performance of historians was not sufficiently exacting. Instead of saying with him that the historian should "answer some of the questions that contemporary society asks of the past," I should say that it is one of the historian's chief obligations to tell contemporary society what questions it ought to ask of the past. In any situation, asking the right questions is half the battle; and so far as the past is concerned, who should know better than historians what the right questions are?

Comment: Freedom for the Historian

BY FRANCE V. SCHOLES
University of New Mexico

WHEN I WAS invited to participate in this session of the Congress I had some misgiving about the topic for discussion. For I felt that surely the essential and basic tasks of the historian are the same in our two countries; that they could not—and should not—be described in local terms; that the role and functions of the historian and the ideals of his profession transcend national definitions and dimensions.

I was pleased and gratified, therefore, on reading the papers of Sr. Villoro and Mr. Whitaker, to find that they cover a considerable measure of common ground, although they approach the question of the historian's task in different ways and with different emphases. Sr. Villoro describes the crisis in historiography in Mexico. Mr. Whitaker's remarks reflect unrest in the field of historical studies in this country. Both of the speakers have discussed, in somewhat different terms or frames of reference, basic problems of methodology and interpretation, the proper range and purpose of historical investigation and historical writing, and other current issues of debate which beset and plague all of us. And having found that they summon as witnesses or examples so many great names, past and present, I could only ask myself: what can I add to the subject in ten minutes?

I have two things to say. First, to applaud the remarks of Mr. Whitaker concerning the role and essential dignity of the individual historian. I hope that this Congress recognizes and will assert the right of the individual historian to pursue his labors in his own way and according to his own lights; the right freely to choose his own subject for investigation; the right not to be placed under pressure, direct or indirect, by any agency, private or governmental (including universities); the right to channel his investigations along lines for which funds may be available, without sacrificing research projects of his own preference or choice. I can only deplore the policies of some agencies which sometimes seem to profess more wisdom than the individual scholar in regard to what should be studied or what merits long-range investigation; and in particular, I wish to register protest against the current emphasis upon and preference for projects which deal with contemporary problems or the contemporary scene. Historians have an obligation, without any doubt, to use their knowledge and talents for the public service. But historians also know, better than others perhaps, that what may seem to be "hot stuff" today may be "cold turkey" tomorrow. And I have serious doubt that very many studies undertaken as a public service at the request or behest of the money-dispensing agencies will be ranked as historical classics.

I also hope that this Congress will recognize the right of the individual historian to resist current trends and emphases in historiography if he wishes to do so, and especially with reference to the insistent demand for interpretations of one kind or another, as that based on that vague and nebulous thing called philosophy of history. In this connection I find great comfort in Sr. Villoro's concluding statement that the great reforms of historiography have not been made by the philosophers of history as such but by the historians themselves. And I assume that this statement refers to classics of historiography, past and present, written by scholars who claimed the right to perform their tasks in their own way.

So let us lift up our hearts in praise of the fact that the individual historian has been—and should be—the master of his craft. Long may he reign

And now my second point. I share Sr. Villoro's view—do not all of us?—that complete objectivity is an illusion. But I also have more faith in the ability of the historian to seek out and establish "objective facts" than have many of our contemporary theorists, some of whom seem to view almost with disdain traditional norms of methodology, including sincere and patient preoccupation with documentary sources. Let us not forget that the master of a craft can be no better than his tools and the materials which he fashions, with love, honesty, and integrity, into a finished product. A revered friend once told me that I spend my time dusting off the "documentary cadavers of the past." Perhaps! But I do believe and know that these "documentary cadavers" often have more life and vitality in them than some of the arid conceptualizations that are sometimes palmed off as history.

It is for these reasons that I wish to question the validity of Mr. Whitaker's remark that facts in and for themselves do not deserve freedom of speech. I doubt that the physicist would agree, and I hope that most historians do not agree. For who has the right to decide what are useless or useful facts? Much of the debate about "facts," "objective history," and the need for vital interpretations reflects, in my opinion, a certain lack of confidence in the ability of the individual historian to make value judgments. We all know that the historical investigator must select those "facts" which he believes deserve emphasis or have significant value, that by this very act he gives interpretation to his data. But again, I plead for recognition of his right to fashion his product as he chooses.

The papers of Sr. Villoro and Mr. Whitaker have demonstrated again the obvious and rather time-worn fact that fashions in historiography are constantly changing, and that what may seem to be new is not so new after all. Mr. Whitaker has quoted Conyers Read's statement that the first prerequisite of a historian is "a sound social philosophy," because he follows the evolution of society with reference to his "concept of what is socially desirable," and consequently his view of the past "inevitably projects itself into the future." If this be a valid measure of what a historian is or should be, then I submit that the "decision" school of Mexican historians described by Sr. Villoro fit this requirement, for they doubtless believed that they had a sound social philosophy, on the basis of which they viewed the past and the future. The same would be true of Mr. Whitaker's "for" and "against" characterization of some United States historians. Moreover, most of the current theories of history reflect "for" or "against" attitudes. Even the "objectivist" or "positivist" school of historiography was not completely devoid of conscious purpose and value judgments. The writing of history has always reflected a vital and human element, if only that of the individual laborer in the vineyard.

So, in closing, let me plead once more for his right to seek out, select, and record his data in his own way and with as much sincerity and integrity as he can summon for his task.

Comment: Classical or Ontological History

BY Edmundo O'Gorman
*Universidad Nacional
Autónoma de México*

The Organizing Committee of the Congress had the goodness to designate me one of the commentators on the remarks which have been presented. In a moment I will set out to fulfill this commission as well as I may in the time allotted. However, it seems to me that I ought first to begin by thanking Messrs. Whitaker and Villoro for the opportunity they have offered to all of us by agreeing to present their opinions concerning this difficult theme, the discussion of which brings us together this afternoon; but, also, I wish to convey to them my personal gratitude for the complimentary manner in which both have been good enough to make reference to my works; and now, let's get down to brass tacks.

My distinguished friend, Dr. Arthur P. Whitaker, began his exposition by pointing out to us that the task of the historian is manifold; that there are a great variety of aspects and problems; and, in addition, that new and unexpected complications are constantly cropping up; and that, on the other hand, there does not exist, nor can there ever exist, a specific way of determining what falls within and what falls without the competence of the historian, because his field cannot be clearly delimited; and, finally, that among historians themselves there does not exist any uniformity of opinion concerning the extent and character of their task, but rather, on the contrary, the greatest discrepancy and variety of opinions reign among them. As the basis for these affirmations, Dr. Whitaker adduces an ample series of pertinent citations, drawn from his vast learning, by which he leads us back to Thucydides himself, the father, if not the grandfather, of all historians.

Without a doubt this way of developing the theme presents a discouraging picture, for if, from Greek times to our own, historians have been laboring without any clear notion of the limits of their discipline, or of what they are doing or trying to do when they cultivate history, or, at least, without having been able to come to any agreement concerning what they ought to be doing, it does not seem very probable that the future will be able to remedy this situation of chronic disharmony.

But Dr. Whitaker, being both a gentleman and a pragmatist, does not terminate his remarks without first offering us a remedy. In fact, in the general statements which he makes concerning the task of the historian as writer, he proposes certain ways of alleviating and simplifying the otherwise insupportable charge, calling to his aid the opinions of many eminent authorities.

Now, this is the heart of his remarks, because if we analyze the ways in which Dr. Whitaker suggests that the historian may succeed in doing his duty, we see that they are not, in the final analysis, anything other than a justification of his dedicating himself, without remorse, to whatever interests him most, instead of drowning in a sea of problems or remaining paralyzed before a labyrinth of doubts concerning the purposes and teleology of his science.

Doubtless we all look with sympathy upon this attitude of Dr. Whitaker's and we all share it, in view of the good dose of common sense by which it is animated; but I fear that, given the way in which he presents the problem to us, far from resolving it, he simply eludes it or denies its existence. For we must make a choice: either the task of the historian implies and demands as much of us as he told us at the beginning, and then it is impossible for the historian to fulfill it; or else he fulfills it by dint of Dr. Whitaker's saving suggestions, but then this task is not what he said it was at first. And should anyone wish to affirm that it is indeed just as complex, just as manifold and just as impossible as Dr. Whitaker said at first, but that it is fulfilled, not by a single individual, but by all historians together, each one doing whatever comes naturally, I propose that we waste no time in adjourning this meeting and reconvening in the nearest church, there to pray that Divine Providence will so inspire the historians of the world that their investigations shall leave not a single problem without having dedicated to it the attention it merits.

Clearly Dr. Whitaker's remarks have been very useful for us, because the dilemma to which he has led us shows that the theme we are discussing here should not be treated from the merely external point of view of the variety or complexity of the themes which may fall within the field of the investigation of the past, and because, in addition, Dr. Whitaker's remarks remind us of something which is absolutely decisive, to wit: that the task of the historian is, above all, an individual task, that is to say, a task in which a man, on his own account and at his own risk, proposes an image of the human past as a truth which entirely contains him and compromises him; this is the fundamental difference between the task of the historian and that of a natural scientist.

This consideration leads us to our commentary upon the remarks of my friend and compatriot, Professor Luis Villoro, with whom, because of similarity of intellectual formation, I find myself more nearly in agreement.

Villoro treats the problem from an internal point of view. For him the task of the historian is not defined so much by objective themes and purposes as by the nature of historical knowledge, and for this reason the central theme of his remarks consists in an examination of the awareness which exists in Mexico, among a small group of historians and philosophers, of the crisis through which the ideas of history and of historical truth themselves are passing. Here I should add that possibly it is not my place to insist at this time upon the correctness of this point of view, because, as Professor Villoro has had the goodness to remind us, I have been connected with this trend of thought for many years. I am, then, entirely in agreement with his central proposition, that the task of the historian consists essentially in trying to answer the questions which man asks himself concerning his temporal condition, or to put it another way, the task of the historian, whatever may be the limits of his field and his personal tastes and interests, should always be to try to understand human life, but specifically in its human—and therefore historical—aspects.

Now, leaving to one side Professor Villoro's remarks with the hope that another of the commentators will deal with them more extensively, these reflections tempt me to present as my own contribution a consideration which may possibly help a little to orient the deliberations of this meeting.

In brief, I believe that nowadays we may speak of two classes of history, somewhat in the same way that a physicist distinguishes between classical Newtonian physics and contemporary physics.

There is, in the first place, the classical historiography founded by Thucydides, which we might call the history of politics, employing this term in the most ample and dignified sense which it possesses. This is the historiography which examines the past and elaborates its image for purposes which are practical, practical once again in the broadest and most noble sense. Basically, and always, it has been a matter of *making the past adequate for the needs of the present*. It is a light which man has with which to orient his action; a sort of sixth sense—we might say the radar which man makes use of in projecting himself into the always uncertain and menacing future. Hence, it is a historiography which is never finished, since the criterion of selection is always changing with life in the process of being lived. In fine, it is a permanent instrument, as defined by Thucydides, at the service of the vital needs of man. Such a conception of historical science contains all the purposes and ends of which Dr. Whitaker spoke to us, and all specializations and personal tastes; thus also is explained the fact, so disconcerting for ingenuous historians, of the permanent variation of historical truth, for although the purpose is always the same, the way of achieving it is always different. The deeds are always the same, but the "facts" are always changing. And just as classical physics continues valid within a limited field for practical purposes, thus also, classical historiography has a permanent value within its sphere of vital operations.

But there is, on the other hand, a different historiography which is hardly beginning to be formally defined, to which I have dedicated my best years and which I have called ontological history.[1] It is a discipline which examines the past in order to recreate the very structure of historical change and to put in relief the processes at play within this structure, seeking in this way to show the dynamic being of the entities produced by these processes. To make use of the same physical simile, I would say that this type of history does not operate, like the other, with substantive concepts, but with the concept of "possibility," which corresponds somewhat to the idea of energy in contrast with the concept of permanently made and constituted matter. It is a type of history which does not seek an image of the past to be used as a basis for work, but rather a description of how the past happened, considered as a form of life, or to put it more concretely, of that unique form of life which is life conscious that it is life, or if you prefer, that it is death. This type of history is, in fine, knowledge of man's being, because as man invents historical entities in his own image and likeness, knowing them we come to know their inventor.[2]

I believe that this distinction between two types of history contributes powerfully to clarifying the problem of the task of the historian, because a moment's thought will show us that, in the light of the two purposes which I have pointed out, the dark clouds which now obscure our notions of that task will be shown to be false problems.

NOTES

1. See Edmundo O'Gorman, "Historia y vida," *Diánoia, Anuario de Filosofía*, Año XI, Número 2 (México, 1956).

2. I have made the attempt to write ontological history in my work *La invención de América* (México, 1958) [published in English as *The Invention of America: an Inquiry into the Historical Nature of the New World and the Meaning of its History* (Bloomington, Indiana, 1961)].

Comment: The "Mestizo" Quality in Current Historiography

BY GUILLERMO CÉSPEDES DEL CASTILLO
Universidad de Sevilla

THE PAPERS to which we have just listened
offer us a varied and, to my way of thinking, encouraging view of the present
multiple directions of historiography in
Mexico and in the United States. For a historian of European education and background, there stands out especially, as far as the
United States is concerned, a general historiographic orientation
that is rather technical and practical and in which the relationships
of history with the other sciences acquire prominence. Even though
similar tendencies exist in Mexico, the work of Mr. Luis Villoro
reflects rather the position of a group of scholars with theoretical
and philosophical preoccupations which tend to conceive history
as a well-defined and clearly differentiated discipline from the other
branches of knowledge.

In short, Professor Villoro has centered his interpretation on the
principles of historiography and the humanistic functions of historical labors. Professor Whitaker offers a more varied panorama
and insists on the diversification of historical labors: I emphasize
the characterization "mestizo," a term by which, he tells us, Irving
Leonard calls himself, and the appreciation of the growing importance of that mixed character among those who cultivate the
historical sciences in the United States. For that reason Dr. Whitaker
also singles out the comprehensive observation by Louis Gottschalk
that there is "still room for all kinds of historians."

The last comment makes me think—if we admit with Professor
Villoro the existence of a crisis in contemporary historiography—

that the crisis is one of development and growth and as such should be contemplated more with hope than with concern. History has gone through many of these crises because it has suffered the successive impact of the development of all the sciences and scientific methods, because it has been sensitive to all the tendencies and advances of the humanistic and philosophic disciplines, and because all the political and literary currents have influenced it. The task of the historian is as old as it is changing; you probably felt as impressed as I did when, scarcely two years ago, Fritz Stern collected a series of essays and reflections of historians on their own work and objectives under the title of "The Varieties of History from Voltaire to the Present." In fact, there is no greater gamut in less than two centuries than that from a Niebuhr and a Ranke to a Pokrovsky and a Barzun. A French historian has said that even within the same culture each generation yearns for and constructs an image of the past in accordance with its preoccupations and its mentality, and for that reason the image always differs from that of the preceding generation.

But through all these changes history preserves its personality and its interest; the variations enrich it instead of destroying it. The concept of a historical job as a literary undertaking has produced outstanding papers and classic works in historiography, and they are full of life and drama—for example, the works of certain Greek and Roman historians, of Spanish chroniclers, and of the North American William Prescott. In our day written or oral historical syntheses have an evident acceptance, a truly suggestive or instructive value, and are effective means for diffusing the advances of historical knowledge. The role of so-called political or external history, so belittled by some, tends now to be reinstated and appraised from new points of view. Juridical studies gave a vital impetus to the development of the history of institutions. The influence of the different philosophical systems has been decisive in the emergence of the history of ideas and also in that "mestizo" discipline which is historiography. Let us not forget that historical concepts which are now used and accepted unanimously, such as "evolution," for example, derive, as do so many others, from the field of the natural sciences. Modern historical methodology owes much to the development of the sciences of economics and politics. And finally, in order not to prolong the enumeration, we are experiencing or beginning to experience the powerful impact which the progress of the social sciences has had on the work and on the formation of the historian.

The subsequent, progressive, thematic specialization, the growing array of technical abilities which is required of the historian, accentuate the "mestizo" character of the historical task. It is only natural that each specialist should tend to overestimate his area of work and for that reason to underestimate others; I personally confess to you that I read historical monographs on economic and social themes with true avidity, while other excellent monographs on diplomatic history or on the history of ideas tend to slip through my hands; and even in the study of the sources something similar happens to me.

It is wonderful that everyone follows his interests and preferences in work. It is deplorable that it leads occasionally to sterile polemics which at best cause us to lose equanimity and time. I again cite Gottschalk: there is "still room for all kinds of historians"—the mere gatherer of documents who later does not utilize them but who puts them at the disposal of others; the cultivator of external history and the meticulous narrator of past events who also offers us his data and discoveries; the historian of institutions who treats them only in their juridical aspect and without insight into their true existence and their evolutionary tendencies; he who approaches historical data with a positivistic and limited criterion; the local erudite who is disinterested in all that is not the history of a town, village, or district; he who limits himself to applying purely analytical methods to the study of the past and lacks all perspective and feeling of the temporality and succession of events; the hack compiler of historical-commemorative discourses. All may teach us something, and in fact they are of more or less use to us.

For that reason, and for the sake of the fruitful discussion which will follow, I would venture to beg that we all abstain from polemics on the virtues of one or another methodological orientation, from dogmas or attempts to prove the superiority of a certain school while despising others. Moreover, in order to avoid the risk of a sterile dispersion of our discussion, I would suggest that we focus it on a concrete matter: examination of the most recent impact on history, that produced by the great advances in the social sciences in understanding the mind and the methods of the historian.

There are some who have already included history among the social sciences as an adjunct or as the focal point of all of them. I believe, as do most of you, or at least as do the authors of the papers of this session, that history is somewhat different from all the social sciences, in essence and in origin. I prefer, with Professor Miranda, to speak of history as more than a science, rather as "a branch of knowledge," even though this vague definition may be judged as a mere convenience, since I lack the time to define its meaning. But on the other hand I do not hesitate to include myself among the large and growing number of historians receptive to close contact with the social sciences. I suppose and I hope that that contact may increase in the future, until it becomes, if necessary, a certain type of "inter-disciplinary work." Further, I believe that we ought to intensify the preparation of our students of history in that which pertains to the social sciences.

During the latest Congress of Americanists three historians (Dr. Magnus Mörner, Professor Charles Verlinden, and I) lamented the isolation into which the History portion of the Congress was evolving with respect to archeology, ethnology, and anthropology. We spoke of the lines of development of ethno-history and planned for a future congress of that series to orient and entitle our papers in such a way that they would perforce especially attract the attention of the ethnologists.

In short, I hope that you will permit me to express my opinion that we historians can gain a great deal from a close relationship with the social sciences. Knowledge of their methods and basic problems will enrich our own methodology; we in turn may feel the obligation to hand on to the social sciences data which will be meaningful and directly assimilable by them. And could we not even attain, as Richard Hofstadter would wish, a kind of historical writing in which the present specialized monograph, which for the nonspecialist is full of unassimilable data, would be converted into a portrait, rather than a mere account, of the human groups—social, national, and so on—of the past?

It is evident that something has been done in this direction. You know this better than I, concerning your respective countries. Allow me, by way of example, to refer to my country, to summarize for you the plan of a recent effort to write this kind of history carried out in the perhaps inappropriately entitled *Social and Economic History of Spain*, directed by Jaime Vicens Vives, of which four volumes have already been published in Barcelona. The study of each historical epoch and region is shaped as much as possible around the following points: (1) demography and economic bases (including statistics on the population, its territorial and social distribution, its relation with the economic conditions of the period and place); (2) property and material values (the property system and its changes; the monetary system and its actual values and their changes); (3) the different estates (or social classes, in accordance with the period), with consideration of their interests and political interrelations, literary and artistic tastes, ethics, ideals, and all that demonstrates the vital characteristics of the estate or social class; (4) the economic accomplishments of the entire society (production, transportation, consumption, finance); (5) the formation of broad social thought on the levels of morality, culture, and politics; and (6) a synthesis of daily life (customs, dress, foods, diversions, etc.), always if they have meaning in and of themselves as cultural elements.

There is no doubt, on the other hand, that the social sciences would gain a great deal from drawing closer to history. Perhaps this approximation would give them a better conception of the temporality and of the succession of events, a more exact, expressive, and clear idea of the complex of factors which the social sciences tend to analyze today in an abstract and perhaps consequently fruitless way, since the lack of historical grasp impedes many anthropologists, for example, from understanding a specific cultural situation because of defective or nonexistent knowledge and study of its antecedents and evolution in time or because of the incorrect use of historical data. That many studies based on field research would have their value multiplied by proper consultation of historical documents is something already evident to not a few anthropologists and I hope it will be so for them all in the future.

And I also hope that in the future we historians will remain free of what could be called "the superstition of the document," a common tendency among us. I hope that we all may come to understand that historical facts, despite their own intrinsic and absolute value, are symbols of certain social and cultural changes, manifestations of something more profound, traces of a spirit which, as Professor Villoro tells us, is what really matters to the historian or—as I would dare to say—matters to the historian as much as the facts themselves.

The Second International Congress of Historians of the United States and Mexico, November 3–8, 1958

Officers

Honorary Presidents
Nabor Carrillo, *Rector,* Universidad Nacional Autónoma de México
Eusebio Dávalos Hurtado, *Director,* Instituto Nacional de Antropología e Historia
Carlos Pérez Maldonado, *Presidente,* Academia de Ciencias Históricas de Monterrey
Logan Wilson, *President,* University of Texas
Walter Prescott Webb, *President,* American Historical Association
Ralph Wright Steen, *President,* Texas State Historical Association

President, Mexican Committee: Pablo Martínez del Río

Secretary General: Archibald Ross Lewis

General Recorders: Israel Cavazos Garza
Ramón Martínez López

Secretary: Helen P. Travis

Program Participants in the Sessions of the Second International Congress of Historians of the United States and Mexico

Gabriel Aguirre—Universidad Nacional Autónoma de México
Arturo Arnáiz y Freg—Universidad Nacional Autónoma de México
Luis Avelleyra—Museo Nacional de Antropología
Geoffrey Barraclough—Royal Institute of International Affairs
Robert E. Bell—University of Oklahoma
Ray A. Billington—Northwestern University
Charles Julian Bishko—University of Virginia

Carlos Bosch García—Universidad Nacional Autónoma de México
Thomas N. Campbell—University of Texas
Antonio Castro Leal—Universidad Nacional Autónoma de México
Alberto María Carreño—Academia Mexicana de la Historia
Guillermo Céspedes del Castillo—Universidad de Sevilla
François Chevalier—Institut Français d'Amérique Latine
Daniel Cosío Villegas—Colegio de México
His Excellency Price Daniel—Governor of Texas
Eusebio Dávalos Hurtado—Instituto Nacional de Antropolgía
    e Historia
Ernesto de la Torre Villar—Universidad Nacional Autónoma de
    México
J. Frank Dobie—Texas
J. C. Dykes—U. S. Soil Conservation Service
John S. Galbraith—University of California, Los Angeles
Herbert Gambrell—Southern Methodist University
Glenn E. Garrett—Good Neighbor Commission of Texas
Luis González y González—Colegio de México
Sir Keith Hancock—Australian National University
Lewis U. Hanke—University of Texas
John H. Hill—Texas A. and M. College
Fritz L. Hoffman—University of Colorado
William R. Hogan—Tulane University
Ernesto del Hoyo—Instituto Tecnológico y de Estudios Superiores
    de Monterrey
Wigberto Jiménez Moreno—Escuela Nacional de Antropología
José M. Lacarra—Universidad de Zaragoza
A. R. M. Lower—Queen's University, Ontario
Robert S. Lopez—Yale University
Carlos Pérez Maldonado—Academia de Ciencias Históricas de
    Monterrey
Pablo Martínez del Rio—Escuela Nacional de Antropología
José Miranda—Universidad Nacional Autónoma de México
Eduardo Noguera—Instituto Nacional de Antropología e Historia
José Ortega y Medina—Universidad Nacional Autónoma de México
Edith Parker—Del Mar College, Texas
William M. Pearce, Jr.—Texas Technological College
Antonio Pompa y Pompa—Museo Nacional de Antropología
His Excellency Raúl Rangel y Frías—Governor of Nuevo León
Harry H. Ransom—University of Texas

Frank H. H. Roberts—Smithsonian Institution
José Honório Rodrigues—Arquivo Nacional, Rio de Janeiro
Claudio Sánchez-Albornoz—Universidad de Buenos Aires
Boyd C. Shafer—American Historical Association
France V. Scholes—University of New Mexico
Ralph W. Steen—Texas A. and M. College
Walter W. Taylor—Southern Illinois University
Alfonso Teja Zabre—Universidad Nacional Autónoma de México
Luis Villoro—Universidad Nacional Autónoma de México
Frank Wardlaw—University of Texas
Arthur P. Whitaker—University of Pennsylvania
Logan Wilson—University of Texas
Philippe Wolff—Université de Toulouse

INDEX

Africa: early trade of, 138; historians of, 136; frontier environment of, 168

Afrikaners: compared to American frontiersmen, 136

Alcaraz: mesta of, 60–61

Alfonso III: decrees of, on resettlement, 32

Alfonso VII: and guarantees of Fuero de Oreja, 41; death of, 28; mentioned, 50

Alfonso VIII of Castile: relationship of, to municipal councils, 43

Alfonso IX: grants of, to his subjects, 42; guarantees of, to Cáceres colonists, 53

Alfonso X: and rebellion of Moors, 43; and moving of frontier to Cadiz, 43; and founding of Real Mesta, 58; authorizes mestas, 60, 61; regulates herdsmen's tolls, 62; mentioned, 45, 63

Almohades invasion: and conquest of Avila, 39; conquest of La Mancha, 50; and expulsion from Guadiana Basin, 50; Castilian plan of defense against, 51–52; final expulsion of, 55; mentioned, 39, 41, 44, 48, 51

Almorávides invasion: of Castile, 28; of Guadiana Basin, 50; French resistance against, 71; mentioned, 38, 39, 41, 48

American Historical Association: tenets of, 183; presidential addresses of, 184; mentioned 185, 194

Americanists, Congress of: 208

Anasazi culture: artifacts, location of, 11; period of, 11; population shift of, 12; Mogollon influence on, 13; mentioned, 10, 22. SEE ALSO Formative Stage cultures

Andalucia: conquest of, 44

antelope: on Flat Top Ranch, 121

Apaches: incursion of, in Northern Mexico, 96

Archaic Stage: characteristics and divisions of, 8; locations of, 8, 9; problems of dating, 22. SEE ALSO Willey and Phillips

archeology, American: themes of, 4

Argentina: pampas of, as frontier, 78

Aridamerica: defined, 95

Arizona: prehistoric cultures of, 9; Anasazi culture in, 11; Mogollon culture, 12; Hohokam culture, 13; Patayan culture, 14, 15

Arkansas, southwestern: Caddo culture, 15

artifacts: of Lithic culture, 6; of Paleo-Eastern Lithic culture, 7; of Desert culture, 8–9; of Anasazi culture, 11; of Hohokam culture, 14; of Llano and Folsom cultures, 22; from Chaco Canyon, 23

Asturias, Kingdom of: natural protection of, 27; diploma of, 33-34; mentioned, 38

Australia: early frontier of, 78, 140; theories of frontier development of,